GARDENING UNDER GLASS AND LIGHTS

The American Horticultural Society
Illustrated Encyclopedia of Gardening

GARDENING UNDER GLASS AND LIGHTS

The American Horticultural Society
Mount Vernon, Virginia

**For The American
Horticultural Society**

President
Dr. Gilbert S. Daniels

Technical Advisory Committee
Everett Conklin
Mary Stuart Maury
Dr. John A. Wott

**Gardening Under Glass and
Lights Staff for
The Franklin Library/Ortho Books**

Editorial Director
Min S. Yee

Supervisory Editor
Lewis P. Lewis

Editor
Ken Burke

Associate Editor
Bonnie Cutler

Art Directors
John Williams
Barbara Ziller

Creative Director
Michael Mendelsohn

Assistant Creative Director
Clint Anglin

Written by
T. Jeff Williams

Contributing writers
Walter L. Doty
A. Cort Sinnes

Major photography by
Michael Landis

Contributing photographers
William Aplin
William Apton
John Blaustein
Clyde Childress
Tony Howarth
Fred Kaplin
Michael McKinley

Illustrations by
Ron Hildebrand

Production Director
Robert Laffler

Production Manager
Renee Guilmette

Production Assistant
Paula Green

For Ortho Books

Publisher
Robert L. Iacopi

For The Franklin Library

Publisher
Joseph Sloves

Consultants

Dr. E. O. Burt
University of Florida
Fort Lauderdale, FL

Dr. Jack Butler
Colorado State University
Fort Collins, CO

Acknowledgments

Michael Kosket
Extension Plant Specialist
Napa, California

Environmental Research Laboratory
University of Arizona

Carl Totemeier
Old Westbury Gardens
Long Island, New York

Filon Corporation
Hawthorne, California

Pacific Aquaculture
Sausalito, California

David Loring
Experimental Gardener
Los Altos, California

Professor Edgar Carnegie
Morro Bay, California

The cover photograph shows a corner of a small greenhouse with a collection of flourishing houseplants—coleus, impatiens, fancy-leaved caladiums, and begonias. Photograph copyright © 1982 by Derek Fell.

A Special Message from
The American Horticultural Society

People have been controlling the environment for centuries in order to raise fruits, vegetables, and other plants under ideal conditions year-round. Today, there are even more and easier ways to do this, and *Gardening Under Glass and Lights* will help you decide which methods can work best for you. There is, of course, the ever-popular greenhouse, with its many variations, but have you ever considered installing a sun pit or a lath house in your yard? What about soilless gardening with a hydroponic system? Apartment dwellers can have a controlled environment in miniature—a terrarium—that will add beauty to their surroundings with very little effort. And with the benefits of glass and light, any window can be transformed into a small but very pleasing garden.

Creating a controlled environment is economical in more ways than one. Besides cutting down your grocery bill if you grow vegetables, you can curb fuel costs—a greenhouse attached to your home shares its collected heat with your living area. And a controlled environment itself need not be expensive. Do-it-yourself construction can be undertaken and mastered with confidence, as you will see when you refer to the different building plans provided for greenhouses and a variety of other systems.

Giving your plants the right amount of light, whether natural or artificial, is of utmost importance. Everything you need to know can be found in the chapter devoted to the subject, including instructions for assembling artificial light gardens that can thrive in dimly lit corridors, basements, or under kitchen cabinets. And to help fill your controlled environment with healthy specimens, there is a chapter on culture and propagation. Even tropical fruits can be grown with little difficulty once you know how.

With this book at hand, you are no longer restricted to gardening in the warm-weather months. When you see how easy it is to grow almost any plant under controlled conditions, your gardening satisfaction will grow as well.

Gilbert S. Daniels
President

CONTENTS

There are many controlled environments that are inexpensive, cost-effective, and space-efficient. Learn about the different types of greenhouses—traditional, solar, and window—plus other systems, from the coldframe to the indoor light garden. Then take a look into the history of the greenhouse; it all started with a Roman emperor's craving for cucumbers out of season.

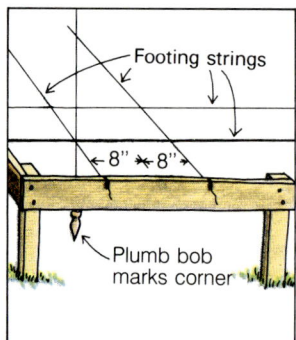

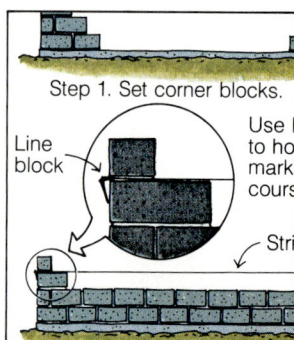

If you want a greenhouse, consider building it yourself. This chapter begins with important questions you should ask before undertaking the project. It then provides guidelines for choosing the greenhouse site, style, covering, and interior design. You're then ready to pour the foundation and lay up the foundation wall. With step-by-step directions, you needn't be experienced.

Copper
Copper nip
Copper fe
bushing
weated
ints
aded
PVC mal
bushing
hented
PVC line
greenhou

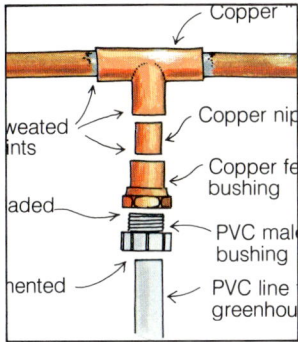

Building a Greenhouse 26

Now you must attach the sill to the foundation, and install the water lines and electrical connections. Learn how in this chapter. Next, review the variety of greenhouse styles and easy-to-follow building plans for each one. If you decide to buy a greenhouse kit, pay special attention to an experienced gardener's advice. For the interior, learn how to design a functional potting area.

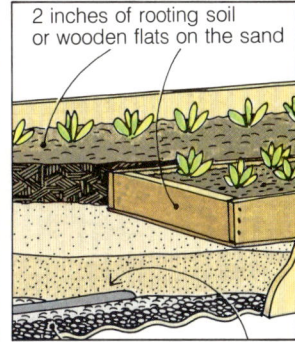

2 inches of rooting soil or wooden flats on the sand

The Greenhouse Environment 50

Help your plants thrive by learning the conditions under which they grow naturally, then duplicate these conditions in the controlled environment. This chapter explains how to maintain the proper temperature and humidity levels, and gives recipes for special container soils. Find out when to water and fertilize your plants; you'll avoid major problems by following a few simple procedures.

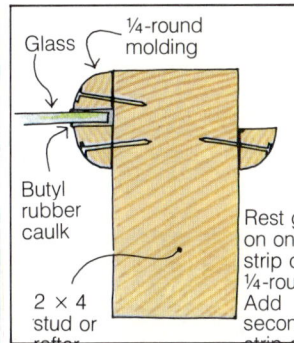

¼-round molding
Glass
Butyl rubber caulk
2 × 4 stud or rafter
Rest g on one strip o ¼-rou Add secon

Solar Greenhouses and Sun Pits 62

By trapping and storing the sun's energy, a solar greenhouse makes a highly economical controlled environment. If attached to your home, it will cut fuel costs by sharing its heat. You'll find some attractive examples of attached solar greenhouses in this chapter, along with instructions for building and insulation. Consider also the sun pit, an efficient below-ground environment.

Labels in diagram: Stomata, Palisade cells, Epidermal cells, Stomata, Mesophyll cell

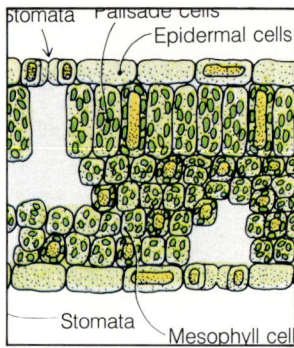

Artificial and Natural Light 78

Here you'll learn how to control the effects of light on plants—too little or too much will prevent healthy growth. See how artificial light can be used as a supplement to natural light, or as your plants' sole energy source. For imaginative decorating ideas, refer to the sections on attractive artificial light gardens and solariums which require a minimum of maintenance.

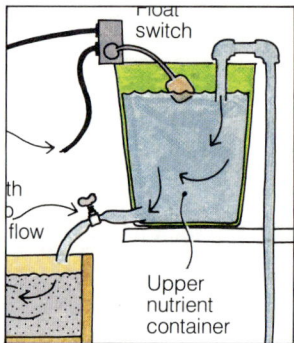

Labels in diagram: Float switch, flow, Upper nutrient container

Hydroponics 96

Growing plants in a nutrient mix rather than soil is an exciting, relatively new, method of gardening. A basic hydroponic system can be constructed from items found in the kitchen, but an automated one will require less of your time. Read here about aggregates, nutrient solutions, growing beds, and sanitation. Instructions for planting are also included.

Other Controlled Environments 106

"Beating the season" can be done in a variety of ways. This chapter offers several devices that will allow you to control temperature, moisture, and sunlight, while affording your plants protection against the elements. You will also learn how to construct a lath house for your yard. If indoor gardens are of special interest to you, see how to plant a terrarium or set up a window greenhouse.

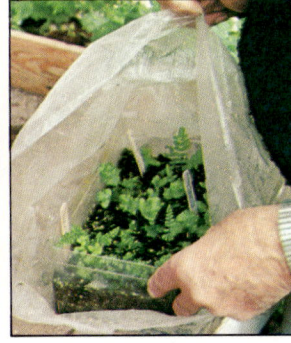

Propagation

You can learn a great deal about your controlled environment by watching the plants in it grow. The easiest way to get plants started is by seed. Here you will find tips on germinating and planting, and a recommendation for a good soil mix. Taking a cutting from the stem, leaves, or roots of a parent plant is another way to propagate. Learn the necessary techniques, plus how to plant.

Special Plants

With a controlled environment, you can grow delicious tropical fruits in the coldest of climates. Pineapple, passion fruit, papaya, guava, and citrus fruits are covered here. But a plant doesn't have to be exotic to receive special treatment—tomatoes do remarkably well in a greenhouse. Read about the four accepted methods of tomato culture. You can also refer to the greenhouse source listing for all your needs.

INTRODUCTION

When you garden under glass or lights, you can garden all year round. The seasons cannot chill your enthusiasm or interrupt your plans.

Seasons pose no threat to a gardener whose plantings thrive in the secluded, nurturing environment of glass or lights. Such an environment creates a special worry-free atmosphere where all kinds of plants and flowers can flourish year-round. For instance, you can harvest orchids amidst snow flurries and have garden-fresh salads in February. This book offers a wide range of ideas for a controlled environment, from a freestanding, attached, or window greenhouse, to a solar greenhouse or solarium. You will also learn about the cold frame, the A-frame, the hotbed, the sun pit, and the basement garden. Other systems, such as the "Hatch Patch," hot cap, shade porch, lath house, and terrarium, are also described. For the more adventurous, a section on hydroponics—growing plants in a solution of nutrients rather than soil—has been included. Since the effect of light is so critical for making plants grow, a chapter has been devoted to that as well.

As you can see, there is a method of gardening under glass or lights to suit anyone's needs. A controlled environment can be purchased, but if you would like to construct your own, building plans for a variety of types are offered, plus details on how to operate the controlled environment at peak efficiency.

Your own house or apartment is a controlled environment by itself, but in many cases, it is too dry and lacks enough light for plants. These problems can be overcome, however, and you'll find many tips on how to do so within these pages. You can redesign entire rooms with the needs of plants in mind; even the smallest of spaces can be adapted to hold them. Look up, down, in closets and along narrow windowsills; almost any place in your home can become a lush garden.

Greenhouses

A greenhouse is a building whose roof and, often, sides are made largely of glass. Inside, the temperature can be regulated so that you can grow out-of-season plants, delicate plants, or virtually any plant. Although the word "greenhouse" may bring to mind opulent Victorian glass buildings, much simpler (and more affordable) versions can be had these days— freestanding, attached, on rooftops, and on balconies. Designs vary according to use and taste but will house your plants equally well. If you want the satisfaction of building your own, you'll find many styles to choose from in this book. At least one of them should fit your needs, whether you live in Minnesota or Alabama. See pages 26–49.

Solar greenhouses. The difference between a traditional greenhouse and a solar greenhouse is that the latter *retains* the sun's heat. The result is a lower heating bill—not only for your greenhouse, but also (if yours is an attached greenhouse) for your home. See pages 62–77 for more on solar greenhouses, and give this section special consideration even if you already have a greenhouse—there are several ways to improve its performance.

Top: This greenhouse in Oyster Bay, New York, rewards hard work with a luxuriant array of blooming plants.

Above: These geraniums, trained into standards, were photographed in midwinter.

Window greenhouses. A window greenhouse is not to be confused with a windowsill garden. The latter is just a ledge supporting plants that are exposed to the open air, while the former is a kind of actual greenhouse: it closes on the inside, so that the plants aren't subject to the drying effects of the house. Some locations are better than others, but fluorescent lighting will make up for whatever natural lighting won't cover. For information on window greenhouses, see page 123.

Other Controlled Environments

Coldframes. These bottomless, covered (usually with glass) boxes are heated solely by the sun. They can be used for rooting cuttings, starting seeds early, growing salad greens in winter, and forcing early spring flowers. Raised beds particularly lend themselves to conversion into coldframes. For more on these handy season-extenders, see pages 106–110.

Hotbeds. These are like coldframes, but with the addition of heat at the bottom. Heat can be supplied via organic matter (rotting manure), a flue, electricity, or the sun. Hotbeds resemble greenhouses in terms of capability. See pages 112–114.

Sun pits. Some people call these "cold frames with head room," and they aren't far off. A sun pit is a dug-out pit that has a clear glass roof. It has a number of natural advantages: it utilizes the ground's natural insulation; the soil around its sunken walls minimizes heat loss; its closeness to the ground protects it from wind; and it will—if placed close to the house— warm the house to some extent. For more information, see pages 75–77.

Basement gardens. You don't need to excavate any extra soil if you already have a basement. Some floor-to-ceiling shelves and fluorescent lights are enough to give you healthy, beautiful plants. See page 87 for more information.

A-frames. A variation of the trellis, the A-frame can be used for vertical growing of vegetables that otherwise take up too much space. It is also easy to position and can be converted into a tent by covering it with plastic. See pages 37 and 115.

"Hatch Patches." Otherwise known as plastic mulches, "Hatch Patches" increase yields and speed up ripening of melons, eggplants, peppers, and summer squash. The debate over clear versus black plastic continues, but the results show that plants clearly benefit from some kind of plastic mulch. See page 116 for more.

Hot caps. Hot caps are most useful where plants are starting to come up but where late frosts may still occur. These coverings can be made quite simply—for example, from the top of a 1-gallon plastic milk jug, or from 3 sticks and a clear plastic bag. For detailed instructions, turn to page 117.

Shade porch, lath house. In the summer, if the sun makes it too uncomfortable for you to enjoy your patio at midday, you can change the environment by building a shade porch or lath house. It can be freestanding or attached to the wall of your house to expand your living area. A myriad of flowering plants will thrive in the cool, indirect light under this structure. See pages 118–122 for more on these.

Terrariums. Perhaps you really don't want to be bothered with the care and feeding of a jungle, but still want something green and growing around you. The terrarium might be just the answer. Small and delicate plants will thrive in this miniature greenhouse. Once it's planted and its self-contained rain cycle is established, you can sit back and enjoy it. See page 122.

Hydroponics. For the more adventurous, this book offers a whole section on setting up and operating a hydroponic garden—growing plants in a solution of nutrients rather than in soil. Gardeners who have been converted to soilless growing claim that their vegetables grow faster than in regular gardens, and even taste better. A hydroponic system is ideally run in a greenhouse because of the greenhouse's ample light and humidity, but it can also be made to work in an apartment under fluorescent lights. See pages 96–105.

Indoor light gardens. Light is critical for making plants grow, whether outdoors or indoors. The indoor light garden is a rapidly expanding phenomenon in this country, where whole banks of plants and flowers, particularly the African violet, are being grown under lights. The wonderful thing about a light garden is that it can be put in the darkest of places.

The pristine pastels of these chrysanthemums warm the central aisle of this greenhouse.

A Look into History

For centuries, man has attempted to improve plant production by controlling the environment. One of the earliest known greenhouses was built around 30 A.D. for the Roman Emperor Tiberius, to satisfy his craving for cucumbers out of season. Glass had not been invented, and the greenhouse, then called a *specularium*, was painstakingly fabricated from small translucent sheets of mica. But Tiberius' greenhouse hardly created a new rage. Aside from the damper of the expense, the technology took centuries to evolve, and it was not until 1599 that the first practical greenhouse was built. Constructed at the University Botanic Garden in Leiden, Holland, it was intended to grow tropical plants for medicinal purposes.

In the 17th century the greenhouse idea caught on and began spreading throughout Europe. The French, who developed a passion for a wonderful new fruit called the orange, began setting up structures to protect their trees from frost. These, naturally, were called *orangeries*. However, these early greenhouses were cumbersome, unrefined structures. The one built by Solomon de Caus in Heidelberg around 1619 had removable shutters on the roof that had to be taken down and put up daily during the frost season. This was no small chore, considering that the roof was large enough to cover 340 orange trees.

Experiments to improve the greenhouse concept, including angled glass walls and heating flues, continued throughout the 17th century. New building technology and better glass spurred the erection of larger and improved greenhouses that contained plants just to please the eyes and palates of European royalty. The *orangerie* at Versailles, for example, was more than 500 feet long, 42 feet wide, and 45 feet high, with south-facing windows for light and heat. It is still in use today.

In Russia, between 1801 and 1805, Tsar Alexander I had built at St. Petersburg three parallel greenhouses, each 700 feet long and connected on each end by two more greenhouses of the same length, with some

Brilliantly colored ranunculus entice visitors into the ornate Conservatory of Flowers in San Francisco, California.

sections for the tropical plants and fruits reaching 40 feet high. The entire structure was heated during the bitter Russian winters by furnaces filled with birch wood.

As elaborate as these were, it was the Victorian Age in England that proved to be the golden era of the greenhouse, with the soaring Palm House at Kew Gardens a prime example of what was erected at that time. (Its replica, the Conservatory of Flowers, can be seen in San Francisco's Golden Gate Park.) By the mid-1800s, glass was being manufactured in great quantity, and the prohibitive taxes on it were repealed. The wealthy immediately began competing with one another to build the most elaborate greenhouse—again, primarily just to grow tropical fruits and rare flowers. Little thought was given to using them for a wide range of food production.

In America, the first greenhouse on record was built around 1737 by Andrew Faneuil, a wealthy Boston merchant. Like his European predecessors, Faneuil used it primarily to grow fruit, but the concept spread slowly, since almost all greenhouses were built for the wealthy.

By 1825, however, greenhouses were more common. Many were heated by furnace-warmed air, although some of the earliest were pit greenhouses heated largely by sunlight flowing through south-facing windows. This is a basic design that remains highly practical today.

Today's Controlled Environments

The modern concept of controlled environments is not restricted to the greenhouse, nor is it in the private domain of the wealthy. Gardening under glass and lights is something anyone can do for relatively little money. It can, in fact, be a very cost-effective undertaking. A sun pit, consisting of a hole in the ground covered with a clear glass roof, utilizes the ground's natural insulation. If placed near the house, it will help keep it warm. Similarly, a greenhouse attached to the home can be used as a solar heat trap, thus cutting fuel bills.

Today's controlled environments fit into virtually any space—from a window, to a balcony, to a little backyard, or several acres. Moreover, they are becoming automated, reducing the amount of time and care owners must spend on them, so that home production of vegetables and flowers is greatly simplified.

The following chapters will provide you with everything you need to know about gardening in a controlled environment. In addition to learning about the various systems and how they're built, you'll read about controlling temperature and humidity, artifical and natural light, soilless gardening, propagation, and plants specially suited to controlled environments. Just as important, you'll discover that this type of gardening is a highly creative and worthwhile endeavor.

Greenhouses can vary in size and complexity. Above: Large greenhouses in the Bailey Arboretum, Locust Valley, New York. Right: "Bubble" greenhouses supported by pressurized air in Zurich, Switzerland. Far right: A home greenhouse on Long Island, New York.

Opposite: The Missouri Botanical Garden's climatron was the first modern structure to provide multiple controlled climates under one roof without the use of partitions.

PLANNING A GREENHOUSE

Planning ahead is important. Learn all you can about different types of greenhouses before you choose which one to buy or build.

Greenhouses have come a long way since they were used as *orangeries* and *pineries* to force growth of oranges and pineapples. The conservatory—a pet project of wealthy Europeans and Americans—developed into a status symbol halfway through the 19th century. But it also was a practical way to produce almost any crop or plant indoors.

Modern greenhouses are modeled after the efficient commercial types rather than the beautiful conservatories of the past century. Now you can choose from dozens of styles and a wide range of prices. Or you can build your own greenhouse at a fraction of what it would cost to buy.

Even if you have no experience whatsoever as a builder, consider putting up your own greenhouse. This book presents several different styles of varying complexity. Building your own does more than save money—it gives you the great satisfaction of having done it yourself. In addition, you can make changes as you go along, which most builders do.

Greenhouses adapt remarkably well to any situation. There is, of course, the traditional greenhouse that's set down somewhere in the backyard. But they also can be found on rooftops or enclosing sunny balconies on houses and apartments. More and more people are discovering the benefits of making greenhouses an extension of the house for people, birds, and plants to enjoy.

First Considerations

Before you actually buy materials for making a greenhouse, ask yourself some serious questions.

☐ "How big a greenhouse do I need?" Greenhouse growers around the country say: Make it larger than you anticipate using. Once you start greenhouse gardening you will want to expand.

☐ "How big a greenhouse can I afford?"

☐ "Do I want a prefab or do I want to build my own?" Consider how much time and money you have available, and what you want the greenhouse to do. If you would like to build your own but feel like too much of a novice, hire an experienced carpenter to help you, or consider buying a prefab type that requires only assembling.

☐ "Do I need a building permit?" You probably will need one, whether you have a prefab or are constructing your own. A simple sketch showing the dimensions and supports is usually all that is required.

☐ "Will a greenhouse result in higher taxes on my property?" Happily, many states are enacting laws to give tax rebates on solar heating devices. Find out whether your model of greenhouse qualifies.

☐ "Are there local design ordinances covering any buildings on residential property where I live?" The building permit office can advise you.

☐ "Are there setback requirements for my property?" In most residential areas, all buildings have to be set back a certain distance from property lines. Check this point so you won't have to move the greenhouse later.

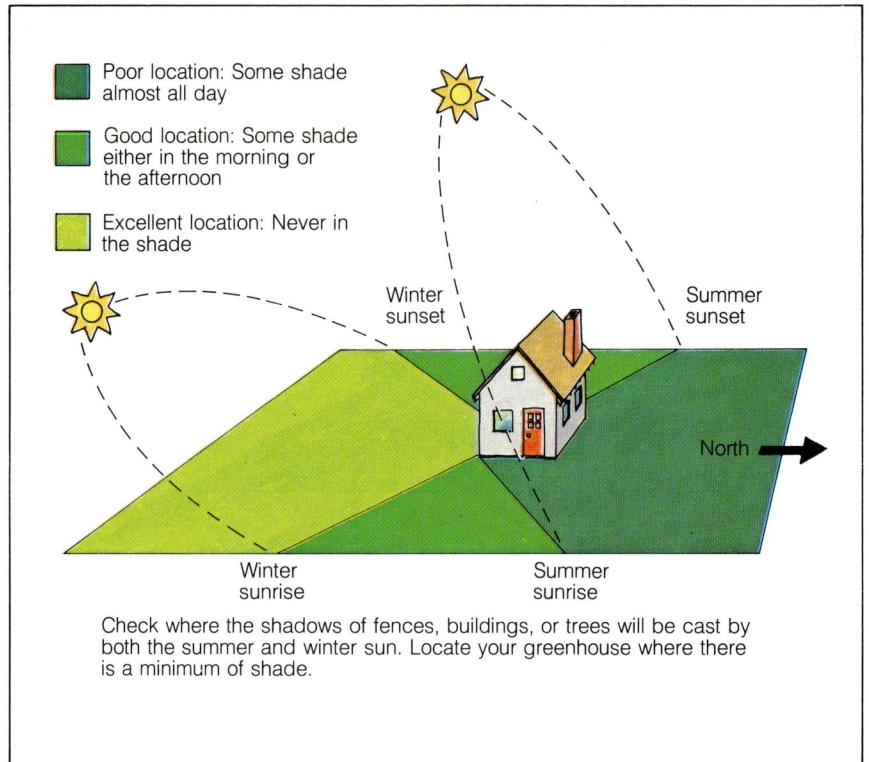

Poor location: Some shade almost all day

Good location: Some shade either in the morning or the afternoon

Excellent location: Never in the shade

Winter sunset

Summer sunset

North

Winter sunrise

Summer sunrise

Check where the shadows of fences, buildings, or trees will be cast by both the summer and winter sun. Locate your greenhouse where there is a minimum of shade.

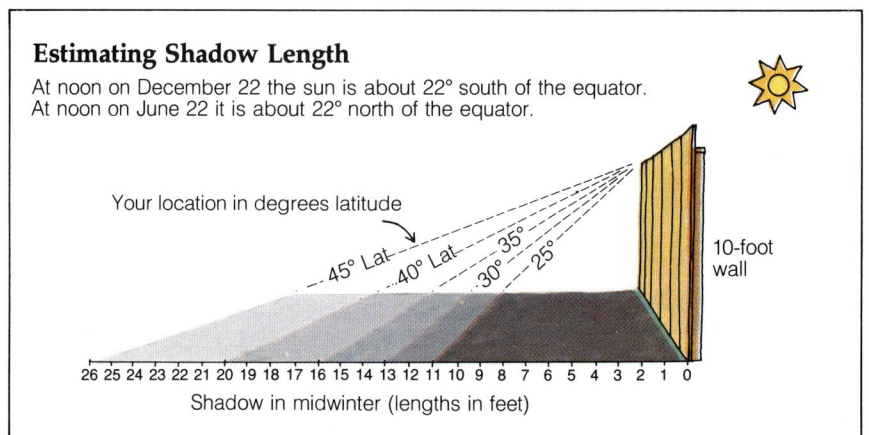

Estimating Shadow Length

At noon on December 22 the sun is about 22° south of the equator. At noon on June 22 it is about 22° north of the equator.

Your location in degrees latitude

45° Lat   40° Lat   35°   30°   25°

10-foot wall

26 25 24 23 22 21 20 19 18 17 16 15 14 13 12 11 10 9 8 7 6 5 4 3 2 1 0

Shadow in midwinter (lengths in feet)

Secondary Considerations

As a prospective greenhouse owner, you should consider these other factors:

☐ *Maintenance costs*. Think about how much you will have to spend to maintain the greenhouse and supply it with water and electric light. Selling some of your flowers or plants might help offset these costs, but don't count on it.

☐ *Heating costs*. Whether you'll be using electricity, oil, or gas, the rates seem to be going up every year. The better your greenhouse is constructed, the less heat you will lose. Installing a layer of plastic sheeting inside to create a thermal barrier can cut heat losses up to 40 percent. Using simple solar heating can, in some cases, not only eliminate all costs of heating the greenhouse, but sharply reduce your residential bill as well.

☐ *Taxes*. Ask either the building permit office or the tax office whether your style of greenhouse will be classified as temporary. If so, you may not have to pay additional taxes, or have to pay only low ones. You may not even need a building permit.

Choosing the Site

Deciding where to put your greenhouse is a critical first step—once it's up, it's there to stay, unless you are prepared to go to a lot of effort and expense to move it.

The first consideration is sunshine. Look around your property. Is there a wall or tree that will put too much shade on the greenhouse? Keep in mind that the sun will be considerably lower in winter than in summer. So, as a rule of thumb, locate your greenhouse away from your home by a distance of 2.5 times the height of any wall or house that might block sunlight.

If you have a deciduous tree in the vicinity, it can provide a double bonus: shade during part of the hot summer days, sunlight in winter when it drops its leaves.

Drainage is the next consideration. Don't build in depressions—these will be catch basins for rain and snow during the winter months. Don't build in boggy areas where the soil is constantly wet and unstable.

Select a site that is relatively level or that can be made level easily. If there is a slope draining toward the greenhouse site, you may have to put in tile or gravel ditches to divert runoff.

Now look at the ground where you want to build. If you expect to plant directly in the soil, examine the ground carefully. If it is too rocky or has too much clay, you may have to create new growing beds. It should also drain well so you don't trap water or turn packed earth into mud.

Water and electricity are two other important considerations. They should be as accessible as possible. The farther the greenhouse is from these connections, the harder it will be for you to run the utility lines there.

Consider, too, the amount of trouble involved in walking to your greenhouse in freezing cold and blinding snow. Something close to the house—or even better, attached to the house—is easy to tend during cold winter months. The most important consideration of all is to maximize the winter sunlight.

What Style of Greenhouse?

There is a wide variety of greenhouses you can build yourself. Which style you choose depends on such factors as how permanent you want it to be, whether it is attached to the house or freestanding, and what type of snow loads exist in your part of the country.

Attached. The attached greenhouse is becoming increasingly popular. It can be heated easily from the house, but solar heat gained in the greenhouse can also be transferred to the main house. Water and electricity are nearby. The greenhouse is within easy reach regardless of the weather outside.

Gothic arch. The gothic roof line is made from laminated wood strips. With wood, permanent coverings such as corrugated fiberglass can be readily installed.

A-frame. This can be built in sections on the ground, then raised into place and covered. It is quick to construct. In areas with heavy snow loads, this shape is ideal. However, it offers only limited head room, except in the center aisle.

Freestanding. This is what usually comes to mind when we think of the greenhouse: the conventional glazed building out in the yard. It can be built to any size and covered with anything from glass to polyethylene.

Greenhouse Coverings

What material you use to cover the greenhouse depends on the cost, the ease in putting it up, how permanent you want it to be, your own sense of esthetics, and how important it is to have a well-insulated structure.

Attached

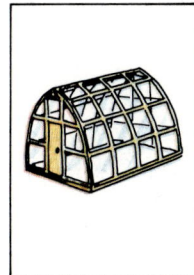

Gothic

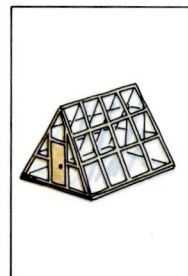

A-frame

Freestanding

Glass. Glass is always popular because it provides an unobstructed view both into and out of the greenhouse. It is also very easy to shade when there's too much hot summer sun. Glass is highly resistant to scratching, and over the years it can be cleaned repeatedly, with no loss in light transmission. It is also usually cheaper than the rigid acrylic plastics on the market. However, glass does present one problem: it breaks. If you live in an area where there are heavy hailstorms, this can be an important consideration. Breakage through vandalism is something else to think about. Glass is also a poor insulator against winter cold.

For roofs, use double-strength glass. Single-strength panes on the walls are sufficient.

Acrylic. Acrylic that is clear and rigid makes a superb covering for a greenhouse. It is only about half the weight of glass and ten times more resistant to breakage. Basic home-carpentry skills are sufficient for cutting acrylic to fit; it can even be curved for special effects. It lets in 90 to 95 percent of the available light and does not appreciably lose this clarity over 15 or more years of exposure to the sun's rays. Double-layer acrylic sheets with a honeycomb interior structure are stronger and are the best insulators against heat or cold.

Fiberglass. Fiberglass covering has proved particularly popular. It comes in both corrugated panels and in flat rolls. Both are a boon because of the ease in handling. Fiberglass panels let you put up simple greenhouses in a day or over a weekend. When choosing these panels, ask your building supplier if they are designed for greenhouse use. They must be specially treated (with Tedlar, for example) to prevent the fiberglass from deteriorating due to sunlight and trapped dirt, which results in a sharp loss of light transmission. Many greenhouse builders prefer to cover the roof with corrugated fiberglass panels because of their strength and ease in application, and cover the sides with flat fiberglass or glass. Fiberglass is not a good insulator, but because it can be easily applied in large sheets, heat loss from air leakage is considerably reduced as compared to a glass-covered greenhouse.

Bottom: The fibergass walls and corrugated fiberglass roof (below) of this attached greenhouse are a good choice for a home-made greenhouse because fiberglass is easy to cut and handle.

Center: Detail of the styrofoam stripping cut to seal the ridges along the roof line.

Polyethylene film. Polyethylene film is the cheapest covering. It is also, unfortunately, the least durable. But it has its advantages if you want only a temporary covering over a simple greenhouse structure during the winter. It can also be applied over large areas rapidly and at relatively little cost. Unless this plastic film is treated, however, it will deteriorate rapidly under the ultraviolet rays of the sun. When buying it, make sure it is ultraviolet resistant and intended for greenhouse use. Some of the special greenhouse plastics will last for as long as three years before they must be replaced.

One of the greatest uses of polyethylene film is as a lining for the inside of greenhouse walls. In this capacity, it creates a thermal barrier that reduces heat loss. Polyethylene greenhouses are the tightest greenhouses, and the use of a double layer of film provides excellent insulation.

Interior Design

When planning the greenhouse, consider what kind of plants you will want to grow. This is crucial. Just as you design your home to suit your family's needs, so should you consider the needs of your plants inside the greenhouse.

Tall plants or vines may require high supports; thus, the A-frame will not

Location and climate are important considerations when selecting your greenhouse design, yet your favorite plants, interests, and budget will dictate individualized style variations as diverse as these shown below and left.

Aisle plan

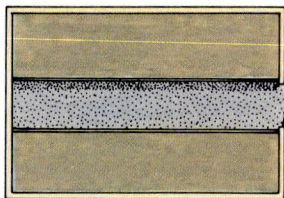

Peninsula plan

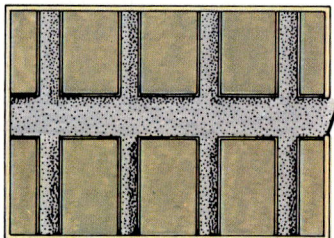

be as usable as one of the other styles. Also, consider whether you will want to grow in ground beds or entirely on benches or tables.

Bench layout is very important. Remember that benches running north and south get an even distribution of light as the sun moves from east to west. The layout for benches or tables usually follows either the aisle plan or the peninsula plan. The aisle plan involves running two rows of benches end to end (usually along each side of the greenhouse, to conserve space), with an aisle between them. The peninsula plan, on the other hand, has individual benches running in from the greenhouse sides, with very narrow aisles between and a wider aisle down the center. If your greenhouse is big enough, the peninsula plan is probably more satisfactory—there's even room in the center aisle to keep plants brought indoors for the winter. But whichever system you choose, bear in mind that it costs as much to heat aisle space as it does the space where the plants grow. Try to plan a layout that minimizes aisle space.

Site Layout and Foundation

Before doing any actual construction, first decide what type of greenhouse you want—attached, gothic arch, A-frame, freestanding, gambrel roof, simplified gambrel roof, or snow-country (see pages 26–43 for detailed instructions on building). After determining how big it will be, you can prepare to work.

First make sure that the site for the greenhouse is level, or almost so. Then—and perhaps most important—put down a foundation that is both level and square. This time-consuming exercise is worth doing slowly; a well-laid foundation will make things much easier for you later on. There's nothing quite as frustrating as ill-fitting walls and roofs resulting from a foundation that isn't square.

Directions for foundations tend to be confusing, involving unfamiliar terms and concepts. If you have an experienced builder to assist you, these ideas will quickly become clear. If you're on your own, read, reread, and follow the drawings and photographs on these pages. Once you begin the actual work, everything will start to fall into place.

This section deals essentially with pouring and making level the traditional concrete footing. But perhaps you prefer a simple, lightly framed greenhouse, with a plastic or fiberglass covering, that does not require an extensive foundation. If so, go ahead and use a light foundation. Simply lay out painted railroad ties and sink them in ditches to just above ground level, or stake them with iron reinforcing rods (also called "rerod bars" or "rebars").

For another easy foundation (in mild-climate areas only), dig a 6-inch-deep ditch the dimensions of your greenhouse, line it with concrete blocks, and fill these with cement. Insert some anchor bolts for your frame and you're set to build. Or sink precast concrete piers every 4 feet around the perimeter, and build up from there.

Once the site is level, put in the footing. This is normally concrete and must go below the frost line. In southern California this need only be 8 inches down, but in New England it must be at least 3 feet. If you put the footing too shallow, the ground below may freeze and heave, cracking both the footing and your greenhouse.

On top of the footing goes the foundation wall. On top of that goes the framework for the greenhouse. The rule of thumb is that the footing should be twice the width of the foundation. Thus, if you plan to make the foundation wall with standard 8-inch concrete blocks, the footing will be 16 inches wide.

Let's assume that the foundation wall will be 2 feet high. To start, drive a 2 × 2 stake firmly into the ground at one corner, leaving 2 feet of the stake above ground. This is point A. Measure off another corner and drive a stake

How to Square Up

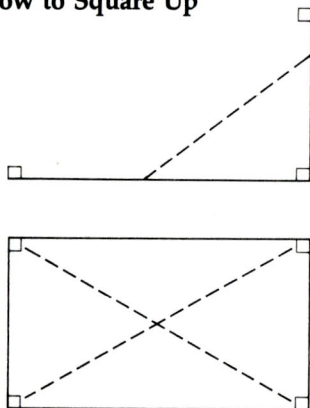

there, creating point B. This is one side of the building, and all the other angles to it must be square. Drive a small nail in the top center of each stake and connect them with a tightly drawn string.

To put in the next point, C, measure the distance and use a carpenter's square to make as close to a 90° angle as you can. Drive a temporary stake in at point C and connect B and C with string.

Now you must make sure that the AB and BC strings form an exact 90° angle. From point B toward point A, measure exactly 8 feet and mark it on the string with a felt pen. Now, from B toward C, measure off exactly 6 feet and mark that point. For the corner B to be square, there must be exactly 10 feet between the marks on the two strings. So with a friend or two helping, adjust the stake at point C until you have that 10 feet on the diagonal.

For the third leg, from A to D, measure it as closely as you can, then drive a temporary stake at corner D. Make sure the distance from A to D is the same as from B to C. Using the same trick of marking the strings at 6 and 8 feet, adjust until square.

Now for the final proof that everything is square: measure both the diagonals, from A to C and from B to D. If they are the same, everything is square. Allowing for slack in the measuring tape and difficulty in measuring the string, a difference of ⅛ inch for a small structure or ¼ inch for a large one is allowable. But if the difference in your diagonals is larger, go over the measurements again.

Batter Boards

The stakes and string you have just put up show the exact outside measurements of the greenhouse. The next step is to lay out the footing. For this, batter boards are needed at the four corners. These batter boards will allow you to remove the stakes and strings when you dig the footing trench and still know exactly where the corners are.

Start by driving a 2 × 4 stake about 2 feet back from the corner stakes and directly on the diagonal from the opposite corner. Drive two more stakes 4 feet from the corner down each side of the building outline to form an approximate right angle. These stakes should be about 3 feet above the ground. Connect with 1 × 4 boards nailed to the stakes at the exact height of the foundation wall. Use a level to check that the boards are absolutely horizontal.

Now construct batter boards at the three remaining corners in the same fashion. These batter boards must all be on the same level. If you don't have a small hand transit to check with, stretch a string tightly and check with a line level.

Now pull another set of strings directly over the four building outline strings and drive nails into the edge of the batter board to mark their line. To make the building outline in string, pull the string tight and tie it to the nails. Remove the original stakes and string, and also remove the string from the batter boards. Since you have marked the positions for the strings with nails in each batter board, you can put the strings back in place quickly when you need them.

Now you're ready to mark the outline for the footing. If you are going to build up a concrete block wall, the footing should be 16 inches wide (twice the width of the standard 8-inch-wide concrete block). If you won't be building the foundation wall but will be putting the greenhouse directly on the footings, 12 inches wide will be ample. For the final word, however, check with the building codes.

For a 16-inch footing, mark off 8 inches on each side of the nail in the batter boards and pull strings all around. Using a plumb bob, drive small stakes at the inside and outside points for each corner. Now snap a chalk line on the ground to mark the footing outline and remove the strings.

For a footing that will be 8 inches thick and have a foundation wall on top,

Laying Out Footings

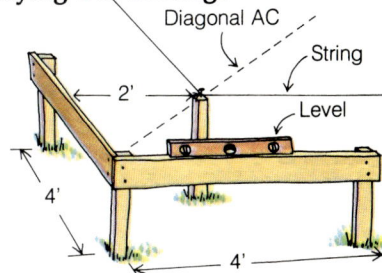

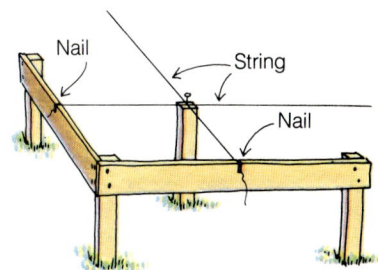

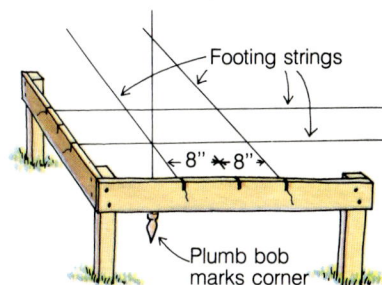

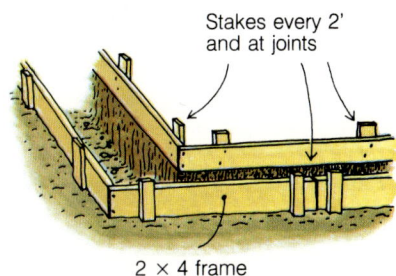

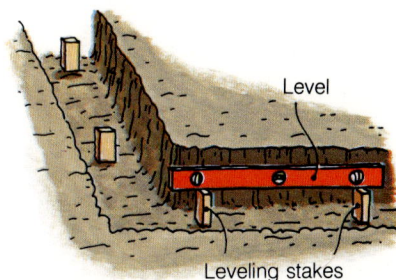

make the trench 10 inches deep. This will keep the footing 2 inches below ground and out of sight.

If, however, you plan to build directly on the footing, bring it up above ground a few inches to keep the greenhouse walls clear of the ground. Do this by nailing together a 2 × 4 frame flush with the edges of the footing trench, inside and out. Stake it every 2 feet for added strength (concrete is heavy and can easily bow out weak frames). This frame must be level all the way around before you pour.

A footing that will remain 2 inches below the ground level must be level when you pour the concrete. Since the sides of the trench are too inaccurate for this purpose, use leveling stakes. For a footing 8 inches deep, start in the center of the trench at one corner and drive a 2 × 2 stake firmly in the ground, with exactly 8 inches showing. Now proceed around the trench, driving stakes every 4 to 7 feet with just 8 inches showing. Use a straight 2 × 4 stud and a carpenter's level to check each one. When you return to the original stake, you must still be on the same level. Now, when you pour exactly to the top of the stakes, you know your footing will be level. Don't worry about removing these stakes: let them stay in the concrete. But before you pour the concrete, plan your water and electricity hookups (see pages 26–29).

Pouring Concrete

Before pouring, line the bottom of the trench with large rocks, if you have any available. The concrete will bind tightly around them, and you will have less of it to pour. Some codes may require you to lay concrete reinforcing rods, called rerods or rebar. Even if you do not have to do this, it is still a good idea. For the slight extra cost you will prevent the footing from cracking at some future date, possibly causing damage to the greenhouse structure.

Using a small concrete mixer or a wheelbarrow, combine 1 shovel of Portland cement, 2 shovels of sand, and 4 shovels of gravel. Blend thoroughly while the mix is dry, then slowly add water. Keep blending, making sure that all the mix gets wet. From this point it takes only a little more water to get a mix that is completely wet and loose without being runny.

After you have filled the footing trench to what looks like the proper level, take a concrete "float" and work the mix vigorously until all the air bubbles are out and the mix has settled. You may then have to add some more. Work this again until all the gravel is below the surface and you have a smooth, level top ready for the foundation blocks. Use a concrete trowel for the final smoothing.

If you're going to build directly onto the footing, insert the anchor bolts now. Leave 2½ inches of the threaded end exposed. Check with a square to make sure that they are perpendicular.

Keep the footing covered at night with plastic, or straw, or both if you are in an area with freezing temperatures. The footing will take at least three days to set enough for you to start the foundation wall. On the second and third days, lightly sprinkle the concrete with water; this will prevent it from drying out too rapidly, which would cause it to crack.

Walls

The foundation or side wall for a greenhouse can be both functional and attractive. This wall (see facing page) is not high enough (usually 24 to 30 inches) to shade much in the greenhouse; but it provides a solid structure at ground level that won't be easily broken as might be the case with a building made completely of glass or plastic.

Before starting the wall, you must find the exact outline and corners again. Put the string back on the batter boards, and pull it tight all the way around. To mark the corners, hang a plumb bob from the point where the strings cross. Next, use a chalk marker to snap lines from corner to corner on the footing.

The walls are usually made from concrete blocks 16 inches long, 8 inches high, and 8 inches wide. (The exact measurements are ⅜ inch less, allowing for ⅜ inch of mortar to bond the blocks.)

Start at one corner and lay the first block very precisely. The rest of the wall will be determined by how square and level this block is.

Use a mortar mix that is 1 part mortar cement (not Portland) to 4 parts fine sand. Mix it dry, then add water until it is smooth and plastic, not runny. Trowel the mortar across the predampened footing and place the first block. Check that it is level and square. Note that corner blocks have one flat end for facing, while the others have two grooved ends for joining. (You get a mixture when you order blocks.)

Lay up the four corners first, extending the bottom layer enough each time to support the next layer at the corners.

To join the blocks, stand one on end and "butter" the exposed end with ⅜ to ½ inch of mortar, then fit it to the adjoining block. To join stacking blocks, butter the top of a block on the inside and outside edges, then lay the next block on top of it. It is not customary to butter the cross web, but note that this web has one wide end and one narrow end. The wide end always goes up so you can apply mortar to it if you want to.

After the corners are up to the desired height, start laying the rest of the courses. To keep these level, use line blocks that hook over the ends of the blocks, with a string stretched tightly between. You can also put perpendicular poles at each corner, with marks every 8 inches for the strings.

Blocks also come in half sizes; request a quantity with your initial order. They are needed on corners and sometimes fit in the middle of the course. More commonly, however, you have to cut a block to fit. Allow ½ inch on each end for the mortar, then cut the block by first scoring it all around with a cold chisel, then snapping it apart with the chisel and hammer. Wear safety goggles.

There are also special blocks recessed to accept door jambs, which you will need for framing the door openings.

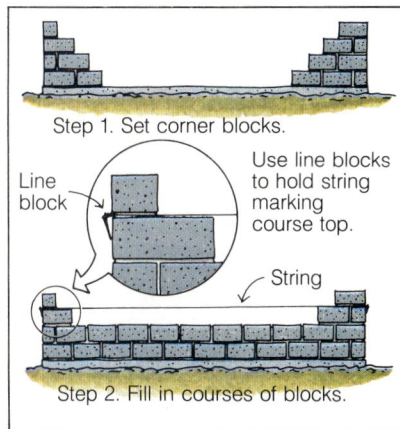

Step 1. Set corner blocks.

Line block

Use line blocks to hold string marking course top.

String

Step 2. Fill in courses of blocks.

Greenhouse foundation walls not only conserve energy by providing insulation and retaining heat but also provide the shade necessary for some tender plants.

BUILDING A GREENHOUSE

You can build your own greenhouse by following one of these clear, economical construction plans.

Once the foundation is finished, you have reached a milestone in the construction of your greenhouse. Now, you are well on the way to growing your first hothouse plant.

This is the time to make the final decision on shape. If you have a basic rectangular foundation, with or without a wall, you can still reconsider ideas you may have gotten while working on that foundation. (Of course, an unusual shape, such as a hemispherical dome or an attached greenhouse, requires an unusual-shaped foundation; it's too late to change your mind at this point.) Review again the basic shapes you could use:

Attached. Easy access from the house, with water and electricity nearby.

Gothic arch. Lovely to look at, but a challenging project—the layout and lamination of the arches takes time unless you are using a prefabricated kit.

A-frame. Easy to build, ideal for areas with heavy snow loads. However, head room is limited at the sides.

Freestanding gambrel. A freestanding greenhouse that is probably the most typical and usable shape to build: the interior-space layout is very practical, and there's easy access for a loaded wheelbarrow through a door at either end.

Once you have decided on the shape and ordered the material, you are ready to move ahead.

Sill

The sill is a board—preferably 2 × 6 redwood, cedar, or rot-proof treated wood—that goes flat around the top of the footing or foundation wall and gives you something to nail the walls to. The sill is bolted to the foundation with anchor bolts. Space them 4 to 6 feet apart, always putting one near the ends of each length of sill. Measure so that a bolt doesn't come to where a stud will stand.

If you have a concrete block wall, hold the concrete in place by pushing wads of paper down each opening where the anchor bolt will go. Fill the top of each opening with concrete and anchor the bolt vertically in place. Leave 2½ inches exposed.

When the concrete has set, place lengths of 2 × 6 wood exactly in line over the foundation on top of the anchor bolts. Then tap the sill with a hammer above each bolt. Using the indentations as a guide, drill holes for the anchor bolts. When the sill is bolted in place all around, you're ready to start putting up walls. (See the individual styles of greenhouses for more details.)

Water Lines

It is best to run water lines to the greenhouse entirely underground, so that they are out of sight and won't freeze in the winter.

Before pouring the footing, lay the pipes in a trench that runs under it. You don't have to install the water lines fully: just lay in a section of plastic

Precast Pier Foundation

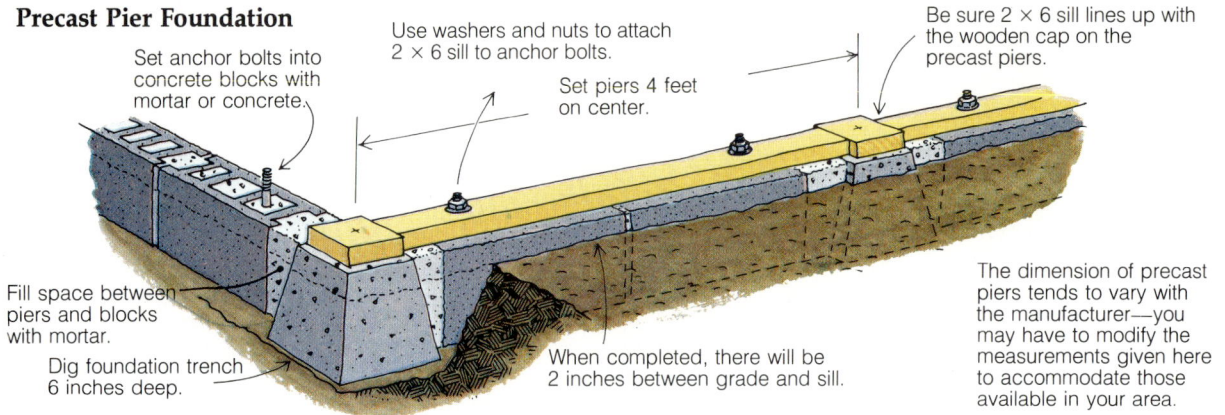

Set anchor bolts into concrete blocks with mortar or concrete.

Use washers and nuts to attach 2 × 6 sill to anchor bolts.

Set piers 4 feet on center.

Be sure 2 × 6 sill lines up with the wooden cap on the precast piers.

Fill space between piers and blocks with mortar.

Dig foundation trench 6 inches deep.

When completed, there will be 2 inches between grade and sill.

The dimension of precast piers tends to vary with the manufacturer—you may have to modify the measurements given here to accommodate those available in your area.

Poured Foundation

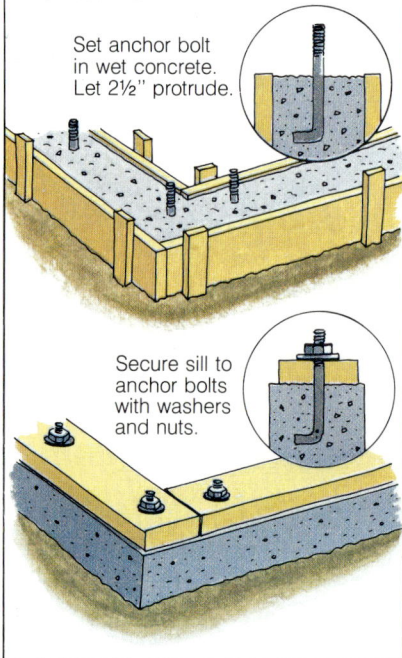

Set anchor bolt in wet concrete. Let 2½" protrude.

Secure sill to anchor bolts with washers and nuts.

pipe (PVC) that you can connect later. If you forget, or if you already have a greenhouse foundation, you can dig down and shove the PVC pipe through, since it is quite flexible. Another alternative is to lay 4-inch plastic drain pipe under the footing. Then you can run any pipes or electrical lines through it if you need to.

If you want to put water pipes through a concrete block wall, first score the block with a circle that is slightly larger than the pipe. Tap it out with a cold chisel and run the pipe through. Use a mortar mix to fill the hole around the pipe.

The only complication in hooking up water lines comes in tying into your main supply line. Whether you do this outside or have to go under the house, the easiest water-pipe material to work with is PVC. The plastic cuts easily and glues together in seconds. It is also flexible, which makes it easier for you to go around curves or under footings. Check your local building code, however. Some communities prohibit the use of plastic pipe.

If you are in an area with little or no freezing and you want only a cold-water tap in the greenhouse, hooking into an outside spigot is easy. (Consider carefully, however; if the exposed line freezes up, the easiest way may not be the best.)

If you do decide to run cold water from an outside spigot, first check the pipe carefully to see what size it is, and whether it has male or female fittings. Then make your purchases. Now, with the water shut off, attach a T-fitting and screw the spigot back on one side.

Cold Water to the Greenhouse

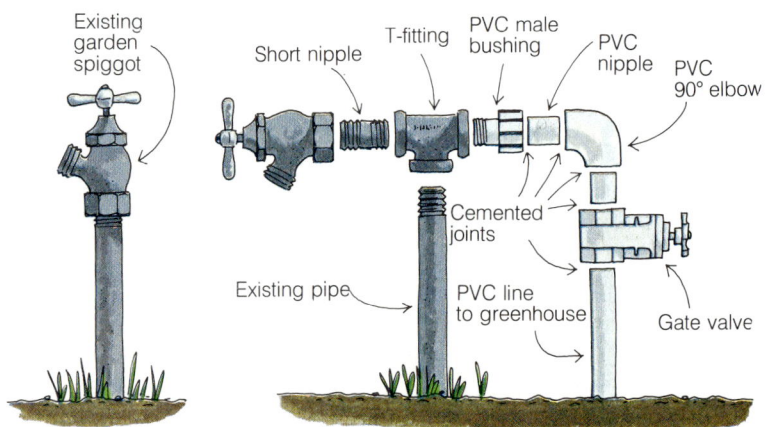

Existing garden spiggot

Short nipple

T-fitting

PVC male bushing

PVC nipple

PVC 90° elbow

Cemented joints

Existing pipe

PVC line to greenhouse

Gate valve

Your greenhouse line will come from the other side. The line can be as small as ½ inch if the water doesn't have to move a long distance. But a ¾-inch line would give more water and probably be more practical. If the water must travel 100 feet or more, you might want to go to a 1-inch line.

To hook up the greenhouse water line, first screw a PVC bushing onto the T-fitting. Glue a short length of pipe into that and then add a 90° elbow that points straight down. From this elbow you can run a line into the ground and over to your greenhouse. Install a PVC gate valve just above the ground. This will allow you to shut off the water to the greenhouse if the line ever springs a leak.

Hot water. If you want hot water in the greenhouse, you have to tie into the hot-water-heater supply lines in your house. In many cases, these are copper pipes. They can be connected to plastic water lines, but be sure you are using a type of plastic that is rated for hot water service. To connect this line you must install a copper T-joint in the pipes. This requires moderate skill in using a propane torch and solder to "sweat" the fittings. However, if you take your water-pipe plans to a plumbing shop, they will give you all the necessary fittings.

PVC pipe. PVC pipe comes in a variety of sizes and strengths to withstand different water pressures. For home use, you will want "Schedule 40," which is more than adequate for residential water pressures. The pipe can be cut with a hacksaw or a regular crosscut saw. After cutting, smooth the inside burred edge with a pocketknife or rough sandpaper. Sand the outside of the pipe and the inside of the coupling to roughen the surface before gluing. When you glue, apply a moderate coat to both the pipe and the coupling. Put them together quickly and give a quarter-turn twist. When putting on an angle coupling, be careful of the alignment—twist it exactly into place the first time. The special PVC glue sets in seconds.

Electric Connections

Unless you are experienced in working with electricity, this phase of your building will require an expert. An electrician's knowledge is needed to determine (1) how much electricity your building will require, and (2) whether a hookup can be made on your existing panel, or whether a separate meter and panel are needed. Fans, extra lights, and heat cables for propagation beds take careful figuring. When all are operating at once, they draw considerable power. Make sure you get help before you start.

You can save yourself considerable expense by doing all the groundwork in anticipation of the electrician. Check with the building code office for the size of wire needed; then buy that size and the length required, as well as the necessary plugs. Lay the wire in plastic conduit tubing at least 3 feet underground from the greenhouse to where it will enter the residence. With everything ready, the electrician can complete the hookups in a minimum of time.

A Variety of Plans

Here are several plans for different kinds of greenhouses. Since this is *your* greenhouse, designed for *your* style of gardening, select the plan that comes closest to what you want. Then use your own ingenuity—and perhaps advice from an experienced builder—to adapt it to your space and circumstances.

The attached greenhouse. The most practical greenhouse of all is one that is part of your own house. This type offers distinct advantages: it's close, which is much appreciated during the cold winter months, and construction is easier, because one wall of the greenhouse is actually your house wall. This also makes the structure better braced.

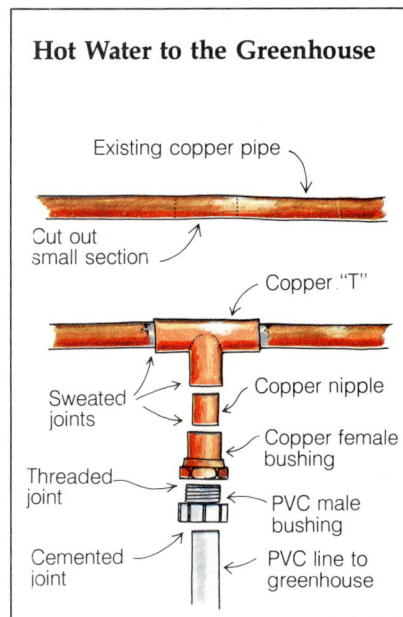

Hot Water to the Greenhouse

Existing copper pipe

Cut out small section

Copper "T"

Sweated joints

Copper nipple

Copper female bushing

Threaded joint

PVC male bushing

Cemented joint

PVC line to greenhouse

An 8 × 12 lean-to model is one of the simplest to put together. Once the foundation is down and all the supplies are on hand, two people can easily put it up in a weekend. It is made from 2 × 4 redwood or treated wood and fiberglass panels treated for greenhouse use.

This section will take you through some of the construction details. Even if you aren't an experienced builder, you can put this greenhouse together. After learning these basics, you can expand on them or build other styles of greenhouses.

This greenhouse is built against a south-facing wall. The first step is to put in a simple foundation. Lay it out and square it, as previously described. Because this greenhouse is so light, you can use a simpler foundation: precast concrete piers spaced 4 feet apart. Once you have put the concrete blocks in place with 2 inches showing, tie them together with a 2 × 4 rot-proof wooden sill. Construct the walls in units and nail them to this sill. The back wall is a house wall directly under an overhanging eave. Fasten a 2 × 6 ledger board 12 feet long to the house wall, using lag screws sunk into every other stud. Set the bottom of the ledger board at 8 feet high.

The next step is the front wall. In these plans, the front wall is 6 feet high and angled back at a 70° slope to catch the winter sun more effectively. This process is described in more detail in the solar greenhouse section, pages 62–77. Angling is not a difficult trick, but if this is your first construction experience, you'll find it easier to make the front wall vertical.

For a 6-foot-high wall, cut the studs 5 feet 9 inches long, which allows 3 inches for the top and bottom plates. The plates are the horizontal members that the vertical wall studs are attached to, top and bottom; the rafters lie across them at the top. The plates can be made from 2 × 4s.

Place studs and roof rafters 2 feet on-center and cover with 4-foot-wide panels of fiberglass (corrugated on the roof and flat on the sides).

To lay out the wall, put the top and bottom plates side by side flat on the ground or driveway. Mark off every 2 feet on the boards, using a carpenter's square to mark both plates at the same time. One of the legs of your carpenter's square is 1½ inches wide, the same as a 2 × 4. Lay it directly over the center of the mark, and pencil in lines on each side.

This attached greenhouse traps the heat of the winter sun, producing an inside temperature of 80°F.

Marking Plates for Studs

Lay the top and bottom plates side by side and mark off "on-center" dimensions, in this case every 2 feet.

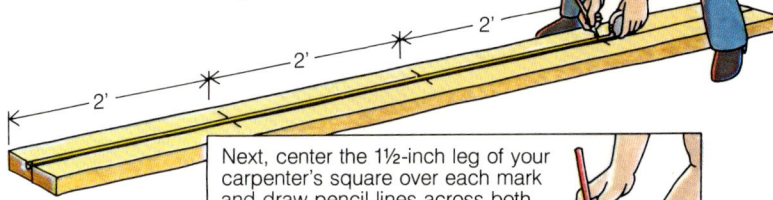

2'   2'   2'

Next, center the 1½-inch leg of your carpenter's square over each mark and draw pencil lines across both plates on each side of it.

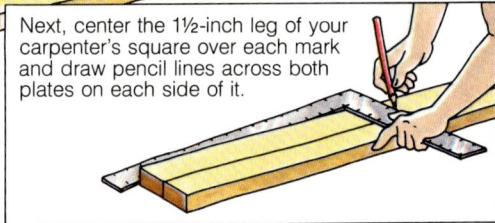

Lay out the wall with plates and studs in place and then nail together. Stand on one stud while nailing on the plate to keep the frame from shifting.

Note that the on-center distance between the first stud and the second is only 23¼ inches. The extra ¼ inch will be taken up outside by overlapping one extra ridge when you put on the corrugated fiberglass.

A vent in the front wall and on the roof is essential to prevent overheating during summer months. You can use a jalousie window, as in this version, or build a wood-frame and fiberglass vent.

You're now ready to raise the first wall. With friends helping, place the wall on the foundation and nail and brace it. Next come walls, which go up in basically the same way as the front wall did.

Allowing for the 3½-inch width of the end studs on the front wall, the plates on the 8-foot end walls will be 7 feet 8½ inches long. The studs for the end walls will be 5 feet 9 inches, the same as the front wall, and again 2 feet on-center. Cut, mark, and assemble the end wall without the door, just as you did the front wall.

For the end wall with the door, mark and construct it similarly; however, leave a space in the center for the width of your 30-inch door plus ¼ inch. Frame it with studs and then nail in cross braces on each side to keep the wall from shivering every time you close the door.

Note that the door on this plan is only 5 feet 9 inches high. You may have to duck a little to go through. If you want a taller door, refer to the alternate (and more difficult to construct) end wall plan that will accommodate a standard 30-inch by 80-inch door.

Nail the end walls into place, as you did the front wall. Again, double check that they are vertical.

With both end walls in place, you're ready to raise the roof. The roof consists of 2 × 4 rafters, 2 feet on-center. Line these up with the studs in the front wall. Attach them to the ledger board on the back wall with metal joist hangers and nail them to the top plate of the front wall.

Start by putting an uncut 2 × 4 rafter in place, mark how it must be cut to fit in the joist hanger, and angle down to the wall. With the rafter held against the end of the plate, use a pencil to mark the angle of the cut so it will lie flush on top of the plate. When you have cut and rechecked that rafter, use it as a pattern to cut the other rafters. Note that if you have a vertical front wall 8 feet out from your house, you will have to buy the standard 10-foot lengths of 2 × 4 and cut them to fit. At each end of the roof, put two 2 × 4

Attached Greenhouse

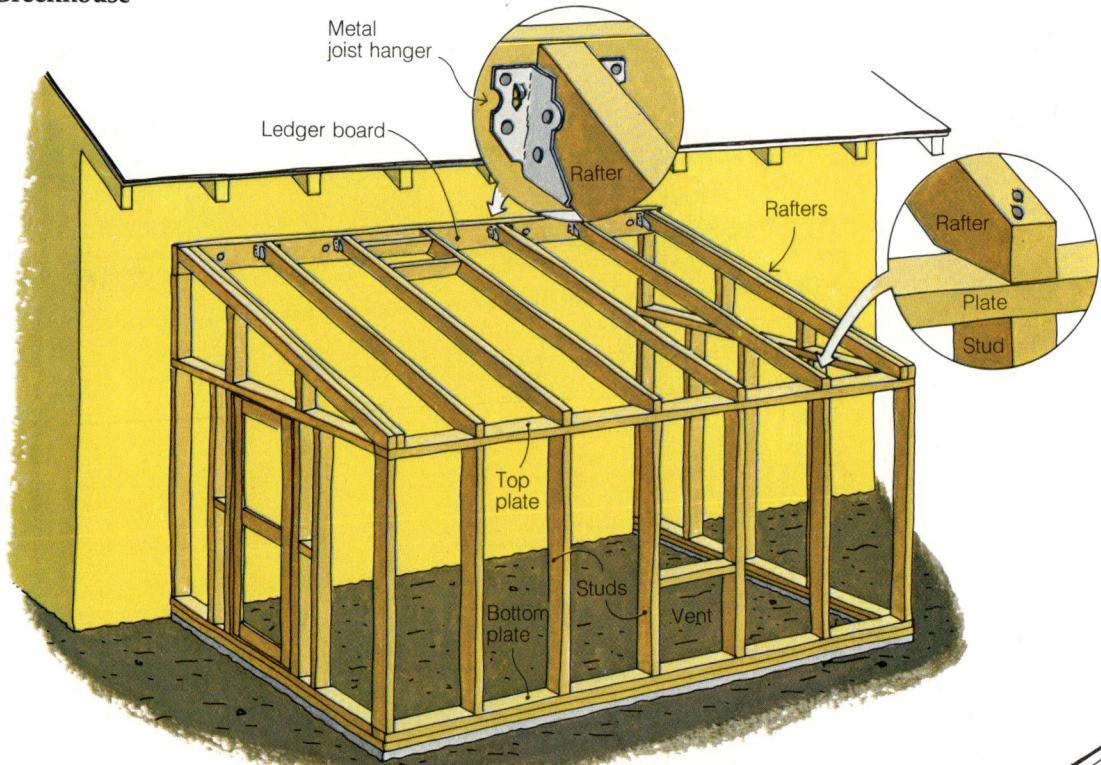

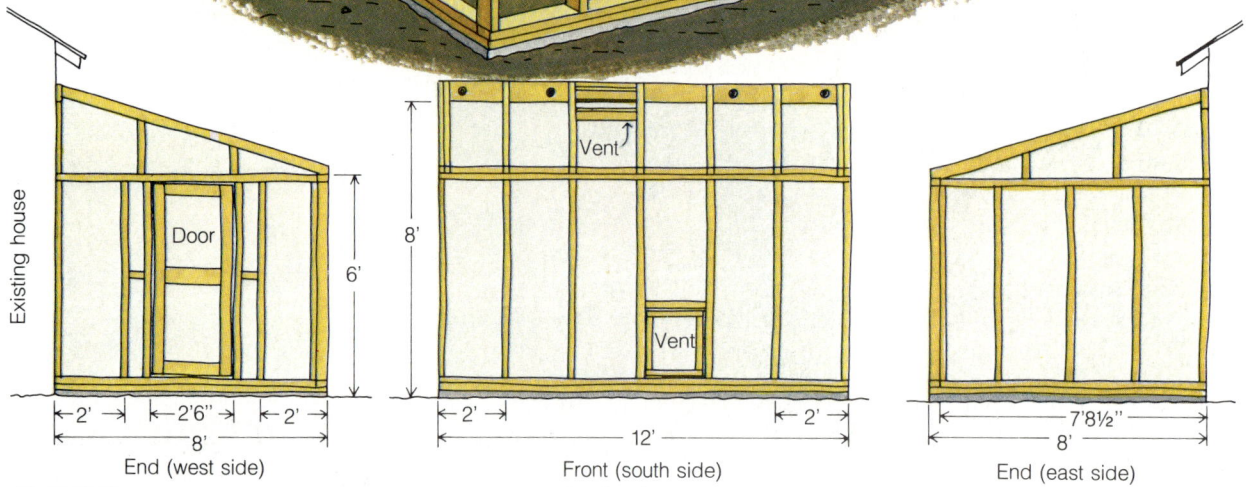

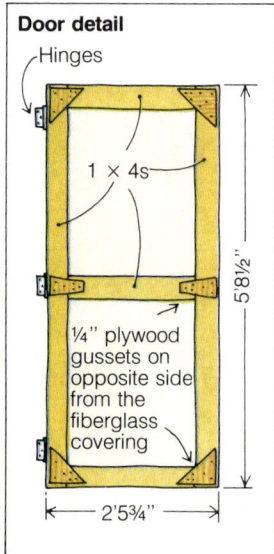

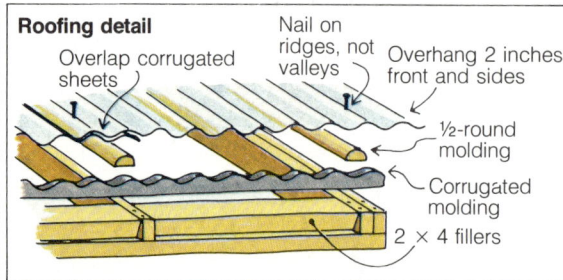

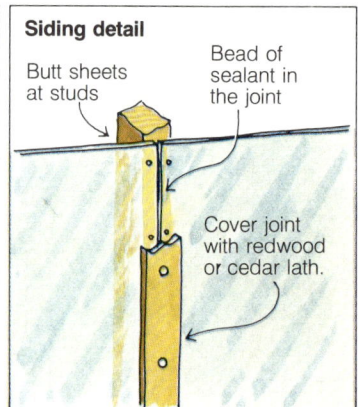

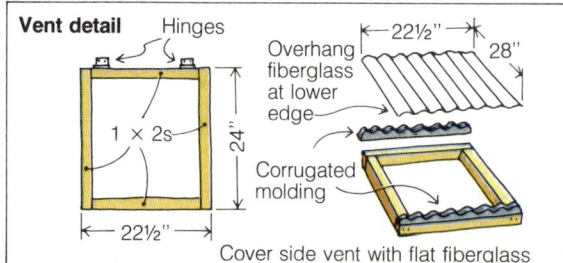

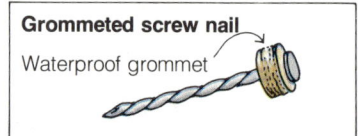

Metal joist hanger

Ledger board

Rafter

Rafters

Rafter

Plate

Stud

Top plate

Studs

Bottom plate

Vent

Existing house

Door

6'

2' | 2'6" | 2'

8'

End (west side)

Vent

8'

Vent

2' | 12' | 2'

Front (south side)

7'8½"

8'

End (east side)

Door detail

Hinges

1 × 4s

5'8½"

¼" plywood gussets on opposite side from the fiberglass covering

2'5¾"

Roofing detail

Overlap corrugated sheets

Nail on ridges, not valleys

Overhang 2 inches front and sides

½-round molding

Corrugated molding

2 × 4 fillers

Vent detail

Hinges

1 × 2s

24"

22½"

Overhang fiberglass at lower edge

Corrugated molding

22½"

28"

Cover side vent with flat fiberglass

Siding detail

Butt sheets at studs

Bead of sealant in the joint

Cover joint with redwood or cedar lath.

Grommeted screw nail

Waterproof grommet

rafters together to make a 4 × 4. This makes it easy for you to nail in the vertical pieces that fill in the angle between the top plate on the wall and the rafters. These pieces are not needed for support, only for something on which to nail the covering. Put one against the house wall between the top plate and ledger board, and one or two others where you see fit.

Next, cut short lengths of 2 × 4s to fill in between the rafters over the front plate. Nail the wide part of the 2 × 4 flush with the top of the rafters just at the front edge.

Vents. The vents are essentially frames to hold pieces of fiberglass that fit in between the studs or rafters. The construction of the roof vent is described here. The vent in the front wall is built the same way, but covered with flat fiberglass to match the wall.

Start by making a frame of 2 × 2s that is 24 inches long and 22½ inches wide, just able to fit between the studs or rafters. Tack redwood corrugated molding, or rubber molding, on the top and bottom widths, and attach a 28-inch length of fiberglass roofing. The 4-inch overhang in front assures no leaks.

Since you cannot nail through the panels without breaking them, lay them in place and drill holes with a 5/32-inch bit, 12 inches apart down the rafters. Use aluminum nails with neoprene washers to prevent any leaks. Nail through every third ridge of the fiberglass on cross braces. The nails you will buy with which to attach the fiberglass are called screwnails. They have a waterproofing grommet attached and a wide screw thread, but you hammer them in. To prevent leakage, always put the nail through a ridge in the plastic rather than a gutter. Don't hammer the nail in too far—just enough so the head and grommet are snug and secure with the plastic.

From the back of the roof frame, where the vent will hinge, measure down 2 feet and put a cross brace. The vent frame should fit smoothly into this opening. With it in place, nail quarter-round molding to the rafters and braces right beneath the frame to support it. Nail the roofing panels in place with an allowance for the vent openings. Then install the vents and hinge them to the back plate. Use a hook and eyebolt fastener to keep them from blowing open.

Alternate Door-Wall Layout

This is an alternate framing layout for the door end (west wall) that you may use if you desire a standard (30" × 80") door.

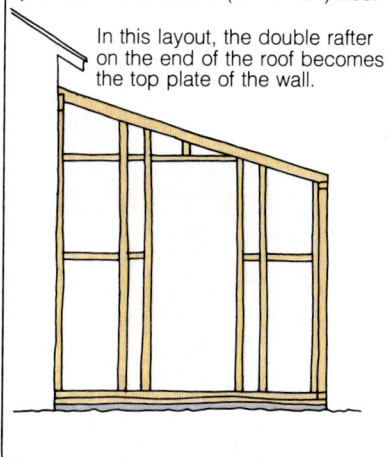

In this layout, the double rafter on the end of the roof becomes the top plate of the wall.

With walls of flat fiberglass (easily cut with tin snips), and a corrugated roof of the same material, this greenhouse will be nearly draft-proof after applying sealant at the joints between panels and insulating foam molding at the top and bottom of the roof panels.

Roof and sides. Once you've done all the framing and completed both vents, you are finally ready to finish the roof and walls.

Nail on corrugated foam molding at the top (along the ledger board) and bottom (across the rafters and filler 2 × 4s). This molding follows the same waves as the fiberglass panels and prevents drafts. If you feel it is necessary you can put half-round molding strips down each rafter to support the corrugated fiberglass. If you use rubber or redwood molding, lay a thin bond of sealant on the molding before you nail the fiberglass panels in place.

Put the panels in place with a 2-inch overhang in front for water runoff. Cut the panels to fit flush with the two vent openings. Across the front, where strong winds may pull the roof loose, put a nail in every ridge for extra insurance.

Its best to cover the walls with flat fiberglass. This makes a tighter fit under the roofline, and is easier to cut than corrugated fiberglass. Measure and cut the front panels first; nail them in place only after you are sure each panel is square. Lay a bead of sealant over each joint and then cover it with strips of redwood lath.

Cover the sides in the same way, using redwood lath to hold the panels tightly under the slightly extended roof.

Floor. The easiest way to floor a greenhouse is to leave the ground bare and use part of it for planting. The problem with this method, however, is that the center walkway generally turns to mud as you water plants and as humidity builds up in the greenhouse. One way to counter this is by laying natural flagstone, large paving blocks, or round concrete pads, available at many garden supply centers.

Many gardeners like to make a simple but effective floor of 3 to 4 inches of gravel. It keeps feet out of the mud, it's inexpensive, and it's easy to apply. You can water freely in the greenhouse and let the water run into the gravel, where it wil help increase humidity.

Some people build on a poured concrete slab, but this is costly and unwise. It means a lot of extra work for you since you have to mop and sweep all the time to keep the floor clean.

One of the most attractive and practical floors is brick on sand. Not only do these floors stay clean because water and fine grit disappear through them, but the bricks catch and hold solar heat during the day and release it back into the greenhouse at night for added warmth. Black bricks will absorb more heat. Buy 3½ bricks per square foot of floor area.

After you've finished framing and glazing the greenhouse, put down a 3-inch layer of sand on the ground. You may first have to excavate the floor a little, so that by the time you finish with the sand and bricks it is not above the door sill.

Or you can place a brick walkway between 2 × 4s down the center of the greenhouse and spread gravel on the rest of the floor.

Before you start laying the bricks, experiment and see what pattern pleases you most. The simplest is the traditional running bond, which has straight, clean lines. The herringbone and basketweave patterns offer more visual variety, but are also more difficult to lay. Experiment and come up with your own patterns, perhaps using combinations of brick and patio blocks, or brick and redwood blocks.

After you put the sand in the greenhouse and spread it around so it is even and fairly level, dampen it thoroughly to settle it. Working on a piece of plywood to prevent your knees from digging up the sand, level a section along the back wall with a 2 × 4. Start laying the bricks in one corner, and keep working out from there. If you have benches down only one side, start opposite them so the less finished edge of bricks will end up under the benches.

As you lay the brick, always check your level. After you finish a section,

Cutting bricks to odd sizes is easy after a little practice. Below: Measure the brick to size and score it. Center: One sharp blow with a hammer and a cold chisel will break the brick. A 2 × 2 redwood baseboard can cover unevenly broken edges. Bottom: Set the bricks in place, leaving a gap of ⅛ inch between bricks.

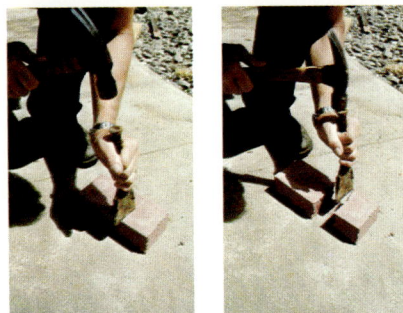

A Few Brick Patterns

Running bond (Traditional)

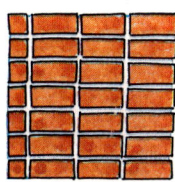
Jack-on-Jack

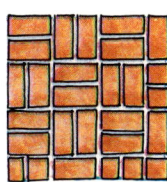
Basketweave

Half-basket weave

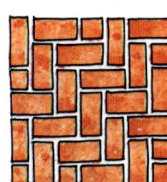
Herringbone

Angled herringbone

lay a 2 × 4 along a row of bricks and hammer it firmly to set and level them.

Set the bricks against each other as snugly as you can. There will still be about a ⅛-inch gap. These gaps will later be filled in with sand.

Bricks do not break cleanly, which is frustrating when you try to fit them into the leftover spaces against walls. To remedy this, you might want to rent a masonry saw. Otherwise, score the brick first with a cold chisel, and then make a single sharp cut. If, when you're done, the edges seem too uneven, hide them by laying down a 2 × 2 redwood baseboard all around.

After the bricks are in place, cover them with a layer of sand. Leave the layer of sand on the bricks for a couple of days while you walk around. The floor will quickly become as tight and firm as if it had been mortared. Then use a broom to sweep the sand back and forth until all the cracks are filled.

You should not wax a greenhouse floor because it should remain porous.

Gothic arch. This model is well suited to areas where there is just enough winter freezing to be troublesome to your plants or small potted fruit trees. It can be easily covered with polyethylene film or, for more permanence, with flat fiberglass panels. This greenhouse is also portable. (While it is designed to be lightweight and portable, it can be placed on a conventional foundation if you want permanence.)

Begin by making a base frame of two 1 × 8s cleated together to make a board 15 inches high. The frame should be 12 feet long and 8 feet 6 inches wide. Use wood treated with copper napthanate or another good preservative.

For the roof supports, cut 20 pieces of ¼-inch exterior grade plywood that are 4 inches wide and 8 feet long. Glue and nail each together in sets of two with galvanized nails, leaving the bottom 8 inches unglued and unnailed. Ten double bands will form the sides.

The next step is to frame in the end-support walls and the doors. At each end, cut an opening 2 feet 9 inches wide in the center of the top board of the frame. Notch two 6-foot lengths of 2 × 4s to fit flush with the bottom board of the frame. Nail on a 2-foot 9-inch door buck at the top; then nail each door frame into position.

For the ridge beam, cut 30° angles on each side of one edge of a 12-foot length of 2 × 10, and toenail it into place on the center of the door buck. To each side of the ridge beam, nail a 12-foot 1 × 6. This is the support for the bands of plywood rafters.

Put the rafters in place with galvanized wood screws on the ridge line, and nail and glue them around the frame. Start at one end with the band nailed and glued on the inside only. Curve it over the door frame and nail it there before screwing it into the ridge boards. Now nail and glue the outside flap to the frame. Complete both ends and then finish at the middle supports.

The gable openings above the doors at the ends are covered with pieces of ⅜-inch exterior-grade plywood cut to fit. Hinge these so they can be opened for ventilation. For additional ventilation, construct roof vents as described for the lean-to greenhouse on page 33.

Cover the sides with one piece of 16-foot-wide polyethylene stapled to the

After you have covered the bricks with sand and walked on them for a few days, use a broom to fill completely the cracks between the bricks with sand.

8'6"

2 × 4 door frame

Exterior view

Interior view

1 × 8s

5'9"

7'

6½"

1'3"

1'3"

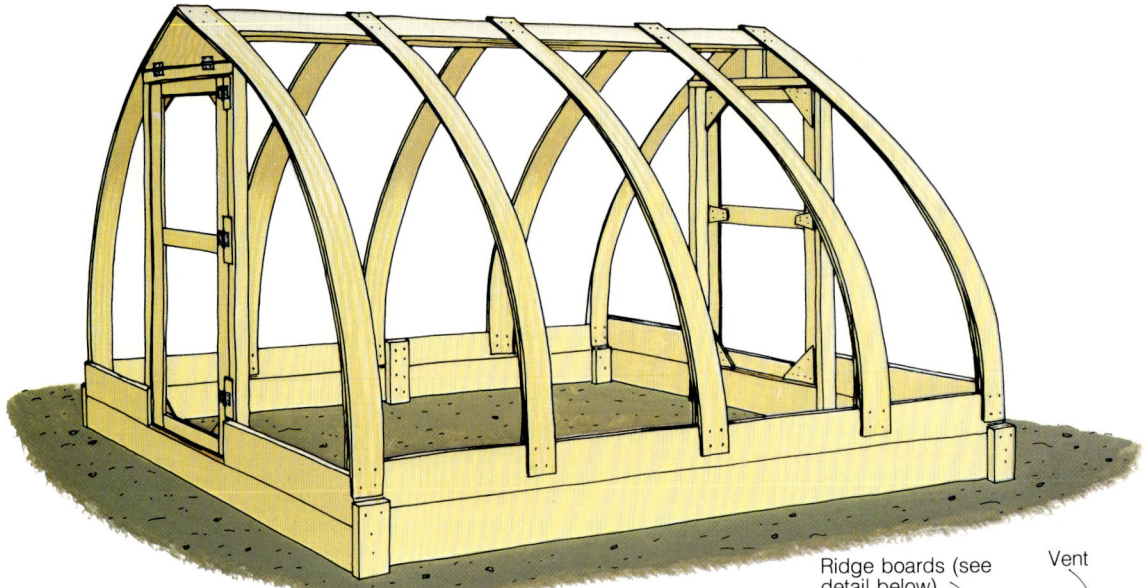

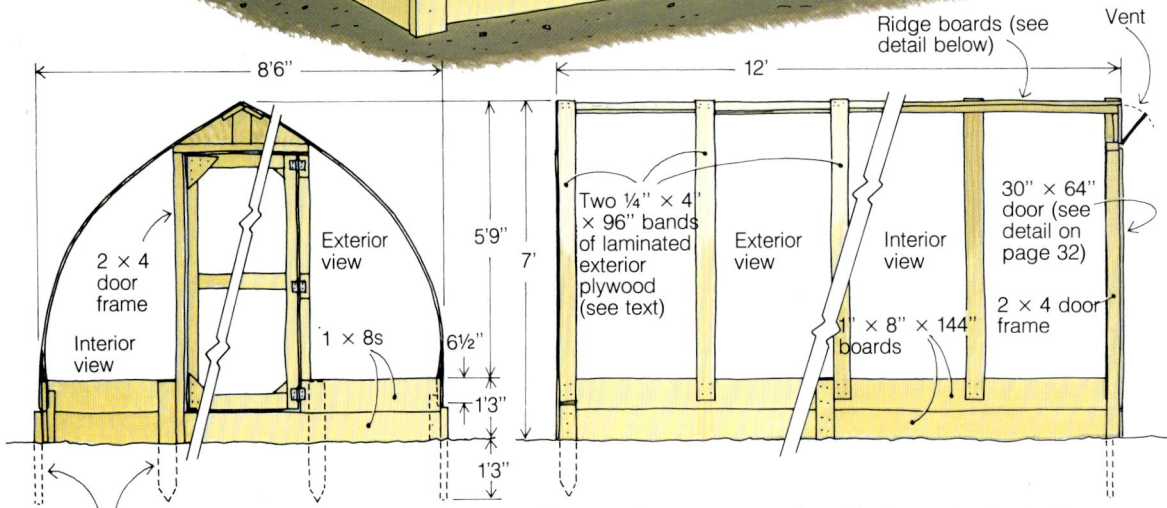

2 × 4 stakes at corners and door frames

Ridge boards (see detail below)

Vent

12'

Two ¼" × 4' × 96" bands of laminated exterior plywood (see text)

Exterior view

Interior view

1" × 8" × 144" boards

30" × 64" door (see detail on page 32)

2 × 4 door frame

Fasten entire structure together with glue and galvanized wood screws unless otherwise noted. Cover with UV-resistant polyethylene film, as described in text.

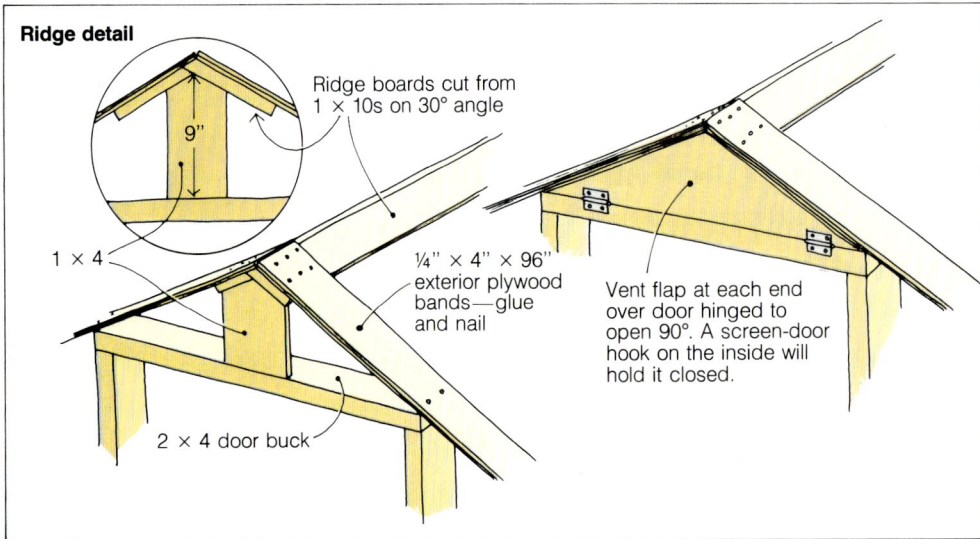

Ridge detail

9"

Ridge boards cut from 1 × 10s on 30° angle

1 × 4

¼" × 4" × 96" exterior plywood bands—glue and nail

2 × 4 door buck

Vent flap at each end over door hinged to open 90°. A screen-door hook on the inside will hold it closed.

base boards and stretched over the ridge of the greenhouse. Then staple smaller sheets of plastic over the ends, leaving the doorways clear.

The doors for this light greenhouse are made from 2 × 2s with one cross brace at the center. To give the door additional strength, nail on triangular plywood braces, or gussets, at each corner. Hinge at the top, bottom, and middle. Now, cover the doors with a polyethylene film that is resistant to ultraviolet damage, and your greenhouse is completed.

In windy areas, this greenhouse should be anchored to the ground. Set the greenhouse in the location you want and then drive two stakes 18 inches into the ground on each side of the doors and two on each side of the framework. Fasten the stakes to the frame with wood screws.

A-frame greenhouse. The A-frame's chief advantage lies in its easy construction. This particular model is also relatively small and lightweight, which makes it portable. It is also useful in areas that get a heavy snow load. This model is often covered on the outside with 8 mil plastic film of a type resistant to ultraviolet rays. For additional protection, essential in snow country, put another layer of ordinary 4 mil polyethylene inside to create a thermal barrier. It can also be covered with flat or corrugated fiberglass.

The base is made from four 10-foot pieces of 2 × 6 redwood or treated wood. (This greenhouse is designed to be portable, but it may also be placed on the conventional foundation described on pages 22–24.) For the rafters and end walls, you need fifteen 10-foot lengths of 2 × 3. The ridge board and door are made from a 1 × 4.

Put the frame together, using plywood gussets at the corners. To build, cut one rafter to fit and use it as the pattern for the nine other rafters. Build one wall with the 1 × 4 ridge board nailed to it, then stand and brace that wall in place. Next, nail the other five rafters in place. With the whole structure still braced, nail in the diagonal braces, then finish the end walls. To provide proper venting, frame in a 10-inch-diameter fan above the door and a louvered opening of the same size at the opposite end of the greenhouse, or use the ridge vent design described for the lean-to greenhouse on page 33. For additional ventilation a second vent can be installed at the base of the side wall.

Glazing of chicken-wire and polyethylene on a 2 × 2-inch-stock frame form the structure of this portable, lightweight A-frame greenhouse.

A-Frame Greenhouse

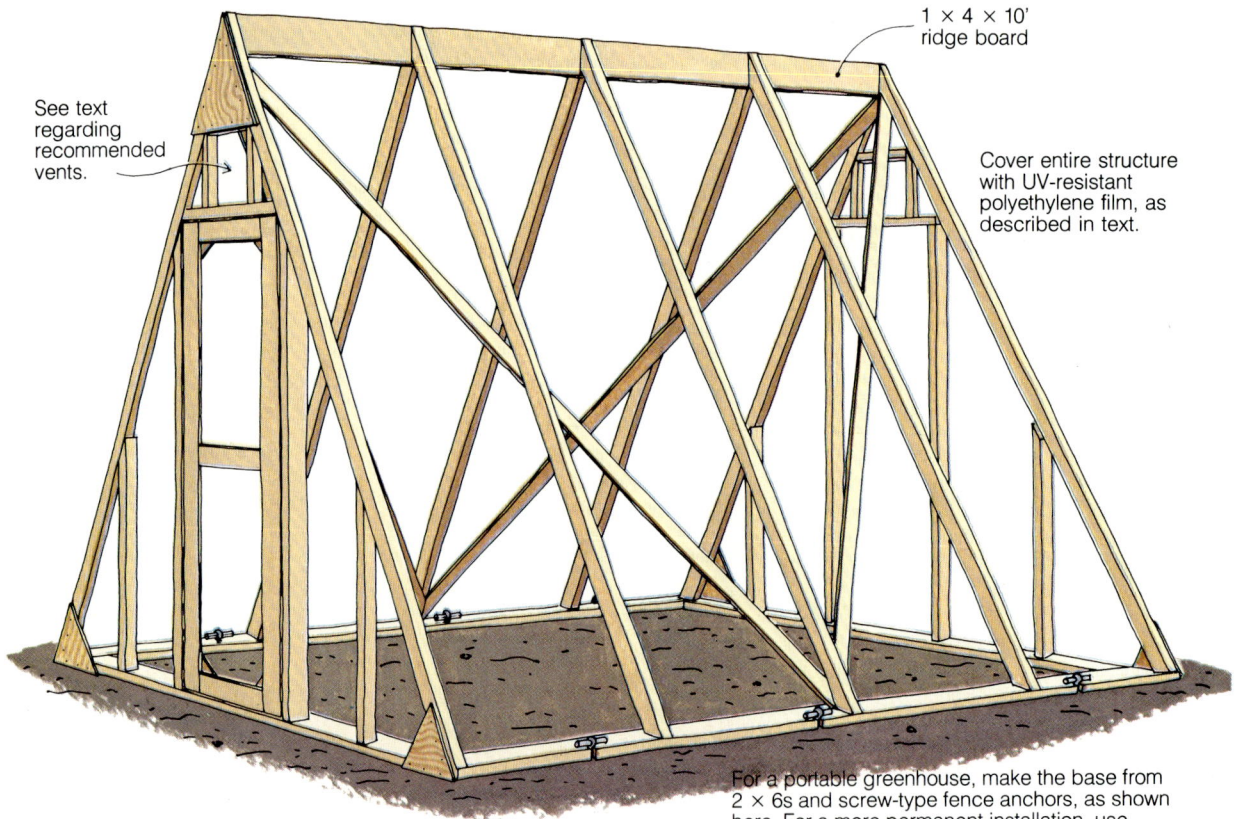

See text regarding recommended vents.

1 × 4 × 10' ridge board

Cover entire structure with UV-resistant polyethylene film, as described in text.

For a portable greenhouse, make the base from 2 × 6s and screw-type fence anchors, as shown here. For a more permanent installation, use a concrete foundation with 2 × 6 sill as described on pages 26 to 28.

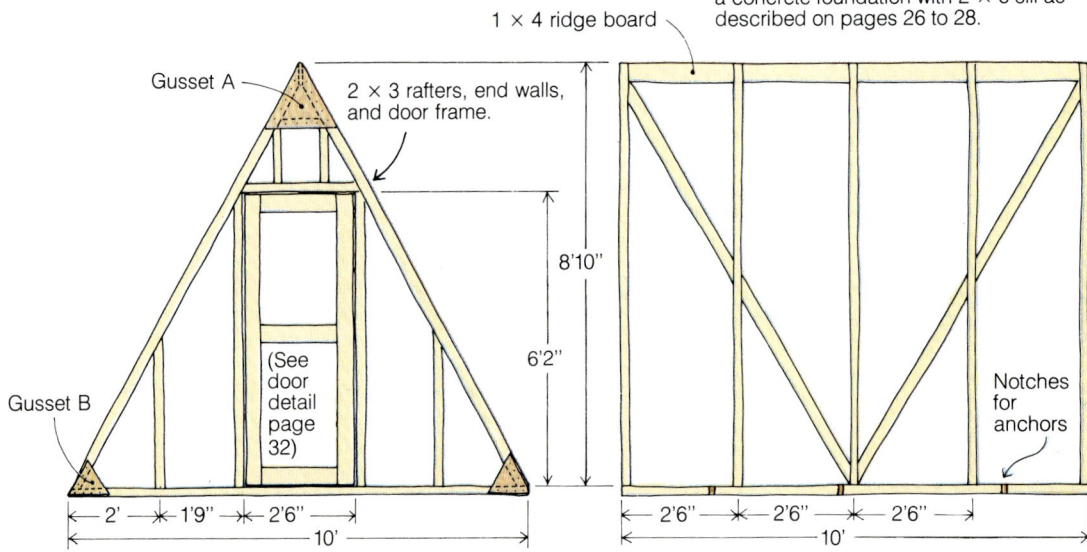

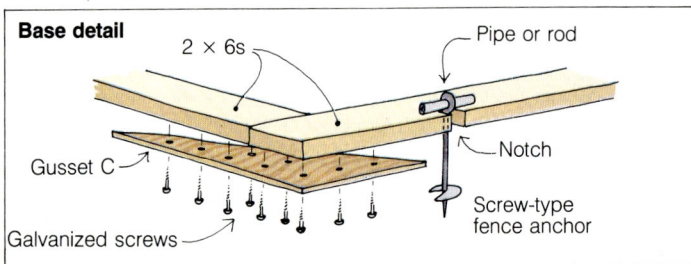

1 × 4 ridge board

Gusset A

2 × 3 rafters, end walls, and door frame.

8'10"

6'2"

(See door detail page 32)

Gusset B

Notches for anchors

2'   1'9"   2'6"

10'

2'6"   2'6"   2'6"

10'

Base detail

2 × 6s

Pipe or rod

Notch

Gusset C

Screw-type fence anchor

Galvanized screws

Cutting diagram for gussets
Use ¼" exterior plywood.

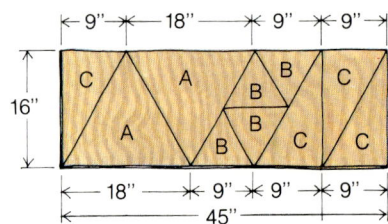

9"   18"   9"   9"

16"

C   A   B   B   C

A   B   B   C   C

18"   9"   9"   9"

45"

A bench across the far end and along the sides makes a good working space with ample headroom in the center.

Anchor the structure securely to the ground. One method is to use a screw-type fence anchor set into notches cut in the base and held with short pieces of rerod pushed through the screw eye.

Freestanding gambrel roof. This type of greenhouse goes up in sections. It lends itself readily to either a polyethylene or fiberglass covering. This type, which is built similar to many barns, has considerable structural strength. It is excellent in areas that have a heavy snowfall. One of the more time-consuming requirements is cutting the plywood gussets. To speed this up, cut one of each pattern, as shown in the cutting diagram, then use these to mark all the others. Also, carefully note the cutting diagram for the legs and rafters. After the legs and rafters are all cut, put them together with the gussets, using galvanized nails and waterproof glue.

For a 10- by 12-foot greenhouse, construct the frame by sinking 4-foot-long 4 × 4s about 3 feet into the ground. This leaves 12 inches exposed on which to nail the 1 × 12 redwood or treated wood frame around the base. (For greater permanence, this unit can also be placed on the foundation described on page 22.) To make the frame level, set the posts in about 30 inches. Then put the 1 × 12 frame in place and adjust it until it is level. Next, cut off any excess from the posts that project beyond the baseboard. The posts go 6 feet apart down the sides and 5 feet apart across the front and back. Across the top of the 4 × 4 posts goes a 2 × 4 sill. Mark the sill where the prefabricated center supports and end supports will go.

To frame up the greenhouse, put the end walls in place first, and brace securely. Put the two 1 × 4 purlins on the ridge, then put in the two center supports and hold them in place by nailing to the purlins. Double check that everything is square before nailing. Further strengthen the structure with 1 × 4 purlins at the middle and lower edge of the roof.

If you are using two layers of plastic, a small squirrel cage fan can be used to maintain the thermal layer of air between them. Install it at one end near the ridge line by mounting it to a plywood panel suspended from the end rafter. Cut a hole in the plywood for the fan to draw in air, and use flexible plastic tubing and a plastic pot with a hole cut in the bottom to direct the air between the two layers of plastic (see drawing on page 42).

Simplified gambrel roof. Here is an excellent style of framing for a small greenhouse. The trick to this one is finding and correctly cutting the angles for the roof.

Start by laying out an 8 × 12-foot foundation. If your climate is dry enough, this lightweight building can go directly on the ground. It would be better, however, to put it on a concrete block foundation. Once the sill is in place, build the two side walls, making them 4 feet 10 inches high so that a 5-foot length of fiberglass siding will fully cover the bottom sill.

To find the angles for the roof rafters, work on a piece of 4 × 8-foot plywood (the greenhouse is 8 feet wide). First, mark the center of the plywood along one of the long sides. Now diagram just one side of the roof.

With a length of 2 × 4 about 4 feet long, trace its outline on the plywood at an angle of your choice for the first leg of the roof. Now trace another outline over to the center of the plywood sheet for the second leg of the roof. Where the two traced patterns intersect, draw a line connecting the two intersection points to give you the angle of cut. The angle where the top leg meets the ridge board is found by drawing a vertical line down through it. The bottom edge of the plywood sheet provides the angle of cut where the rafters rest on the side wall plate.

Once all the rafter legs have been measured and cut, nail on a 1 × 4 at their tops and bottoms, just as if you were constructing a wall on the ground. When you're done, you'll have four roof sections. Put both lower sections on

Gambrel Roof Greenhouse

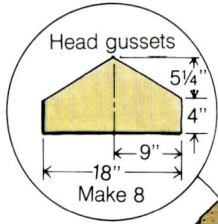

Head gussets

5¼"
4"
9"
18"
Make 8

Cover roof with corrugated fiberglass and the sides and ends with flat fiberglass. Or cover it all with a double layer of plastic film inflated by an electric blower (see text).

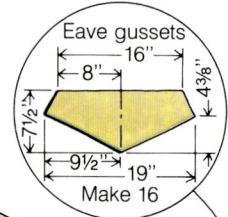

Eave gussets

16"
8"
4⅜"
7½"
9½" 19"
Make 16

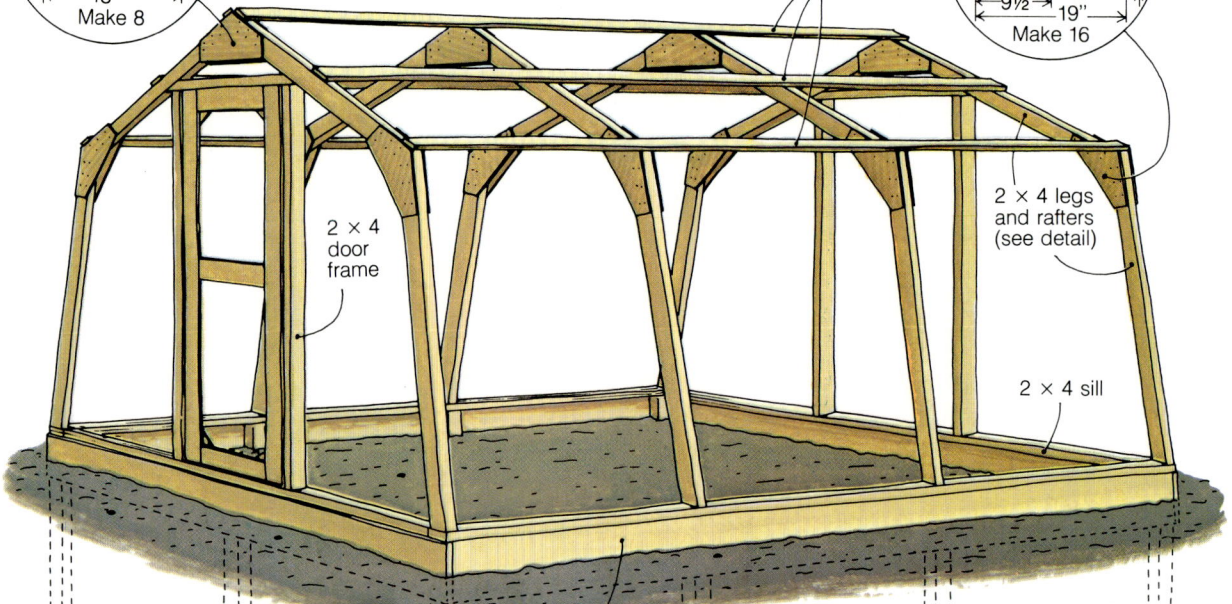

1 × 4 purlins

2 × 4 door frame

2 × 4 legs and rafters (see detail)

2 × 4 sill

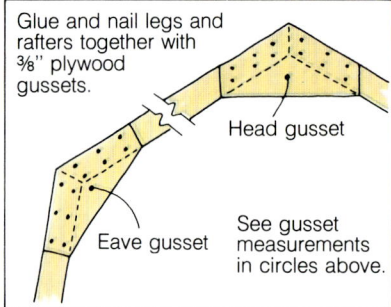

Glue and nail legs and rafters together with ⅜" plywood gussets.

Head gusset

Eave gusset

See gusset measurements in circles above.

1 × 12 board buried ½ below grade

4 × 4 posts set 30" deep and cut off 6" above grade

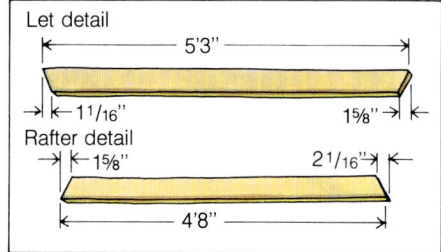

Let detail

5'3"
1¹¹/₁₆"
1⅝"

Rafter detail
1⅝"
2¹/₁₆"
4'8"

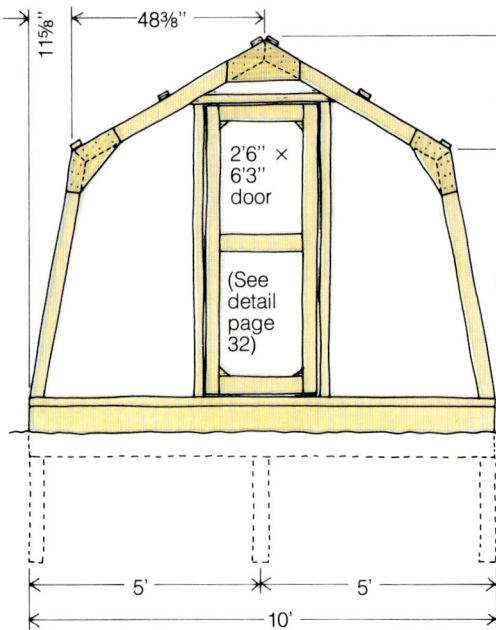

11⅝"
48⅜"

2'6" × 6'3" door

(See detail page 32)

61"

5'
5'
10'

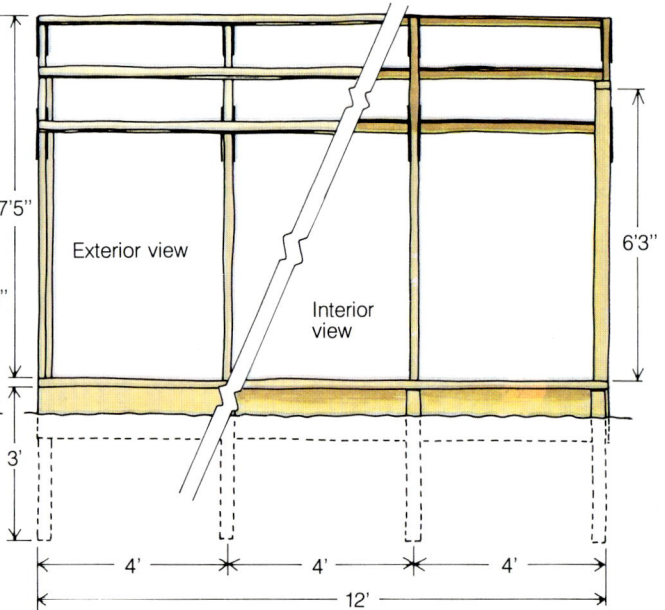

28"

7'5"

8'2"

Exterior view

Interior view

6'3"

3'

4'
4'
4'
12'

Simplified Gambrel Roof

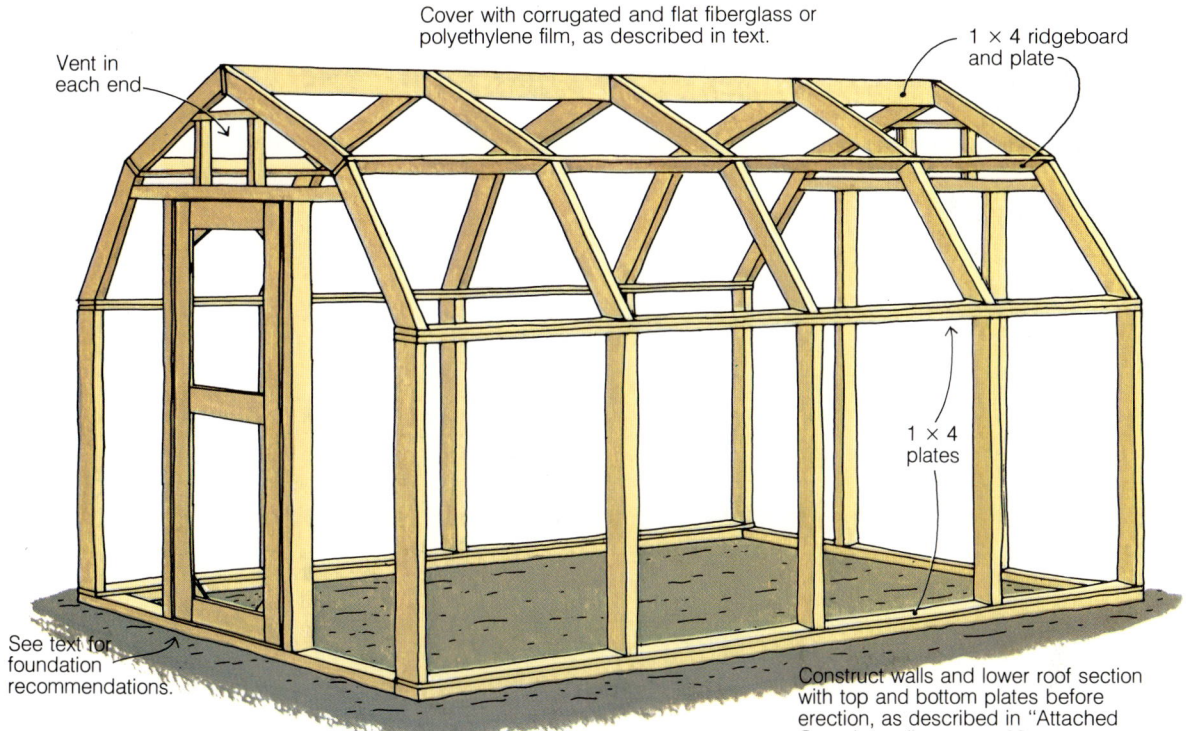

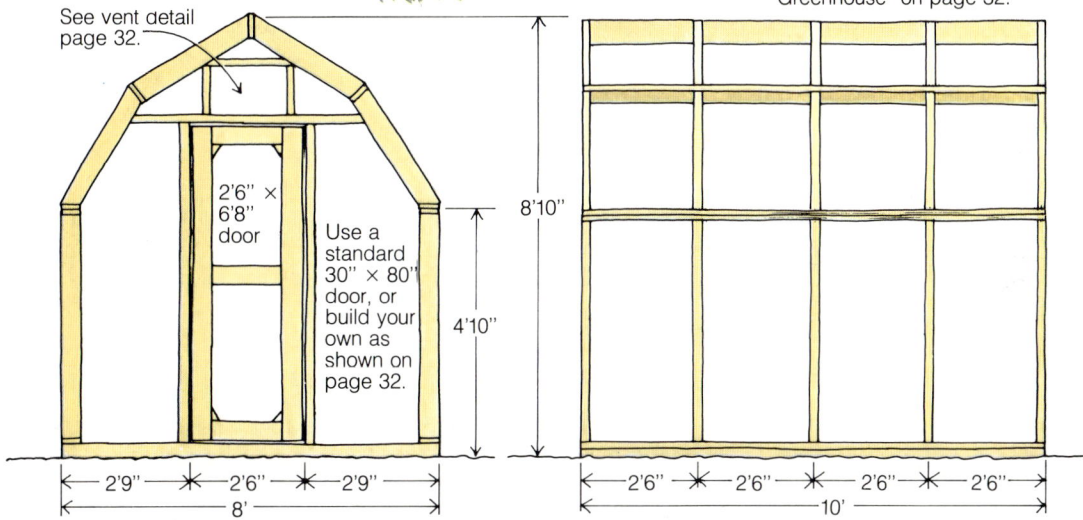

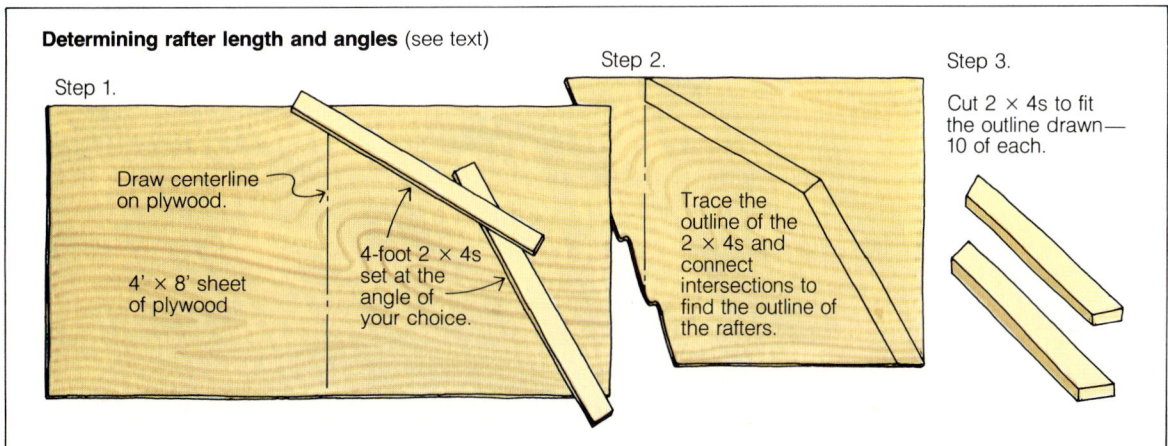

Cover with corrugated and flat fiberglass or polyethylene film, as described in text.

Vent in each end

1 × 4 ridgeboard and plate

1 × 4 plates

See text for foundation recommendations.

Construct walls and lower roof section with top and bottom plates before erection, as described in "Attached Greenhouse" on page 32.

See vent detail page 32.

2'6" × 6'8" door

Use a standard 30" × 80" door, or build your own as shown on page 32.

8'10"

4'10"

2'9"   2'6"   2'9"

8'

2'6"   2'6"   2'6"   2'6"

10'

Determining rafter length and angles (see text)

Step 1.

Draw centerline on plywood.

4' × 8' sheet of plywood

4-foot 2 × 4s set at the angle of your choice.

Step 2.

Trace the outline of the 2 × 4s and connect intersections to find the outline of the rafters.

Step 3.

Cut 2 × 4s to fit the outline drawn— 10 of each.

Inflated Plastic Film Covering
(*An alternative to fiberglass covering*)

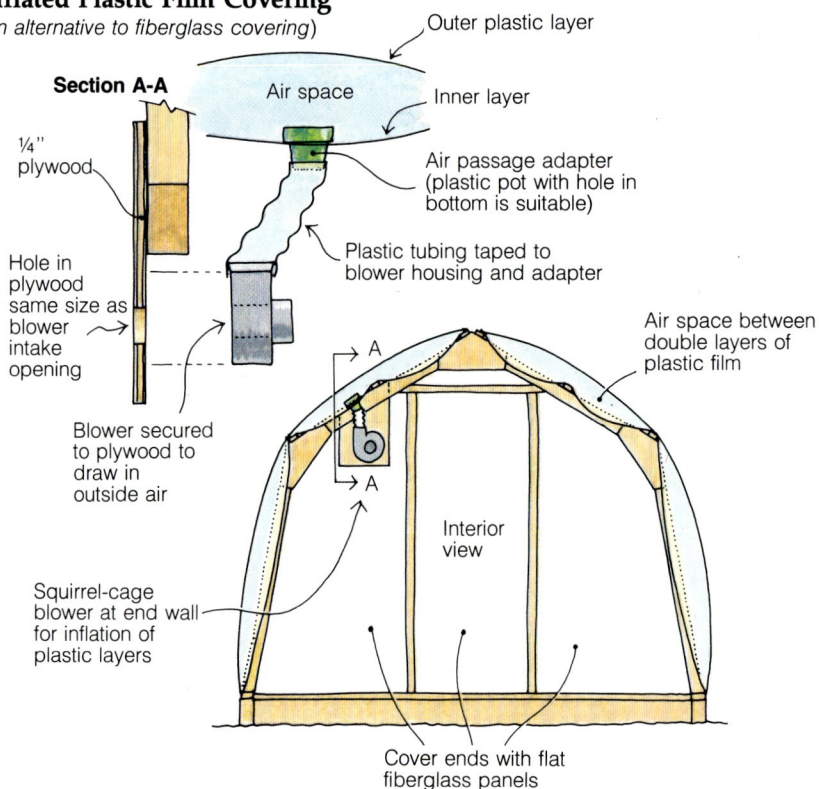

Outer plastic layer

Air space

Inner layer

Section A-A

Air passage adapter
(plastic pot with hole in
bottom is suitable)

¼"
plywood

Plastic tubing taped to
blower housing and adapter

Hole in
plywood
same size as
blower
intake
opening

Air space between
double layers of
plastic film

Blower secured
to plywood to
draw in
outside air

Interior
view

Squirrel-cage
blower at end wall
for inflation of
plastic layers

Cover ends with flat
fiberglass panels

top of the wall and brace them temporarily in place. To tie them together and support them, run a cross brace between each one at the top. Now put the two top components in place and nail. The end walls are made with 2 × 4s under each roof angle and under the center. Ventilators can be in the end walls or can be constructed in the upper sections of the roof, as described for the lean-to greenhouse on page 33.

A door can be cut to fit from 1 × 4s and covered with fiberglass. The structure can be anchored, if not on a foundation, then by drilling holes every 4 feet through the bottom plate and sill and driving a 3-foot length of rerod into the ground through the holes. Bend the top 2 inches at a 90° angle.

Snow-country greenhouse. This greenhouse has a steep A-frame roof that will shed snow quickly. It also has a continuous line of roof vents for natural cooling in the summer. The University of Connecticut plan calls for ten pressure-treated posts to be sunk about 2½ feet in the ground, with 3 feet 9 inches left above ground. To get these exact measurements, first sink the posts and then use a line level before cutting the tops off to the required height. If the rafters are to fit smoothly, it is important to set the posts accurately with the required distance of 8 feet 3¾ inches apart. Each 2 × 4 rafter is 6 feet long, with a 45° angle at both ends. Alternate 1 × 4 rafters are 4 feet long, with a 45° angle at the bottom and the other end cut square.

After the posts are in place, put the 2 × 4 continuous top plate all around on top of the posts. Next, put on the 2 × 4 side plate, which helps support the rafter ends.

Now frame in the doors at both ends and use that frame to support the end rafters. After nailing the end rafters to the 1 × 8 ridge board, put up the other rafters, spaced 3 feet 1⅜ inches on-center.

Add the 2 × 4 blocking to frame the vent openings. Then toenail the 1 × 4 rafters into place, centered on the blocking.

Frame the vents with 2 × 2 and cut according to the diagram to fit between each rafter.

Snow Country Greenhouse

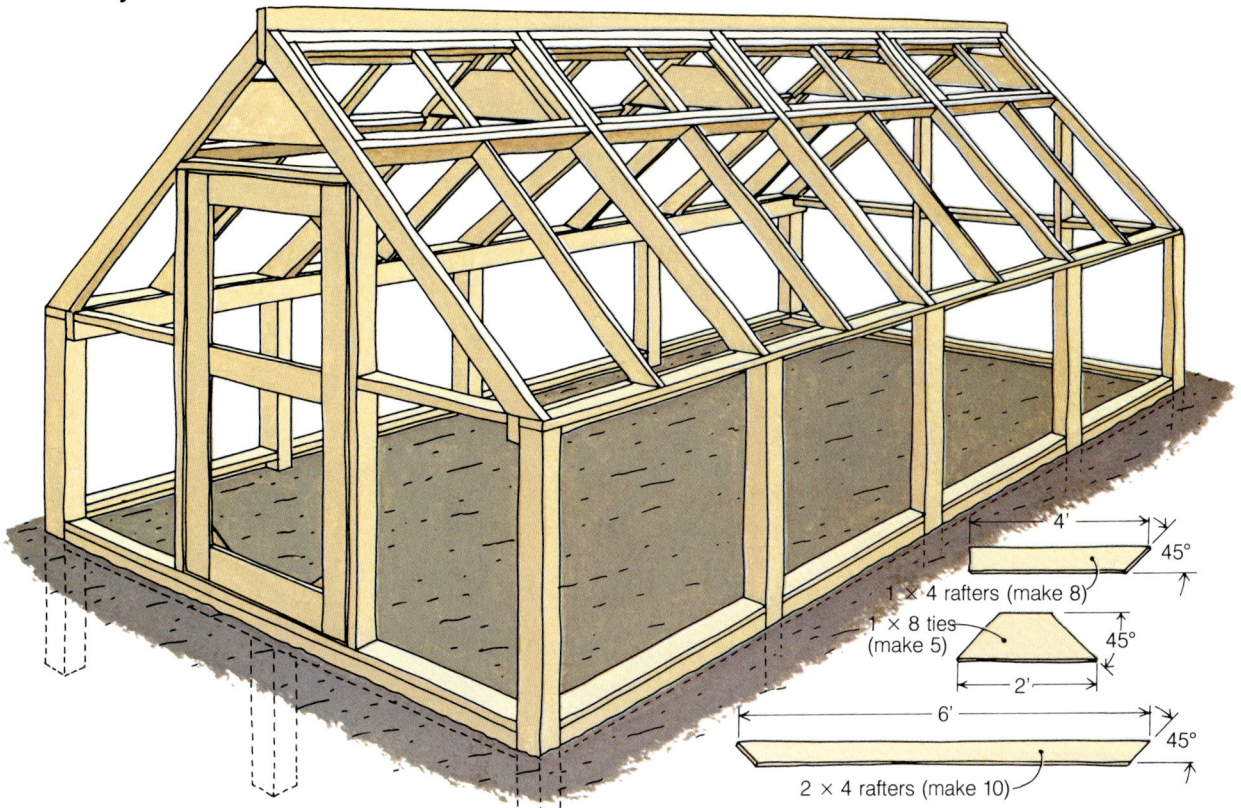

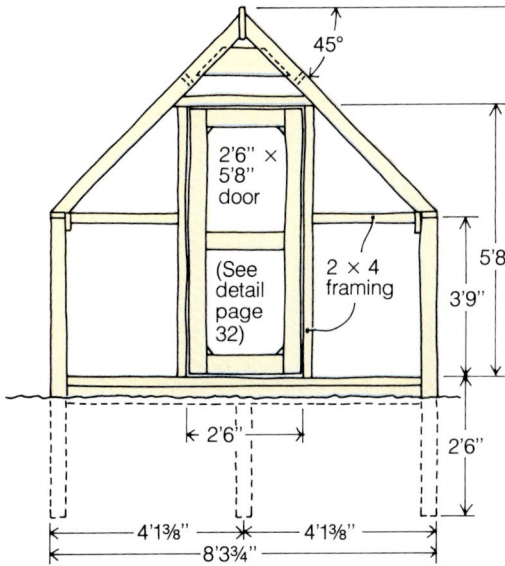

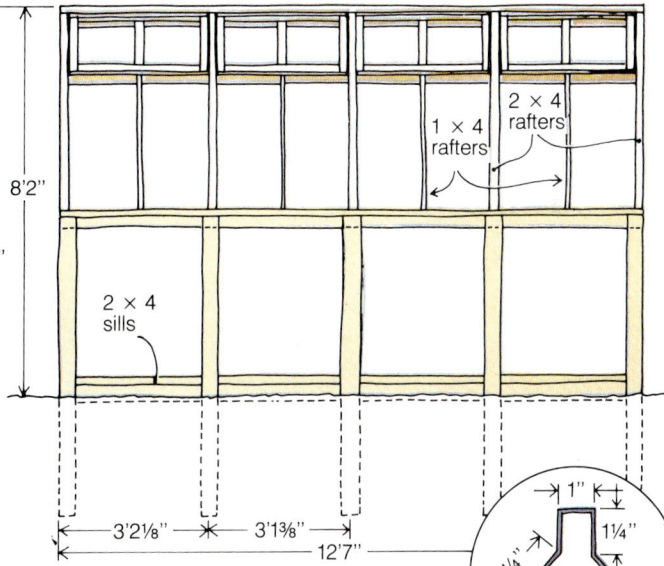

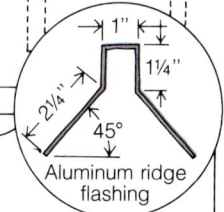

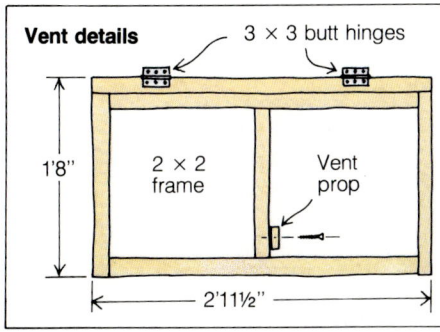

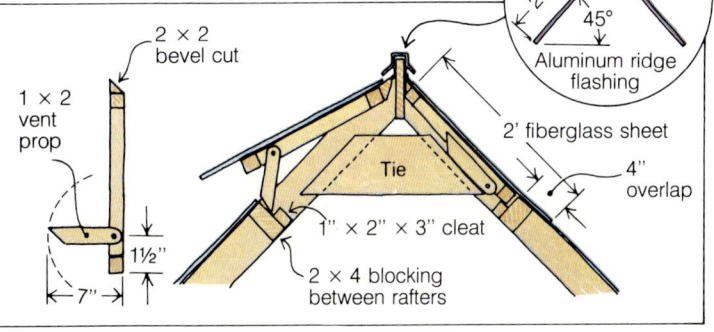

1 × 4 rafters (make 8)

4'
45°

1 × 8 ties (make 5)

2'
45°

2 × 4 rafters (make 10)

6'
45°

45°

2'6" × 5'8" door

(See detail page 32)

2 × 4 framing

8'2"

5'8"

3'9"

2'6"

2'6"

4'1⅜"

4'1⅜"

8'3¾"

1 × 4 rafters

2 × 4 rafters

2 × 4 sills

3'2⅛"

3'1⅜"

12'7"

1"

1¼"

2¼"

45°

Aluminum ridge flashing

2' fiberglass sheet

4" overlap

Vent details

3 × 3 butt hinges

2 × 2 frame

Vent prop

1'8"

2'11½"

2 × 2 bevel cut

1 × 2 vent prop

1½"

7"

Tie

1" × 2" × 3" cleat

2 × 4 blocking between rafters

This indoor gardener gives her hanging *Cattleya* orchid special care.

Greenhouses You Can Buy

You may want a greenhouse but lack the time, tools, or desire to build one from scratch. You needn't be left out in the cold because there's a wide range of greenhouses you can purchase. (See page 141 for a list of greenhouse sources.)

Two factors to consider are how much (or little) work you want to do, and how much you can spend. If you feel particularly energetic, get started with a plan from this book or purchase a less challenging, prefabricated type that requires only assembling. Or you may choose a model installed by professional contractors. Lance Walheim, an experienced greenhouse grower, offers these comments on buying a greenhouse of very high quality:

"I would always have a cement floor contoured toward drainage holes leading to the outside. I think it's important to keep a greenhouse clean and to be able to hose it out as often as possible. Debris or soil can be hosed through large, closely spaced drainage holes. Cement floors also eliminate the problem of disease generated by damp open soil areas.

"Strong benches are essential. They should allow for maximum drainage or somehow prevent buildup of water, which can harbor disease and promote wood rot.

"For glazing, I prefer corrugated fiberglass. It is durable, lightweight, and easy to handle.

"Propagation is easiest with a mist system and electric bottom heat. A separate compartment in the greenhouse is best for this purpose—it is much easier to control the environment on a smaller scale.

"Heating and cooling are the keys to successful greenhouse growing. Even heat distribution is best achieved by the perforated plastic sleeves or tubes underneath the benches. Actual placement of the heater becomes secondary because the heat can be directed by the tubes. Keep the heater low but not blowing directly on the plants.

"Cooling is a bit tougher. The three most common methods are wet-walls (evaporative cooling), ventilation, and shading. A combination of the three usually works best. Evaporative coolers push cool air generated by the evaporating water. Another arrangement is to have the wet-wall and exhaust fans on opposite ends of the greenhouse—cool air is then pulled from one wall to the other."

Right: Corrugated fiberglass and a redwood frame comprise the basic elements of this freestanding prefabricated greenhouse. This style is affordable and not difficult to assemble.

Below: Adjustable shade-cloth blinds are a feature of this attached style prefabricated greenhouse.

Greenhouse enthusiast Floyd Pick chose a greenhouse kit. If you are considering this type, let his experience be a guide.

"I ordered the 12 × 6 model. It arrived in three packages. One package contained the fan, heater, and thermostat. The other two contained the redwood, fiberglass, and hardware. The total weight of the three boxes was about 270 lbs.

"The first stages of construction were probably the most difficult. I did 95 percent of it myself, but I needed to get help a couple of times until the ridge brace connecting the frame sections was in place. My wife held a section in place until the connection could be made.

"Before the fiberglass panels were installed, I treated the frame with a stain and sealer. The frame is redwood, which is decay- and insect-resistant to some degree. I believe this step will extend the life of the frame considerably. Where the wood braces are close to the earth, I painted with copper napthanate, a greenish-colored wood preservative.

"The benches were bought separately. I ordered two that run the length of each side. Mine are stacked one on top of the other resembling bunk beds. The opposite side of the greenhouse is for a raised bed. On the shelves will be my cactus and succulent collection, plus a few house plants. Seed propagation (heat cable, mist, and Gro-light fixture) will also take up some bench space. The raised bed is for vegetables—tomatoes, cucumbers, etc. I'm especially looking forward to growing vegetables next winter.

"Back 15 or 20 years, I remember commenting that I'd like a greenhouse. It always seemed too expensive and time consuming. (So far my total costs have been only $520.) The rising cost of supermarket produce is one reason I finally bought one. It may take a while, but someday I expect to reduce my grocery bill.

"For me, the actual assembly was not difficult. It took about 50 hours in total. I believe anyone who is methodical and patient can do as well."

Benches and Potting Areas

The benches and cabinets inside a greenhouse can be both functional and beautiful. Design them to suit your own needs, taking into consideration your height and your reach. You should be able to reach comfortably across or under a bench to care for plants there.

The benches should also provide a good display area for the plants and be open to the maximum amount of light. They should be constructed in a manner that lets air circulate freely through them and among the plants. You should keep a space between the back of the bench and the greenhouse wall for good air flow.

Generally, benches are 30 to 36 inches wide if they can run along only one side, and 48 to 60 inches wide if they run down the center of the greenhouse. For the sake of efficiency, the aisles should take up as little space as possible. Again, adjust dimensions to your special needs.

Bench styles. The most common arrangement is a continuous bench that runs around the sides and ends of the greenhouse. A small sink and potting area often are built into one end of the bench.

One variation on the straight and level bench is the stairstep, which allows more display room. The steps should face south to catch the most sunlight, but this could result in too much direct light. Unless you put your plants against a white wall to get reflected light, you'll have to turn them regularly. Shade-loving plants can go under the stairstep bench.

A different bench arrangement is the "peninsula"—a series of benches protruding toward the center, resembling fingers or peninsulas. Although time-consuming to build, these are better for larger greenhouses because they provide the greatest amount of bench area. In this style, the center aisle may be 3 to 4 feet wide for easy movement and the side aisles kept to only 18

An early-morning misting of the gravel floor (top) increases the humidity for Mr. Floyd Pick's flourishing young peppers (center). Above: Mr. Pick installed this fan and electrical hookup in his prefabricated greenhouse.

Benches installed in the greenhouse shown under construction on page 33. The bench at right is built with 2 × 4s and 1 × 4s. The bench at left is simply two 1 × 2s laid on two oil drums. The drums are filled with water which absorbs heat during the day and releases it at night.

to 24 inches wide. The bench tops, accessible from both sides, are 48 to 60 inches wide. When installing benches, make sure the legs rest on firm supports, such as bricks or concrete pads—never directly on the ground.

Some basic benches. An attractive and practical greenhouse bench is made from 2 × 4s with a top of 1 × 4s. The top can be as much as 36 inches wide, but the support structure is no more than 30 inches wide to keep the legs out of your way. Lay the 2 × 4 legs on a flat surface, such as a driveway or garage floor. Put them 4 feet apart on-center and nail a 2 × 4 rail flush with the top. Use a square to make sure the legs are perpendicular to the rail. If your bench is under 16 feet long, you should be able to use one board for the rail. Otherwise, use notched joints over one of the legs to connect two or more boards.

Make a duplicate of this side, and you have the front and back supports for the bench. Put them in place in your greenhouse and tie them together with a 2 × 4 brace inside the top of each leg and another halfway down. Remember, for a 36-inch bench this substructure should not be more than 30 inches wide.

If you cannot tie this bench to either end of your greenhouse, use more braces underneath. Use diagonal 2 × 4s running from the bottom of the back leg to the top of the front leg.

Once the frame is in place, cover the top with 36-inch-long redwood or treated 1 × 4s spaced an inch apart. Allow a 6-inch overhang in front to keep the legs away from your feet. Give the top a finished look by nailing a strip of 1 × 1 half-round molding along the protruding ends. If you want to provide a lip to prevent pots from being brushed off, use a 1 × 2 for the facing.

For an attractive variation on this bench—one with a smoother appearance—use lap joints to tie the legs and top rail together. If you don't have a table saw with a dado blade, make laps by marking each piece, cutting halfway through with a saw, and then chiseling out the lap area. The top cross braces can be nailed directly to the inside of each leg where they are hidden, but the lower cross braces should be lap jointed for a truly finished effect.

The component bench. This type of bench can be built with components and adapts readily to any length. Build the support structure with 2 × 4s for the front and back legs, and fasten each leg at the top between two horizontal 2 × 4s extending 6 inches beyond the front leg. One-third the distance up from the bottom of each leg, cut lap joints on the inside to accept 2 × 2 rails. These will strengthen the bench and provide lower shelf supports. When all the units are cut and together, place them in the greenhouse and use finishing nails to attach the top made of 1 × 4s running lengthwise and spaced an inch apart.

If the bench is too long for single lengths of the 1 × 4 top, put the joints on alternate legs for added support.

Other bench styles. There are numerous other types of benches, including some that use 3/8-inch cement asbestos board, either corrugated or flat, to provide a solid top. These are primarily used for planting directly into soil on top of the bench. However, there are problems with this practice, including water-logging of plants and spawning of disease in the wet soil. Some gardeners use this type of bench to hold soaked vermiculite, keeping the potted plants resting on top wet for several days.

If you want to use benches filled with soil, use corrugated asbestos boards because of their strength. When the benches are not filled with soil, wire is laid across these boards to provide a flat, stable surface for pots. In either case the boards are sloped slightly toward one end to carry away water.

Pipe-framed benches commonly have 1¼-inch galvanized pipe embedded in concrete piers. These pier forms can be made with half-gallon milk cartons. Set the complete framework in the forms and brace it while you check the level before pouring the concrete.

Benches can also be quickly installed using cinder blocks on-end and a framework of pipe or 2 × 4s. The top can be asbestos board; or, for a very simple bench, unroll a length of snow fence onto the rails.

Wire mesh top is widely used in many greenhouses. It provides excellent circulation but tends to sag if not properly supported. To help minimize such problems, put 2 × 2 cross supports every foot. Cover the exposed ends of the wire with a 1 × 4.

The greenhouse potting area. A greenhouse and a potting area go hand-in-hand. Some people prefer the potting area to be outside but near the greenhouse, such as some type of lath structure. Others, especially those in cold winter areas, want their potting area protected and warm—in the greenhouse itself. If this is what you require, put the potting area in the northeast corner, where it will block the least amount of sun.

The potting area should provide a flat and solid place with sides 4 to 6 inches high to keep soil from spilling over; storage for tools; and room under the bench to keep soil mixes, fertilizers, and pest sprays. A small sink is convenient, but not necessary. If you do put in a sink, get a used one. It will meet your needs for about a third of the price of a new one.

Set the sink directly into the bench by resting it on two 2 × 4 braces. Place the sink edge flush with the bench top for easy cleanup. Most codes require that the sink drain be tied into your house system, but since so little water is normally run through there, you may be able to let it run directly onto a nearby plant or tree. In snow country, the drain will have to stay below the frost level, and you may want to run it into a dry well filled with stones. Check your local code requirements before installing the sink.

Shelves can be constructed underneath a bench by running 1 × 4 slats across the lower braces. Keep them spaced for good air circulation.

It's a good idea to keep the lower shelves out of the reach of small children by installing cabinet doors. They can be constructed as a gate and from the same material as the bench top. Lay out two 1 × 4s about 18 inches apart and put on vertical 1 × 4 strips, leaving a 1-inch space between each. Don't nail until everything is laid out to allow for adjustments in spacing.

The vertical slats should fit under the bench top and against the top rail. Use a carpenter's square as you nail the slats in place with finishing nails.

After they are on, turn the door over and check the square again. Cut a diagonal bracing and put it in place, with one end against the lower hinge. After it is hung on hinges, use magnetic catches or a bolt to fasten it in front.

Overhead cabinets can be made from 1 × 12 redwood cut to fit between the bench and the eave of your greenhouse. A handy cabinet is 3 feet wide and made as a box, with simple butt joints that are nailed and glued. Put several shelves 6, 12, and 18 inches apart to handle your different storage needs. When the shelves are in, back the boxes with a piece of Masonite or other rigid material. If you want the back open for more light, use galvanized angle braces inside all corners.

If you have an outside wall to mount these boxes on, you do not need a backing or braces. Cut a 2 × 4 to fit across the inside of the box at the top. Fasten this 2 × 4 to the wall with lag screws sunk into the studs, and then hang the box from it. Put another 2 × 4 support under the lowest shelf to keep the box from swaying. Hold it in place with one screw through the top of the box into the wall support. Do the same at the bottom. If you want cabinet doors, cut them to fit from ½-inch plywood and install with butt hinges.

Portable work bench. If you don't have a great deal of working room in your greenhouse, try a combination of two collapsible tables and a portable potting bench.

The folding tables are cut from ¾-inch exterior-grade plywood that has been painted and treated with a water seal. Each table is no wider than the height of the potting bench. The table, when folded down, should clear the floor by at least an inch. You also need to get by the table when it is folded out.

The plywood top is hinged to the top rail of the bench. Under the front of the table, screw in a 2 × 4 and then use hinges to attach two legs made of 2 × 2. Put a cross support between the legs halfway down, using screws and glue. When you are not using the table, the legs fold up and the top drops down. If necessary, use magnetic catches to hold the legs up when the table is folded.

Put two of these tables beside each other, with a 20-inch space in between. The portable potting board may be 24 inches wide, allowing a 2-inch overlap on each side. All dimensions can be reduced if your space is tight.

Make the base of the potting board from two 1 × 12 pieces of redwood. Tie the base together with 2 × 2 cleats underneath that are set in 2 inches from each side. This will keep the potting board from slipping when set between the two foldout tables. Make the sides from 1 × 6 redwood.

Tool rack. A good storage space for tools is above the potting area between the hanging cabinets. Here, the tools are accessible yet out of the way.

One type of tool rack is made by cutting a piece of peg board to fit the area and framing all the edges on the back with 1 × 2 furring strips, including one down the center. This keeps the peg board away from the wall so you can insert the metal tool hangers. Put vertical 2 × 2s on each side and then glue and nail a 1 × 2 across the bottom to make a narrow shelf. Six inches above that, put a 2 × 2 across the front as the retainer for the tools. These racks are ideal for holding the variety of small trowels, shears, scissors, spoons, and brushes that go with potting. You can add one more shelf above, if necessary, and hang the heavier and less frequently used tools and supplies there.

Greenhouse shelves. Once you've filled all the benches in the greenhouse, start looking for more growing room. Plants are commonly hung in individual pots, but a few suspended shelves will give you much more room.

One simple but effective way to hang several pots of the same size at once is to build a rack from 2 × 2s. Each rack should be at least the length of the spacing between the overhead supports, usually 2 or 4 feet on-center.

The controlled environment of a greenhouse, with its humidity and good light, can be revitalizing for ailing house plants.

To make the racks, lay out two lengths of 2 × 2 and then nail them to 2 × 2 crosspieces just long enough and spaced just enough apart to catch the top rim of your pots. Suspend the framework from eyebolts, using thin wires. If the shelves are longer than the greenhouse support spacing, run support wires down from each cross-frame of the greenhouse.

A variation on this shelf is a rack 8 to 12 inches wide and made from 2 × 2s and lath strips. For a shelf 8 inches wide, cut the 2 × 2 supports 12 inches long and space every 12 inches. Nail on the lath strips with ½ inch of space between each. To keep the pots from tipping over, put vertical pieces of 2 × 2 on the end of each undersupport, using a lap joint for added rigidity. Add a lath rail across the top.

One readymade shelf that will support small pots is a length of aluminum roof gutter. Leave the ends open and support it from wires fastened to the greenhouse frame.

THE GREENHOUSE ENVIRONMENT

Growing in a greenhouse requires some knowledge about watering and misting methods and how to control temperature and humidity.

Growing plants in a controlled environment is different in several respects from growing plants outside. A greenhouse is subject to wide extremes in temperature on the outside but must maintain a good climate inside if the plants are to grow well. In summer, sunlight can increase the temperature to suffocating levels unless the greenhouse is properly ventilated and cooled. In winter, it's hard to know just how much heat you need. Unless the greenhouse has been sealed tightly, with its outside insulated or a double wall used inside, heat will flow out of it at an alarming—and costly—rate. Maintaining a proper level of humidity compounds these problems.

Several other factors also have to be considered: the kind and amount of ventilation; the amount of light, natural and artificial; and the soil and air moisture. These variations and combinations will determine your success in producing big, beautiful tomatoes, or poinsettias for Christmas. The controlled environment is a place to raise plants that have originated in different parts of the world and grow naturally under different conditions.

It is best to learn as much as you can about the origin and preferences of the plants you want to grow. You should find out what the best natural conditions are for each variety, and duplicate them in the controlled environment as nearly as you can. If you want to grow a plant from a tropical rain forest and another from the desert, you must make as good a compromise with these natural conditions as you can.

Whether you live in the North, East, South, or West, heating and/or cooling the air will require understanding and careful planning.

Heating the Controlled Environment

In heating a greenhouse, two basic considerations must be attended to: providing enough heat, and distributing it evenly—both at a reasonable cost.

The entire system should be automatic, to save time; it should also be as simple and straightforward as possible to minimize problems. The system's ability to use the cheapest available fuel is of obvious importance.

In considering the above, use as many solar heating techniques as you can. Sunlight is free, so make use of it. Several means of capturing and storing solar heat are discussed in the solar greenhouse section, pages 62–77.

Preparing for installation. Before you install any type of heat system, double check for cracks around vents, doors, and glazing panes that allow great amounts of heat to escape. Line the vents, doors, and glazing panes with 4 mil polyethylene film. The inner layer should be 1 to 6 inches away from the glazing for good results.

Estimating heating needs. Use this method to determine the size of heater your controlled environment needs:

First, figure the total surface area (SA) by multiplying length times height of each wall and the roof. For instance, one 6×8-foot wall has 48 square feet.

Tomato seedlings thrive under conditions regulated by two thermostats; one for heating, and another for a cooling fan.

(Don't count the floor.) Add all the other surfaces together, and the result will be the total area in square feet.

Second, calculate the degree rise (DR), which is the difference between the coldest outdoor temperature recorded in the past several years and the temperature you want to maintain inside. Get the low temperature from the weather bureau. If you want to maintain a temperature of 55°F. and the lowest expected temperature is 15°F., you have a rise of 40 Fahrenheit degrees.

Now consider the insulating factors (IF) for the type of glazing you choose, given in the accompanying table. Start multiplying: SA × DR × IF = heat loss per hour in British thermal units (Btu). The heater output should be equal to the heat loss you just calculated.

Most heaters are labeled with their rated Btu output, but you can convert your Btu finding to kilowatts for electric heaters by dividing by 3,413.

In making the final decision on your heater, remember that very low outside temperatures don't happen every year; you can probably get by with a smaller heater and save some money on the initial installation. You can also install a battery-operated alarm in case the temperature does fall suddenly or your heating system fails.

Whatever type of heater you have—coal, wood, gas, oil, or electric—you must keep the air moving to prevent all the heat from collecting at the top of the roof. That is why a heater with a combination fan is so widely used. Otherwise, use the cheapest heating fuel available to you and install a small fan near the top of the roof to circulate the air downward.

The thermostats that will run both the heater and the summer vent fans should be located where they will not be in direct sunlight. They are commonly mounted on the wall under a shelf or in a small box for protection.

A relatively new concept in heating is the use of infrared waves. One commercial greenhouse has used gas-fired overhead infrared heaters since 1976, with an estimated fuel savings of 60 to 65 percent compared with normal gas-fired heaters. Infrared heating is totally different from conventional heating. Conventional heaters warm the air, which in turn warms the

Glazing Insulating Factors

Glazing	Calm	Windy
Glass	1.5	1.8
Fiberglass or polyethylene	1.2	1.4
Double layer (glass/plastic)	0.8	1.0

Far left: Greenhouse workmen at Planting Fields Arboretum, Oyster Bay, New York, provide additional wintertime insulation by installing polyethylene sheeting.

Top left: An automatic gas heater typical to greenhouse use.

Bottom left: Basic indoor environmental control is provided by a sun-shielded thermometer, thermostat, and humidistat.

plants. Infrared radiation travels in a straight line through the air until it hits a solid object, which then absorbs that energy. In a controlled environment, the energy hits and warms plants, not the surrounding air. The units look something like fluorescent fixtures and can hang close to plants without harming them. Reflectors direct the heat in uniform patterns to ensure that all corners are covered.

For small greenhouses some type of space heater will usually be quite adequate. For larger greenhouses, however, an oil- or gas-fired boiler can be used to heat water, which is then circulated through thin tubing located on the outside wall below the benches. If you already have hot water heat in your house, you may be able to tie into the existing system.

Cooling

In much of the country, it's more difficult to cool a greenhouse in summer than it is to heat it in winter. In the northern latitudes, you may not have a cooling problem: open vents in the wall and roof may be enough. This is probably true if the summer temperatures around your area rarely exceed 80°F. (27°C.). But if you have long periods with higher temperatures, plan to install some cooling devices.

There are two basic rules for cooling: first, minimize the heat buildup by shading; second, use fans to draw the cooler outside air in while blowing the hot inside air out.

Like heating, the entire fan system should be automatic. Fans should all be hooked to thermostats so they will kick on when the temperature rises beyond a certain point. It's better to buy a two-speed fan so you can set the air exchange to the slower speed during the less extreme months of spring and fall. The thermostats should also be made especially for greenhouses (or barns) so they will not be damaged by high humidity. Some thermostat settings are not too accurate; check them by placing two or three thermometers around.

In addition to the fans, use thermal pistons to open and close vents automatically. These pistons expand with heat to open vents and then

An electric powered, thermostatically controlled vent is set to automatically regulate air circulation.

Top: A thermal piston type self-regulating vent.

Above left: Rising hot air is circulated by this small fan placed near the top of the greenhouse.

Above center: Thermometers at various locations in the greenhouse, especially at plant level, will give accurate temperature readings.

Above right: Mercury in this maximum/minimum thermometer pushes pins which set and "record" the highest and lowest temperatures.

contract when the temperature drops. They come with dials so you can set them to your needs.

Shading. Greenhouses are sometimes shaded during the hot months. Opaque plastic, bamboo, or aluminum screens can be mounted on the roof and rolled down when protection is needed. These are also useful to protect glass roofs in areas with heavy hailstorms. Green vinyl or special reflective coatings come in rolls and can be cut to fit inside your windows. Wet the windows, then apply the plastic with a squeegee.

For more exact shade protection buy Saran or other shadecloth from greenhouse supply stores. These cloths are rated by the density or thread count to provide shade ranging from 30 to 92 percent. For most purposes 50 percent shade will be about right. The edges of the cloth are equipped with grommets to tie them securely over greenhouse roofs.

Other gardeners whitewash their greenhouse roofs in the summer, or use special shade paint, counting on the winter rains to wash it away. However,

Above: Direct midday sunlight is filtered through an aluminum shading screen.

Left: When plants have been trained to this sturdy trellis, the greenhouse interior will benefit from the natural shading.

the results are not particularly attractive. Other solutions are to build lightweight lath covers to place on the roofs, or to lay on panels of green fiberglass framed with 2 × 2s. For a more natural shade, plant sunflowers or pole beans on the south side of the greenhouse or train quick-growing vines over the roof.

Cooling devices. Shading helps, but it often isn't enough. In many parts of the country, a greenhouse needs some artificial cooling in order to be really effective. One of the best inexpensive systems is the evaporative cooler, commonly called a swamp cooler. You can buy one, or make your own for a fraction of the price. The basic principle is simple: a fan draws outside air through a constantly wetted pad, which further cools the air and simultaneously increases the humidity.

Setting this up will involve some basic math. First, fans are rated in cubic feet per minute (cfm), which indicates how many cubic feet of air is moved every minute. To find the cubic feet of space in your greenhouse in order to

Swamp Cooler

PVC pipe with many small holes, clamped to the 2 × 4 frame above a sheet metal strip that directs water onto the pad

2 × 4 frame built into greenhouse wall

Rain gutter, sloped slightly toward the sump and pump

Screws and large washers hold the sandwich of wire mesh and pad to the 2 × 4 frame.

Garbage can sump with submersible pump wired to a thermostat and fan

A thermostatically controlled cooler.

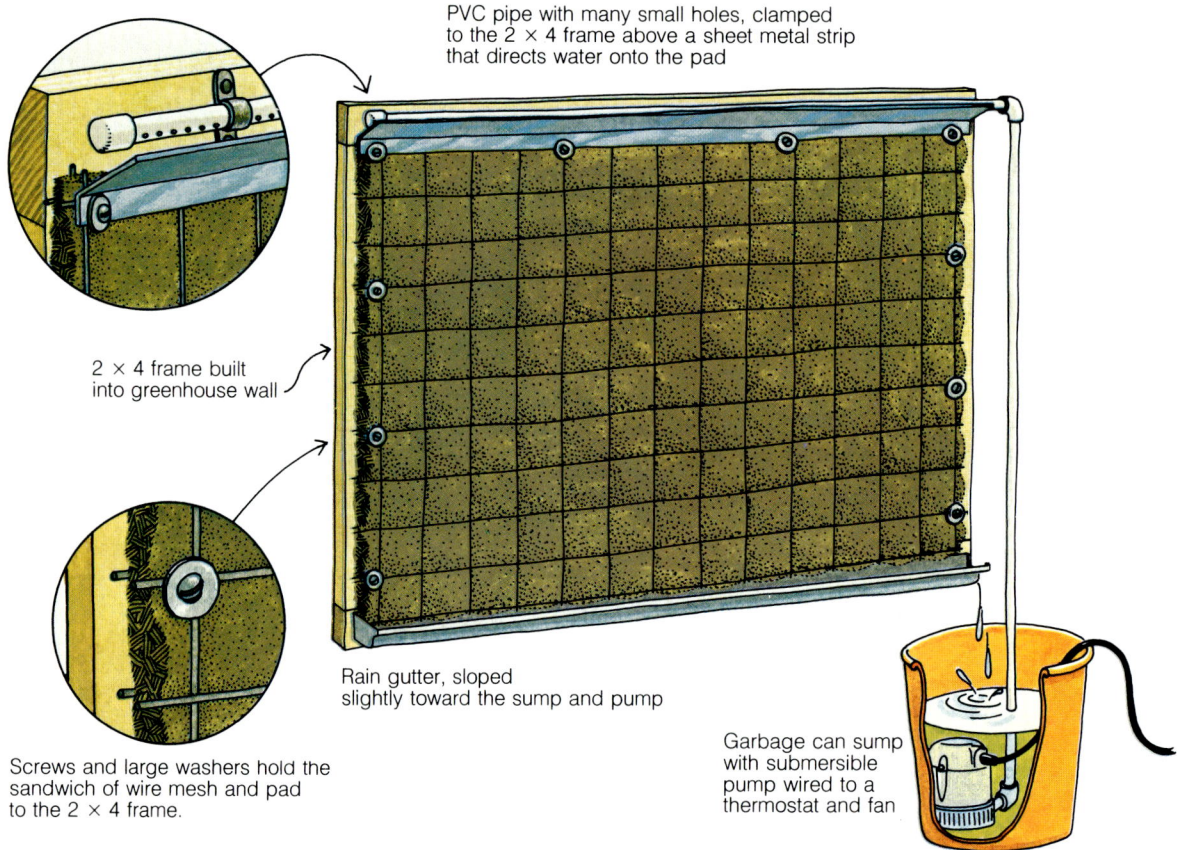

buy the right size fan, multiply the length and the width of the structure by the *average* height of the roof. (This height often comes close to 10 feet, which makes the calculation a little easier.) An 8 × 12-foot greenhouse would have 96 square feet of floor. Multiply this by the average roof height, say 10 feet, which yields a volume of 960 cubic feet.

Commercial greenhouses exchange the inside air every minute. But since the home greenhouse has a smaller volume that heats up much faster, it should exchange the air twice a minute. So if your greenhouse has a volume of 960 cubic feet, you will need a fan that will move twice that amount of air every minute, or about 2,000 cfm.

The fan should be mounted close to the top of the roof, usually over the door, to pull out the hottest air. The cooling pad should be located at the opposite end of the greenhouse and, ideally, at the same level as the plants or lower. The cooling is done by pulling air through a constantly wet pad of aspen shavings, excelsior, or plastic.

The site of the pad for your greenhouse is important. It is determined by dividing the needed air flow by 150. Thus, the 8 × 12-foot greenhouse needing air exchange of 2,000 cfm would require about 13 square feet of pad (2,000 ÷ 150 = 13.3). An effective pad should run across the entire wall.

Aspen pads can be purchased anywhere replacement pads for swamp coolers are sold. Cut the pad to size and clamp it between wire mesh to prevent it from sagging. Cut the greenhouse wall opening to size, and frame it with 2 × 4 redwood or some other wood treated with a preservative. On the lower support, mount a section of rain gutter, angled slightly for water runoff. Fasten the screen and pad in place between the frame with screws and washers, for easy removal.

At the lower end of the rain gutter, stand a plastic garbage can with a circulating pump that will supply about ⅓ of a gallon per minute per linear foot of pad, regardless of the pad's height. The sump, or garbage can, should have a capacity of 1¼ gallons for each linear foot of pad in order to hold the water that drains back when the system stops.

The water is distributed by a PVC pipe clamped to the 2 × 4 just above the pad. Drill a close series of ⅛-inch holes and, for better distribution of the water, put a small strip of sheet metal under the pipe to spread the water onto the pad.

The pump and fan are generally hooked to the same thermostat so they will start at the same time. A slightly more sophisticated hookup is in two stages: the fan starts when the temperature hits 70°F. (21°C.), and the water starts moving when the temperature reaches 80°F. (27°C.). Remember that the fan will draw air through any opening or crack in the greenhouse, so make sure that the door is closed and the house is tightly sealed to ensure that all the air comes through the pad only.

Don't forget to recover the fan and pad openings of the greenhouse wall for the winter, and seal them well.

Humidity Control

If the humidity in the greenhouse is too low, the plants will suffer by developing poor growth patterns. High humidity makes many plants grow better, but too much humidity is not an improvement—when it is over 90 percent for any length of time, there is a high risk of disease.

Low humidity is generally corrected by misting or watering the floor two or three times a day to build up water content in the air. Only in severely dry areas would a humidifier be needed in a greenhouse, particularly if a pad or swamp cooler is used.

Too much humidity is the usual problem as evidenced by roof and walls so covered with condensation that it seems to be raining inside. If the level is high during the day but the leaves have a chance to dry out at nightfall, the risk to the plants is not too severe. It is when the leaves are damp through the night that real problems can arise.

Condensation problems often occur during cold weather. The air in the greenhouse flows along the cold windows and cools so rapidly that it can no longer hold its moisture. It then condenses out onto the plastic.

This problem can be reduced by putting in a thermal layer of polyethylene film or insulating the windows on the outside at night to prevent the collision of warm and cold air. A small fan to keep the warm air circulating will also reduce condensation.

Mist systems. If you are in an area that has high temperatures and low humidity much of the year, a misting system may be a good solution. A mist system is also excellent for propagating new plants, minimizing plant moisture loss, and cutting greenhouse temperatures. Most important, mist systems lower the leaf temperature and allow photosynthesis to continue at a good rate.

Mist systems are normally set up with two timers—one to turn the entire system on during the day and off at night, and another to run the spray nozzles a few seconds every few minutes. You should set the timing sequence yourself, based on what your plants need. Spray nozzles should be activated when the leaves are dried and should be on only long enough to thoroughly wet all the leaves. (This can be as much as twenty times an hour in very hot and dry areas.)

The problem with clock-type controls is that they don't consider the time when the sun is behind clouds and there is less evaporation from the leaves. This produces a tendency to overwater. Newer systems use a balance rod with a piece of screen on one end and the on-off switch hooked to the other. When water builds up on the screen, as it would on a leaf, the rod dips and

An automatic mist sprayer (top), regulated by a solenoid valve (above), maintains high greenhouse humidity.

Below: A dry/wet bulb humidistat.
Bottom: This dripless humidifier increases greenhouse humidity.

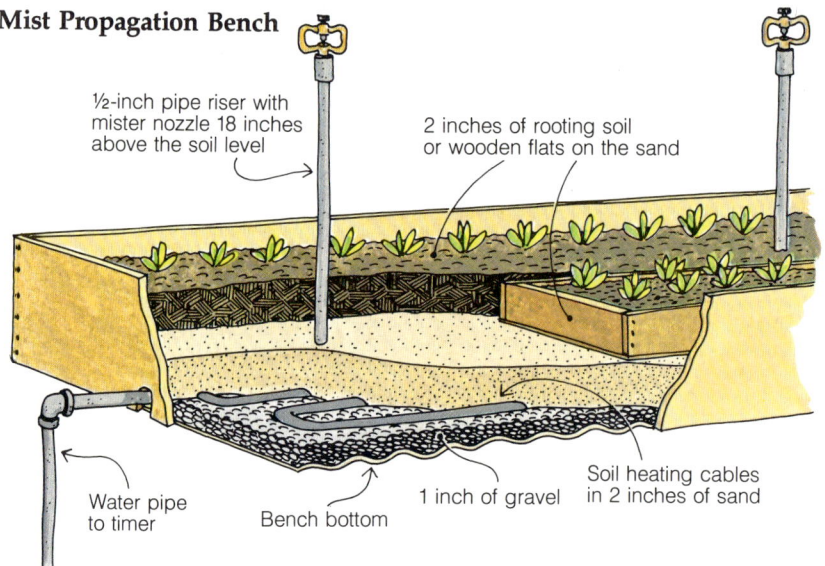

Mist Propagation Bench

½-inch pipe riser with mister nozzle 18 inches above the soil level

2 inches of rooting soil or wooden flats on the sand

Water pipe to timer

Bench bottom

1 inch of gravel

Soil heating cables in 2 inches of sand

shuts off the misters; when the water has evaporated, it rises and switches the misters back on.

Contrary to expectation, misting does not promote diseases but actually retards some, such as powdery mildew.

Mist propagation bench. A mist propagation bench can be set up in any part of your controlled environment. The bench should be made of a material that's impervious to water, such as corrugated cement asbestos covered with 1 inch of gravel and topped with 2 inches of sand to provide quick drainage. This sytem is excellent for rooting cuttings in flats. If you want to root directly into the bench, you will need another 2 inches of soil mix on top. For best results, the growing medium should be warmed with electric cables, since the misting tends to lower the soil temperatures.

To bring the water for misting to the bench, a ½-inch PVC pipe is usually more than adequate. The pipe can either be suspended overhead or built into the bench with ½-inch PVC pipe risers. Either way, the spray nozzles should be about 18 inches above the cuttings.

The spacing of the misters will depend on their size and make. Follow the manufacturer's directions carefully. All areas of the bench should be covered, which means some overlap, but no excess.

If you are misting only in a small section of the greenhouse, you can hang curtains of clear plastic film around the misters to keep other areas dry. If you grow a lot of hanging plants, mount your misters just under the greenhouse roof so that everything lower in the greenhouse will be covered by the mist.

A misting system is only one step away from an automatic watering system. For automatic watering you want more water, but only for a brief period every day or two in the summer and only once or twice a week in the winter. Use PVC pipe, lawn sprinkler valves, and lawn sprinkler heads high in the greenhouse. A single timer set to water for approximately 5 minutes at a time on the desired days will work well. If you water around noon you will also take advantage of your system to provide effective cooling inside the greenhouse. A lawn sprinkler timer with four or six zones will allow you to set up an elaborate system that can accommodate almost any combination of plants.

A sophisticated timing system controls misting operations. One clock regulates the master on/off switch; a second clock times misting frequency. The third controls supplementary lighting.

Soil and Water

The relationship between soil and water is so close that it makes sense to talk about them together. The rate of a plant's photosynthesis, and therefore growth, depends on the plant's having a constant supply of minerals and water to take through its roots. If the plant can't get the minerals—either from the soil itself or from added fertilizer—and there is not enough water, growth will be stunted or stopped altogether.

Is special soil mix needed? If you take the word of the most successful commercial growers of plants in containers, the answer is "yes."

If you take the word of the hundreds of thousands of home gardeners who have bought and used a container mix, again the answer is "yes." Garden stores everywhere sell special container mixes under a wide variety of trade names—Redi-Earth, Jiffy Mix, Metro Mix, Super Soil, Pro-Mix, Baccto, and many others.

The mixes are referred to as "soilless mixes" or "synthetic soils." (Synthetic does not mean "artificial.")

Basic ingredients for container soils. The organic portion of the mix may be peat moss, redwood sawdust, shavings, hardwood bark, fir bark, pine bark, or a combination of any two or more of these ingredients.

The mineral portion may be vermiculite, perlite, pumice, builder's sand or granite sand, or a combination of two or three of them. The most commonly used minerals are vermiculite, perlite, and fine sand.

Vermiculite (Terralite), when mined, resembles mica. Under heat treatment, the mineral flakes expand with air spaces to 20 times their original thickness.

Perlite (sponge rock), when mined, is a granitelike volcanic material that pops like popcorn and expands to 20 times its original volume when crushed and heat treated (1500° to 2000°F.).

The mix you buy may be 50 percent peat moss and 50 percent vermiculite, or 50 percent ground bark and 50 percent fine sand, or other combinations of the organic and mineral components. The ingredients in the mixes vary, but the principle behind all mixes is the same. Soilless "soil" must provide:

☐ Fast drainage of water through the "soil."
☐ Air in the "soil" after drainage.
☐ A reservoir of water in the "soil" after drainage.

Most important in any container mix is the air in the "soil" after drainage, since plant roots require air for growth.

Making your own container mix. Before you begin gardening with large containers for shrubs and trees, consider the advantages of buying the prepared commercial mixes. What do you plan to do with the mix? Few home gardeners need large quantities of a mix designed for seedlings and small pots. And, when growing seedlings or growing seed in pots, sterilization of the growing medium is all-important.

If all you need is a few cubic feet of container "soil," it is best to buy one of the commercial mixes. However, if you'll want more than a few cubic feet, consider making your own. These are the components you would blend together for 1 cubic yard of very lightweight mix for seedlings and pots:

  9 cubic feet of peat moss
  9 cubic feet of vermiculite
  9 cubic feet of perlite
  5 pounds of 5–10–10 fertilizer
  5 pounds of ground limestone

For a heavier mix for seedlings and pots:

  7 cubic feet of fine sand
14 cubic feet of peat moss
  7 cubic feet of perlite
  5 pounds of 5–10–10 fertilizer
  8 pounds of ground limestone

In all these formulas, a fertilizer mix of 5–10–10 is substituted for combinations of super phosphate, calcium, or potassium nitrate in the amounts called for in the Cornell Bulletin #43. Check this bulletin if you wish to duplicate their procedure in producing the Peat-Lite mixes.

A mix recommended for indoor foliage plants is composed of the following:

14 cubic feet of peat moss	5 pounds of 5–10–10 fertilizer
7 cubic feet of vermiculite	1 pound of iron sulphate
7 cubic feet of perlite	8 pounds of ground limestone

A mix for most shrubs and trees is made of:

9 cubic feet of fine sand
18 cubic feet of ground bark or
    nitrogen-stabilized sawdust

or, for a coarser mixture

9 cubic feet of fine sand
9 cubic feet of peat moss
9 cubic feet of ground bark

Add to either of the above:

5 pounds of 5–10–10 fertilizer
7 pounds of ground limestone
1 pound of iron sulphate

Converting garden soil into container soil. The organic materials used in the commercial mixes are almost stabilized in their decomposition. Peat moss, redwood sawdust, fir bark, and pine bark "stay put" in a container mix—some for five years or more.

In conditioning a garden soil, you can add various types of organic material—peat moss, ground bark, manure, leaf mold, and compost, in all

While premixed potting soils are available from most nursery centers (right), you may prepare your own soil mix, using such ingredients as (clockwise from top right): perlite, vermiculite, fir bark, peat moss, and coarse builders' sand.

stages of decay. All organic materials help make heavy soils more friable and sandy soils more retentive of water and nutrients. If the manure and compost add to the fertility of the soil, so much the better. When using such organic amendments or organic mulches of leaves, straw, or grass clippings, it is common practice to add the organic material to the soil every year to replace those that break down.

Materials that shrink or disappear do not belong in a container mix. You'll get the most satisfactory mix from a garden soil—clay loam or sandy loam—mixed with either peat moss, nitrogen-stabilized sawdust, or ground bark.

Watering. The watering of plants is probably the least understood and most mismanaged aspect of gardening. Water has several functions. It is the solvent that carries the minerals from the soil through the plant; it is a raw material used by the plant in synthesizing other, more complex, compounds; it is an essential item in the process of photosynthesis for the production of food; and it cools the plant through transpiration into the air. Water is taken into a plant as liquid through the root hairs, used by the plant, and given off into the atmosphere from the leaves as a vapor.

The usual controlled-environment plant has to grow in a very confined space and a limited amount of soil. To compensate for this, such plants must be assured of good drainage, a porous soil that will retain moisture, and plenty of water. But whenever the plant is watered, some of the available nutrients are leached out of the pot or soil, and should be replaced with a suitable fertilizer.

Be careful with thick, hairy-leaved plants such as the African violet (*Saintpaulia*). Water can cause spots on their leaves if its temperature is not very close to that of the leaves. Such plants are better watered directly in the pot or from saucers of water under them.

Fertilizer—When and How Much

When using a mix containing a 5–10–10 fertilizer, you will usually begin feeding 3 weeks after planting. If frequent watering is necessary after planting, start the feeding program earlier.

Because fertilizers are leached through the mixes when water is applied, the frequency of watering determines the frequency of fertilizing. Fertilizers will leach from a mix containing perlite faster than from a mix containing vermiculite. Therefore, plants grown in a peat moss-perlite mix will require more frequent applications of fertilizer.

Some container gardeners prefer to fertilize with a weak nutrient solution, applying it with every irrigation. When watering plants with a nutrient solution in this manner, a safe concentration would be 1/10 the amount called for on the label for a monthly application. If the label calls for 1 tablespoon to 1 gallon of water, make the dilution ½ tablespoon to 5 gallons or approximately ¼ teaspoon to a gallon of water.

Plants growing in containers demand closer attention than the same plants growing in a flower border or in a vegetable patch. When you restrict the root zone in a container, you must compensate for the smaller root area by both watering and feeding more frequently.

The amount of fertilizer needed at any one time is very small, but the need is continuous. The nutrient solution applications, as described above, satisfy the need for a constant supply of nutrients. The use of the time-release fertilizers is another popular solution to this problem. The need for constant availability is taken care of by applying nutrients in a form that continues to become available in small amounts over a long period of time as the plant is watered. Check the label for rate of application. The use of a time-release fertilizer mixed with the soil just before planting is the easiest method to follow.

SOLAR GREENHOUSES AND SUN PITS

These two types of controlled environments may suit your particular needs. The basic facts about them are here.

If you've had second thoughts about starting a greenhouse because of the cost of heating it, consider the solar greenhouse. If you already have a greenhouse, consider solarizing it. Solar greenhouses offer several ways to cut your heating bill, not only for the greenhouse but for your own house as well.

The Solar Greenhouse

Calling a greenhouse "solar" is somewhat redundant. A more accurate term is "a greenhouse with a solar heat sink." The greenhouse itself traps the heat each day (as anyone knows who has been in one for a few minutes on a sunny day, regardless of the outside temperature). But the greenhouse can't retain that heat by itself. It needs some means of storing heat, whether it be barrels of water, piles of rock, or a pumice block wall that has been completely filled with concrete.

Objects with the ability to store heat serve two purposes: during the day they soak up the heat, including some of the excess that would otherwise overheat the greenhouse. At night, this stored heat emanates back through the greenhouse. This is a highly successful principle. A case in point is a redwood and glass greenhouse in Santa Fe, New Mexico. At an altitude of 7,000 feet, Santa Fe has frigid winters and considerable snow. Yet no outside source of heat was required in this greenhouse, which uses a 14-foot-long, 8-foot-high pumice-block wall poured full of concrete as the heat sink. The lowest nighttime greenhouse temperature recorded was 42°F. (5.5°C.) when it was 4°F. (-15°C.) outside. During the day, excess heat from the greenhouse was pumped into the residence to help reduce the fuel bill.

There are two types of solar energy systems: active and passive. The most widely used in home greenhouses is the passive system. (The greenhouse in Santa Fe, just described, uses this.) The active system requires electricity to pump heated air into a storage area, such as a basement, that is filled with rocks or water drums. The system is more efficient than the passive, but also more costly and complex.

Solar heat storage. Heat arrives from the sun in the form of short infrared waves, which strike and heat objects in the greenhouse. The heated objects re-radiate warmth back into the greenhouse in the form of slightly longer waves, which do not readily penetrate the greenhouse covering. This builds up heat in the enclosed space. Whatever style of greenhouse you have, or want, solar heat storage principles can cut your heating costs.

Probably the most widely used heat sink is water in a common 55-gallon drum painted a dark color to better absorb heat. Piles of rock are also popular. Water, however, is much more efficient—55 gallons can store up to 15,000 Btu when the surrounding air temperature rises by 33 Fahrenheit degrees (or about 18 Centigrade degrees).

Whatever type of heat sink you choose, it won't eliminate artificial heat-

The barrels absorb low-angled winter sunlight and retain the heat. Because the sun is at a higher angle in the summer, it does not hit the barrels and the cooler temperatures of the water-filled barrels cools the greenhouse.

ing totally unless your greenhouse can operate under ideal conditions. A backup unit is necessary; however, you may not need to use it very often.

To calculate the minimum heat storage capabilities required, allow 2 gallons of water (16½ pounds) or 80 pounds of rock for each square foot of greenhouse that admits sunlight directly onto the storage units. Generally, calculate only the south-facing roof and wall. For example, if the combined area of the roof and wall is a total of 200 square feet, you should have 400 gallons of water or 16,000 pounds of rock for an effective heat sink.

You can buy drums for under $20 at most wholesale gasoline distributors, or more cheaply through the want ads. Set the drums where they will collect the most heat and fill them with water. Leave 3 or 4 inches of room at the top to allow for expansion. Space the drums slightly apart to allow air to circulate around them freely. If you don't want black drums, paint them dark brown or green, but always use a flat, nonreflective paint.

One caution: do not let the barrels touch any exterior wall or glazing. Heat can be transferred by conduction, and if barrels touch some glazing, the heat will be pulled from the barrel directly to the outside air.

If you have rocks instead of barrels, use chicken-wire cages to hold them. And since mass is required to hold heat effectively, the larger the rocks, the better the storage. Place them as you would barrels, wherever they will receive maximum sunlight. Unless they are naturally dark, spray them a dark color.

Some greenhouse gardeners use discarded plastic milk jugs set along the back of the bench to soak up heat. Although a small number of these is not efficient, every little bit helps. At worst, it's a good way to warm the water for your plants instead of running a hot water line into the greenhouse.

Another efficient heat sink is either a brick wall or cinder blocks poured full of concrete. To use a brick wall as a heat sink, if you already have a lean-to greenhouse against your own house, cover your back wall with bricks. Buy black bricks, or paint them dark for maximum heat absorption. Firmly affix this brick facing to the side of the house with steel braces set in the mortar and screwed to the house studs at regular intervals. This will keep the wall from toppling over after it is completed.

Pumice or cinder blocks poured full of concrete are worth considering if you are going to build your own greenhouse. In that case, consider making a lean-to style, using the north wall as a heat sink. When the outside of this wall is heavily insulated to prevent any heat loss, it becomes a highly effective heat sink (see the Santa Fe greenhouse on pages 70–72).

Solar Heat Sinks

Here are several materials and methods used for solar heat storage in greenhouses as well as other solar heating applications. See text for specific recommendations and some construction details.

Stacked water-filled steel drums

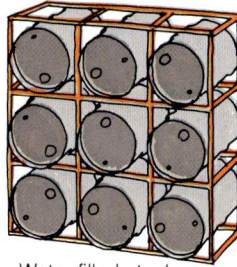

Water-filled steel drums on metal racks

Water-filled plastic containers on shelves

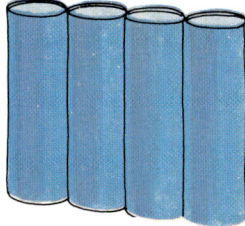

Commercially made water-filled metal or plastic cylinders

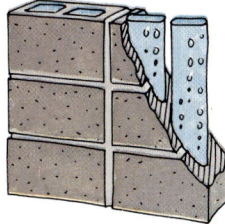

Water-filled vinyl bags in concrete block cavities

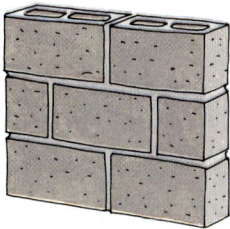

Concrete-filled cinder or pumice concrete blocks

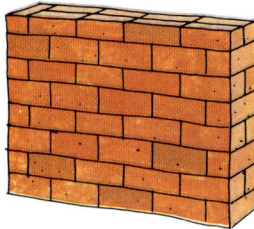

Brick, stone, or adobe wall

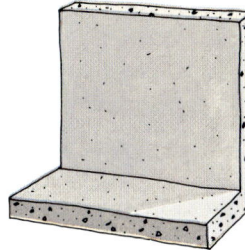

Concrete wall or slab floor

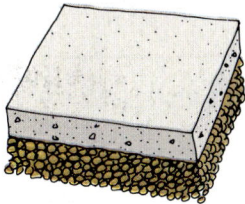

Concrete slab with bed of rocks beneath it

Bin (or loose pile) of rocks

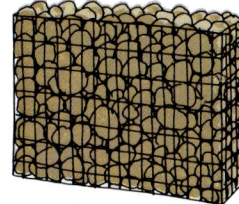

Rock wall held in place with wire mesh fencing

Passive System

The sun's warmth is deposited and held in the thermal-mass heat sink (in this case, concrete-filled cinder blocks of the north wall and the brick floor) during the day. At night, this heat radiates back out of the heat sink and keeps the area warm.

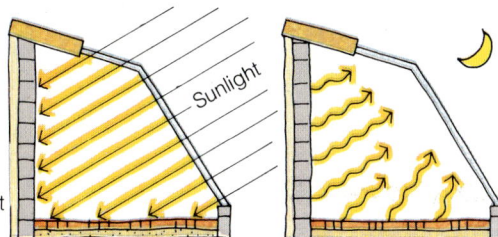

Sunlight

Active System

The sun's heat warms the transfer fluid (water or air) in a solar collector. This fluid is pumped to another location, such as the basement, and stored in a thermal mass heat sink. Another pump moves this heat again, as warm air, when needed.

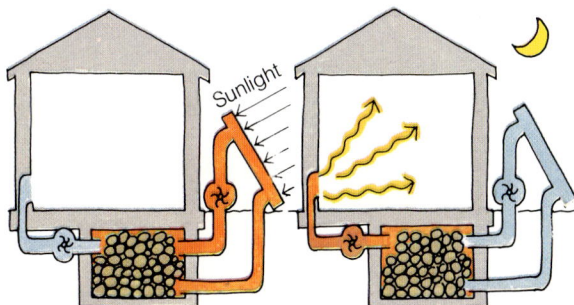

Sunlight

The Environmental Research Laboratory at the University of Arizona experiments with different kinds of solar collectors. Top: These solar panels collect heat for both living areas and a greenhouse. Below: Warm air trapped in this attached greenhouse is used to heat a residence.

The solar-heated greenhouse/residence. The combination of a solar greenhouse and a living area is a highly energy-efficient system many have experimented with. Greenhouses are heat collectors; homes are heat users. Combining the two makes good sense. Two such combinations are described here. Both store the heat trapped by the greenhouse during the day to warm the greenhouse and the home during the night. Both heat air in collectors, then duct it to rock beds for storage. Both use the energy of the sun for two purposes—to grow plants and to provide heat.

At the Environmental Research Laboratory at the University of Arizona, solar engineer Dr. John Peck and research horticulturist Dr. Merle Jensen have developed a home solar collector that doubles as a year-round vegetable garden.

The entire south wall serves as the collector. It consists of two layers of thermal pane glass (usually 6 inches apart) with venetian blinds in between. The blinds are coated on one side with dark, heat-absorbing paint. Sunlight heats the metal blinds, which, in turn, heat the air.

Their patented "Clear View" collector provides a virtually unobstructed view even when adjusted to collect heat. At night, these collectors can be closed for privacy and reduction of heat loss. They absorb 650 to 700 Btus per square foot per day.

The rock bed used for heat storage has a 300-cubic-foot capacity, and is filled with 3- to 6-inch rock. Air is circulated through the rock bed (and the entire system) at about 60 cubic feet per minute. To make use of the heat at night, the direction of air flow is reversed.

A method of insulation using foam is still in development at ERL. In conjunction with double-layer polyethylene, it can reduce heat loss up to 70 percent. The three photographs above show the foam being injected. The foam lasts a few hours, becomes a liquid again, and then is collected and reused.

The greenhouse/residence is cooled by an evaporation-type cooler. When humidity is high, the rock bed is precooled at night. The air drawn through the rock bed the next day is cool and not humid. Precooled air from the rock bed can be further cooled by evaporation. Experimenting with such a system (dubbed "two-stage cooling"), Peck and Jensen cooled air an additional 5 degrees. Where high humidity prevents effective use of evaporation cooling, Dr. Jensen suggests inserting a partition between the growing area and the living area, using refrigeration-type air conditioning for the latter.

A wide variety of edible plants have been grown here. Lettuce, other leafy vegetables, and herbs are grown at ground level. Fruiting vegetables are grown in hanging pots near the roof of the chamber.

Fruiting plants, such as tomato, eggplant, pepper, and cucumber, require at least 6 hours of direct sunlight. Exotic fruits also have done well, including bananas of the dwarf 'Cavendish' type and the low-growing 'Solo' papaya. A peat moss/vermiculite-type soil mix is used, fertilizer is slow release, and irrigation is by a drip system. Yields have averaged over 2 pounds of vegetables per day since the first plantings in 1976.

Another combined greenhouse/solar collector system was designed by and installed at the home of Professor Edgar J. Carnegie of Morro Bay, California.

The system consists of a south-facing, single flat plate solar collector 4 feet wide and 38 feet long. The collector is mounted flat on the edge of the roof.

The outside air is preheated 10 to 20 degrees by traveling through the greenhouse. It is then sucked into the solar collector inlet and further

An experimental application of liquid foam made at the Environmental Research Laboratory is being tested as an insulating agent. Pumped from large barrels (left), it is gradually applied over the exterior surface (center and above).

The solar greenhouse (shown opposite, bottom) produces tomatoes (below) and crowder peas (bottom).

Edgar J. Carnegie of Morro Bay, California, designed and built the rock storage solar collector/greenhouse shown on these pages. Right: An exterior view. Below right: The interior. Below: The exhaust fan.

heated. From there, it moves through an 8-inch, insulated duct to the rock storage area.

The rock bed used for heat storage is 300 cubic feet in volume and filled with ¾-inch crushed gravel. Professor Carnegie figures that these rocks, when heated at 140°F., contain approximately 1,400 Btus per cubic foot. In practice, this is enough to maintain the greenhouse area at a 55°F. minimum and still provide about 20 percent of his home-heating needs.

Professor Carnegie grows a variety of plants in his greenhouse, both ornamental and edible, including tomatoes year-round. The system, which is automated by use of thermostats and drip irrigation, costs $2,600.

Left: An insulated air conditioning duct moves heated air from the solar collectors to rock storage.

Above: A solenoid valve attached to "spaghetti" tubing waters each plant individually.

Insulation. No matter how much heat your greenhouse can store, it will be lost if you can't keep it from escaping as soon as it is radiated from the heat sink. One little draft in a greenhouse will render the heat sink almost useless. The basic solution? Make the greenhouse as airtight as possible. Put weatherstripping around the doors and vents, and use a flexible sealant to close all joints between the roof and walls. Check to make sure all the glazing fits snugly.

Even in a tightly sealed greenhouse, however, heat will continue to escape through the glazing material. The quickest way to cut this loss is by stapling 4 mil polyethylene plastic (the ultraviolet-resistant type lasts longer) around the inside of the greenhouse. When kept at least an inch away from the wall, it can reduce heat losses by 30 to 40 percent, yet cut light reception by only about 10 percent.

For a smooth, even pull when stretching the film, staple one end to a stick the same width as the plastic. Don't stretch it too tightly—the plastic expands and contracts with temperature changes. In wood-framed greenhouses, staple over heavy twine. This will prevent the staple from cutting through the plastic and make removal of the staples easy (just pull the twine). Be careful to seal the bottom of the plastic film tightly against the bottom wall plate. Otherwise, a chimney effect (air being drawn up through the gap) will rapidly cool the greenhouse. If your greenhouse is made of aluminum, you can buy reusable clips from any of several manufacturers for putting up the polyethylene.

Greenhouse glazing can also be covered with plastic bubble pack. Some varieties are practically self-adhesive. Apply them simply by wetting—

Reflection Capabilities

Material	Percentage of Reflection
White plaster	90–92
Mirrored glass	80–90
Matte white paint	75–90
Porcelain enamel	60–90
Polished aluminum	60–70
Aluminum paint	60–70
Stainless steel	55–65

they will stick with hundreds of tiny suction cups. Other types of bubble pack may require two-sided tape or spray-type adhesive in order to be secure against the glazing.

An effective but more time-consuming method of insulating is to cut pieces of rigid, inch-thick insulation material, such as styrofoam or urethane, to fit each panel of glazing. Use small magnets and pieces of metal glued to the corners to fasten them in place. Finding an area to store the insulation pieces during the day can be a problem, but white pieces will offer the added advantage of reflecting more light around the greenhouse.

Reflection in the greenhouse is an important compromise with some solar-heat storage principles. It takes a dark color to trap the heat rapidly, but that can result in phototropism problems, causing the plants to lean away from the darkness toward the windows. To help counter this, place reflective material strategically. Installing insulated plywood panels on the outside walls of the greenhouse can help insulate the greenhouse. During the day, lower them by a pulley system and angle them to reflect the maximum sunlight into the greenhouse. At night, raise them to cover the walls. But take great care not to overdo this and similar reflected-light arrangements; otherwise the plants in the greenhouse will get overheated.

The north wall. The north wall of a greenhouse is the greatest escape route for heat. Heat gained in the greenhouse where the sun comes through the glass simply flows out the north wall. Some studies show that a conventional glass wall may have up to 15 times the heat loss of a conventional frame wall with 4 inches of fiberglass insulation.

If you already have a greenhouse, you can improve its performance by covering the north wall with a material that will both insulate and reflect light back into the interior. For an aluminum and glass structure, one effective method is to seal the north wall with panels of white, rigid insulation cut to fit each opening.

If you have a frame greenhouse, fill the north wall with batts of fiberglass insulation and then cover it with exterior-grade plywood. First, apply a coat of water seal; then paint it white. This bounces back additional light and may make the north bench one of the best propagation areas, instead of one of the poorest.

Foundations and floors. When thinking about insulation, don't forget the floor and foundation. During the winter months in cold areas, the ground is frozen many inches deep. That subsurface cold is a severe drain on greenhouse heat. To block it, put sheets of rigid insulation 1 or 2 inches thick around the outside of the foundation, from the footing to the top of the wall. Or dig a 4-inch-wide trench down to the bottom of the footing and fill that with pumice stone.

The floor, particularly if made of brick, flagstone, or concrete slab, is an effective heat sink. But if it isn't insulated, its heat gain will be quickly lost. Counter this by laying 4 inches of pumice rock beneath the flooring to insulate it. Water will still drain through.

If you build a cinder-block wall for the north side of a lean-to greenhouse, be sure to insulate the outside so that heat radiating from the heat sink goes only to the greenhouse.

An attached solar greenhouse. Santa Fe, New Mexico hosts a solar greenhouse that is both beautiful and efficient. The owner, John Moseley, is a landscape architect as well as a talented builder and student of solar techniques. This greenhouse is attached to the residence not merely for convenience but to utilize the excess greenhouse heat during winter. In summer, cooler air in the house is vented through the greenhouse to the outside.

The glass and redwood greenhouse is 8 × 14 feet, and the roof is angled for maximum utilization of the summer sun. It is very similar in construction to the attached greenhouse described on pages 29–35. But in this case

the top third of the roof is covered with insulation to provide relief from the overhead summer sun. Vents are installed as necessary.

The 14-foot north wall, the heat sink, is 8 feet high. It's made from pumice block poured full of concrete, and the outside is insulated with 4-inch-thick rigid insulation that was stuccoed to protect it from the weather. The low foundation for putting up the polyethylene wall in front—also insulated on the outside below ground level—is topped with bricks to follow the line of bricks on the territorial-style main house.

The front wall and roof were originally designed to have only one pane of glass in each opening, but a local code required two. The code also required that the glass windows be separated at the corners, so the block wall was extended and a work area formed beside the outside entrance.

Construction started by laying out the area and setting up batter boards, as detailed on pages 22–24. The ground was then excavated to make the brick floor of the greenhouse level with the floor of the residence. After the greenhouse was finished, the two were connected by a sliding glass door.

With the excavation completed, concrete forms of 1 × 4s for the footing were put around the inside perimeter and leveled all the way. The outside of the footing was formed with rigid insulation braced against the outside of the excavation.

When the footing had hardened, the walls were built with standard-size pumice blocks, and insulation was brought up to the ground level in front and on the sides. The front and side walls were poured full of pumice rock for insulation. The back wall—the heat sink—was given maximum insulation on the outside.

In the frame, each vertical stud, plus the top and bottom plates and the crosspieces, were rabetted to receive the panes of glass. (If you don't have access to a table saw for rabbeting, you can put the glass in with quarter-round molding or 1 × 1 redwood strips as stops nailed to the studs and rafters.)

The west wall, with the exterior door, was framed piece by piece. The 2 × 6 door frame went in first; then the top plate, the door header, and the window and vent frames.

Once the front and side walls were in place, the next step was building the roof. This was done a little unconventionally: instead of placing each rafter individually, the roof was measured and laid out as it would be for building a wall. The front ends of the rafters were first cut so they would be in vertical line with the front wall. Like the front wall, each piece was rabbeted to accept the panes of glass; then the entire roof section was nailed together. Once it was lifted into place and toenailed to the top plate of the front wall, a 1 × 6 was used to cover this seam. At the back, where the roof extended above and slightly over the wall, the area was covered with plywood and insulated inside and out.

In Santa Fe, New Mexico, landscape architect John Moseley designed a heat-collecting pumice-block-and-concrete north wall to warm both residence and greenhouse.

Attached Solar Greenhouse, Santa Fe, N.M.

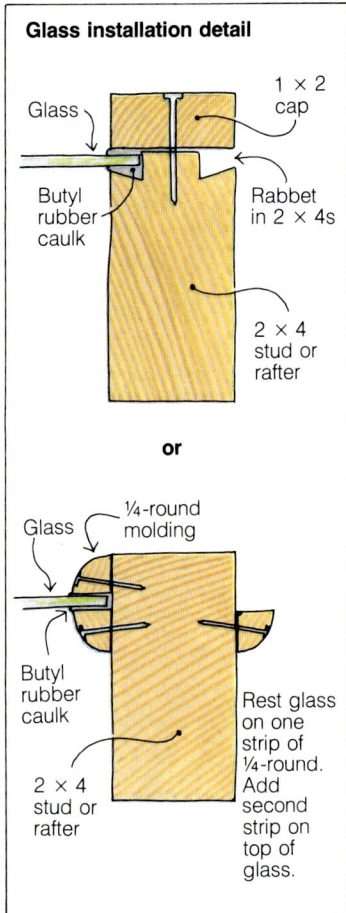

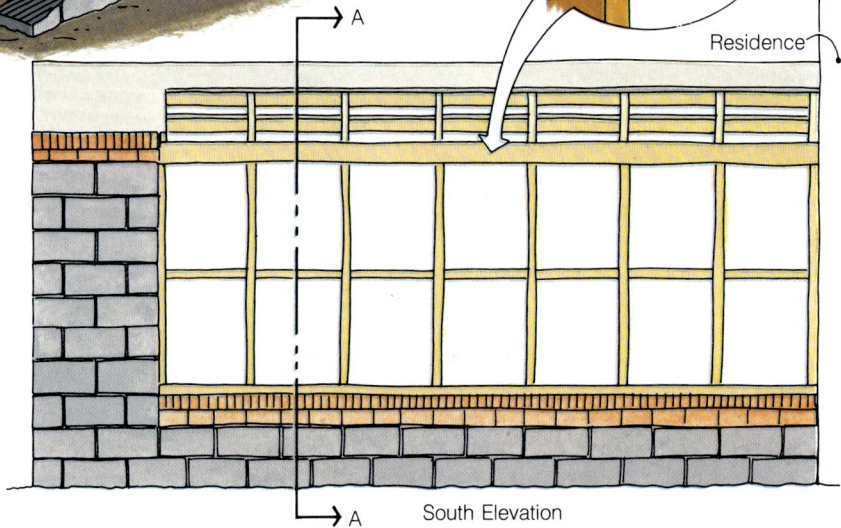

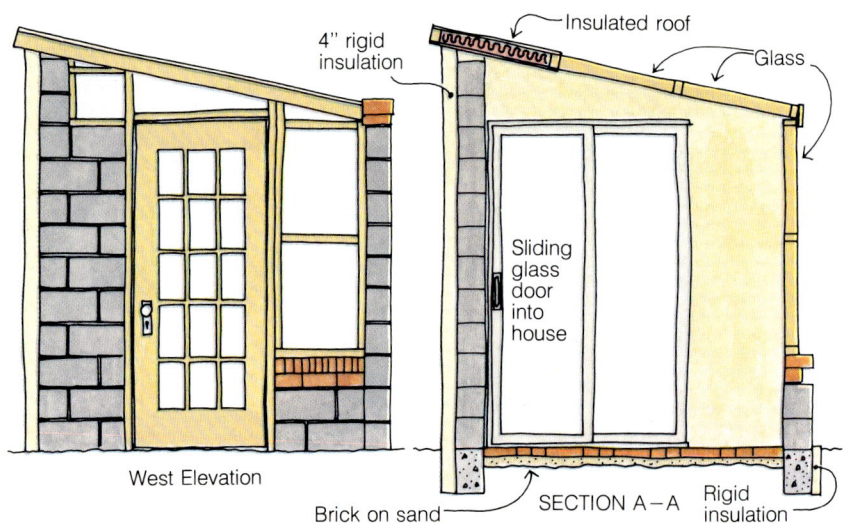

4" rigid insulation covered with stucco

Pumice blocks filled with concrete

Block wall cut away on drawing to show more of end wall

1 × 6 covers joint of roof and wall

Residence

A

A

South Elevation

Glass installation detail

Glass

1 × 2 cap

Butyl rubber caulk

Rabbet in 2 × 4s

2 × 4 stud or rafter

or

Glass

¼-round molding

Butyl rubber caulk

2 × 4 stud or rafter

Rest glass on one strip of ¼-round. Add second strip on top of glass.

West Elevation

4" rigid insulation

Insulated roof

Glass

Sliding glass door into house

Brick on sand

SECTION A–A

Rigid insulation

The glass went in quickly; then each piece was sealed inside and out with butyl rubber. The glass was held in place with strips of 1 × 2.

For the flooring, sand dug from a nearby dry stream bed was laid 3 inches thick over the ground. The sand was then dampened and leveled. Each brick was laid, tamped, and leveled, as described on page 34.

With the floor down, all that remained was to finish the benches and sink area before bringing in the plants and seedlings. By February—a month after it was completed—the greenhouse was filled with flowering plants and vegetables.

Angled-wall solar greenhouse. First designed by Bill Yanda, a New Mexico builder, this type of greenhouse is useful in areas with hot summers and cold but fairly sunny winters. The south wall is angled to directly face the low winter sun. But again, the top third of the roof is covered and insulated to give some respite inside from the summer sun. The angle of the front wall is generally 60°. To calculate the optimum angle for your own location, follow this rule of thumb: put the wall at an angle equal to the geographical latitude, plus 35°.

The amount of roof covering is important. In calculating this, bear in mind that you want the winter sun to strike high on the back wall, which will be absorbing and storing heat. In the summer, about a third of the greenhouse will be shaded, but there can still be enough reflected light for good growing. Plants that love heat and sun should be moved to the front of the greenhouse in summer.

Once the foundation is down and the sill is in place, the next step is to build the front walls. In this model, the south wall and roof have studs and rafters at intervals of 2 feet on-center.

Before laying out the wall, cut the studs at the angle you wish. For a 60° slope, use a protractor to make a 30° angle on the bottom of the stud. The angle of the cut is always the difference between the vertical of 90° and the angle you want the wall to be. Cut the top of the stud parallel to the bottom so the top plate will lie flat. When the wall is all cut, lay it out, nail it together, and put it in place with bracing at both ends.

The next step is to put up the rafters. If you can bolt one end to the overhang on your house, fine. Otherwise, put up a ledger board on the house and support each rafter with a joist hanger. You can cut expenses a little here by notching each rafter 1¼ inches and fitting them over the ledger board and then nailing them into place.

To get the front of the rafter to lie flat on the wall plate, you must cut an angle called a "bird's mouth." To find this, hold one rafter in place at the outside end of the wall and mark where it needs to be cut. Use this rafter as a pattern board. When all rafters are cut, toenail them into place directly over each wall stud.

Now measure off the top third (more or less—depending on geographical latitude) of the roof rafters and mark, using a chalk line to snap all rafters at once. Nail 2 × 4 bracings straight across on this line; this is where you will join the clear and solid portions of the roof.

Before going any further, put the end walls in place. The top plate on the end walls ties directly onto the front wall plate. From this junction, run a stud down to the bottom plate. On the end where the door will be, use two studs nailed together on the side of the opening where you want to hang the door. Once the door is hung, measure off the door opening, allowing ¼ inch additional space for clearance, and put in the other side of the door frame.

This stud should be cross-braced midway up the wall to either the adjoining stud or to the endwall stud that is tied to the side of the house.

On the front wall between each rafter, nail in a 2 × 4 so that it is flush with the top of the rafters. You may have to use a ripsaw here for an even, tight fit. Now cover all crosspieces on the roof with strips of corrugated molding—

Angled-Wall Greenhouse

(An alternative to the attached greenhouse on page 32)

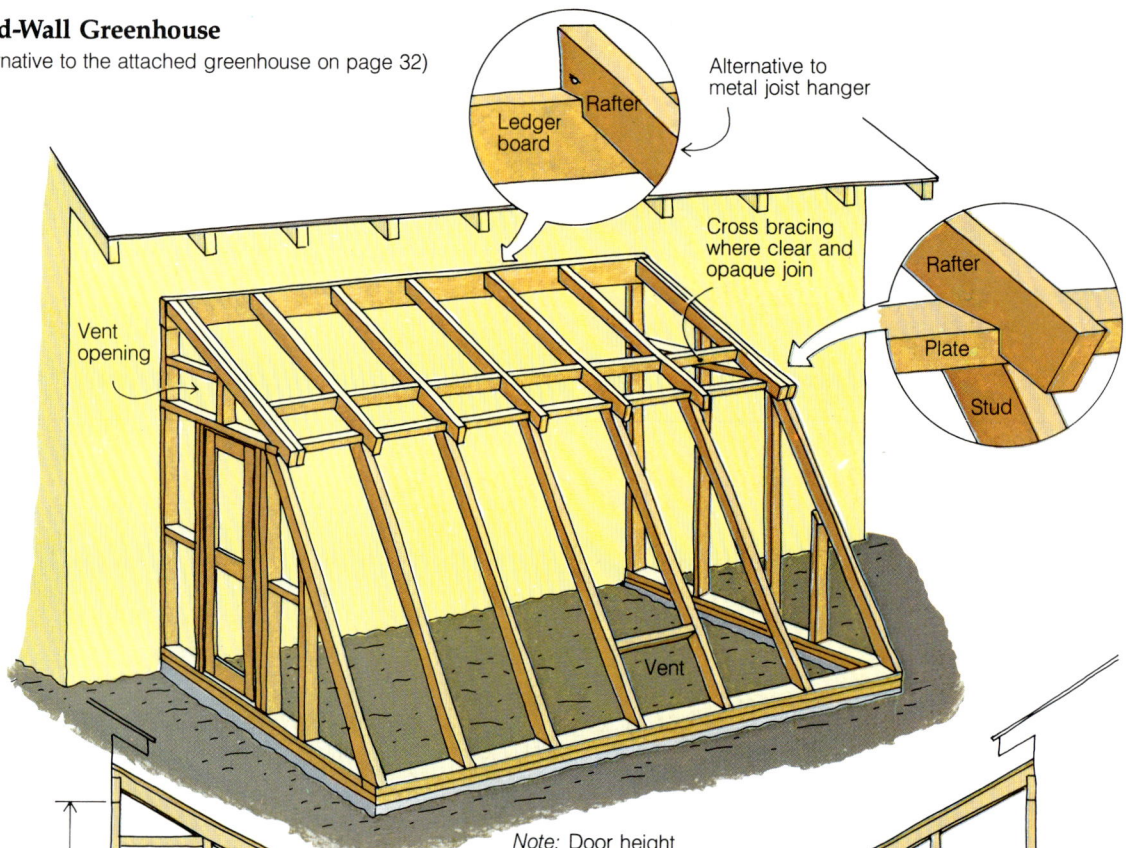

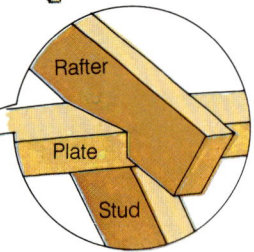

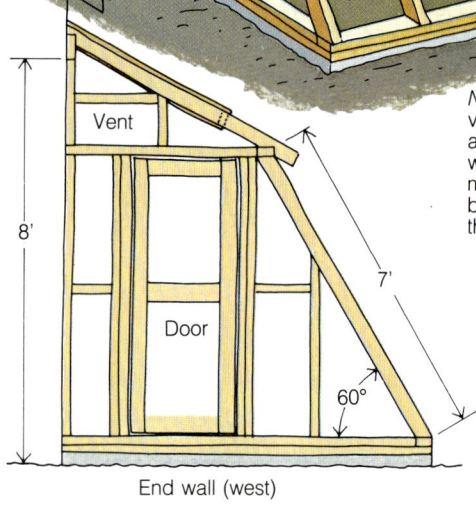

Ledger board

Rafter

Alternative to metal joist hanger

Cross bracing where clear and opaque join

Rafter

Plate

Stud

Vent opening

Note: Door height varies with height and angle of front wall. Be sure to measure opening before building the door.

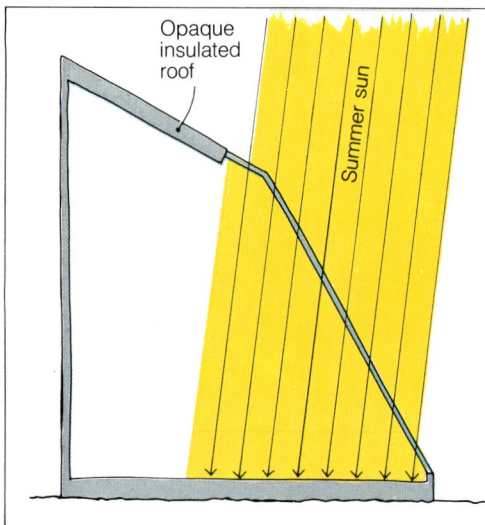

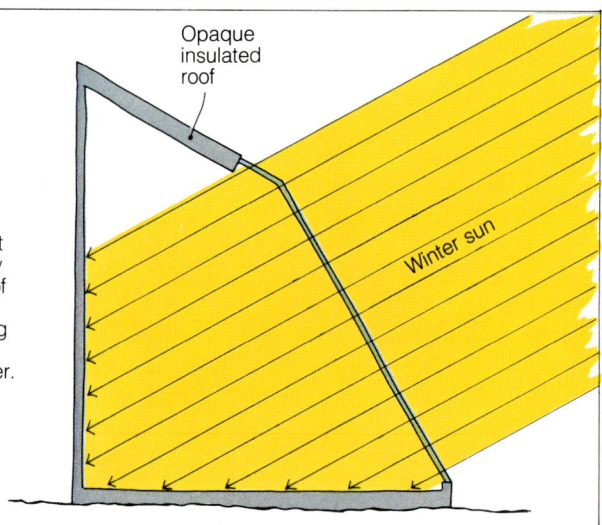

Vent

Vent

8'

7'

Door

60°

End wall (west)

End wall (east)

Opaque insulated roof

Summer sun

Opaque insulated roof

Winter sun

Angled front and partially covered roof allow more solar heating in winter than summer.

foam, redwood, or rubber. You are almost ready to put up the corrugated panels on the roof.

First, drill out the nail holes in each panel. Along the top edge (which will be covered by the solid portion of the roof), put holes on top of every third ridge. Along the bottom (which will be pulled at by winds), nail every ridge with an aluminum nail that has a neoprene washer.

Now, across the upper edge of the fiberglass roof, lay in another strip of molding, right on top of the fiberglass, and add a bead of sealant. Then put the solid panels of ⅜-inch exterior-grade plywood in place. Allow it to overlap the fiberglass by 4 inches, to keep rain from blowing in. You can use corrugated steel as the opaque part of the roof, which will mesh evenly with the corrugated fiberglass; however, this is difficult to vent and is a poor insulator.

If the back of the roof is not under an overhang, use metal flashing between it and the house. At any rate, seal this area tightly. Then you can cover the plywood with composition or cedar shingles, or paint.

On the front and side walls, use flat fiberglass panels. Before nailing in each panel, put down a bead of sealant and make sure the panel is square. Nail it every 6 inches with flathead galvanized 4d nails. When all pieces are up, lay another bead of sealant along the joints and cover with a strip of redwood lath.

To the solid roof inside, staple in fiberglass insulation. Then cover with wood or paneling of your choice. This area, like the whole interior, should be painted white to reflect light back into the greenhouse.

Finally, to create the dead-air insulating barrier, cover the interior with ultraviolet-resistant 4 mil polyethylene film.

The Sun Pit

Ordinarily, plants grow *above* the ground, not *below* it. But the sun pit—a below-ground environment with a clear roof overhead—is a particularly efficient way to grow plants year-round. Sometimes called a coldframe with head room, the sun pit requires little or no additional heating. It takes advantage of the ground's natural insulation and loses little heat through the walls to the soil. In fact, if the excavation is deeper than the frost line, the pit can actually gain heat from the ground. Its low profile protects it from the wind. And if you put it close to your house, you can use the extra heat from the pit to warm your home.

Like most greenhouses, a sun pit soon proves too small, so build in plenty of room. A bare-minimum size is 8 × 12 feet, but 12 × 18 feet would give you growing space on both sides of the pit and down the middle.

First, mark out the area where you want the sun pit, locating it on the east-west axis, with one length of the roof facing south. Do not dig the pit

Sun Pit

Detail of north half of roof

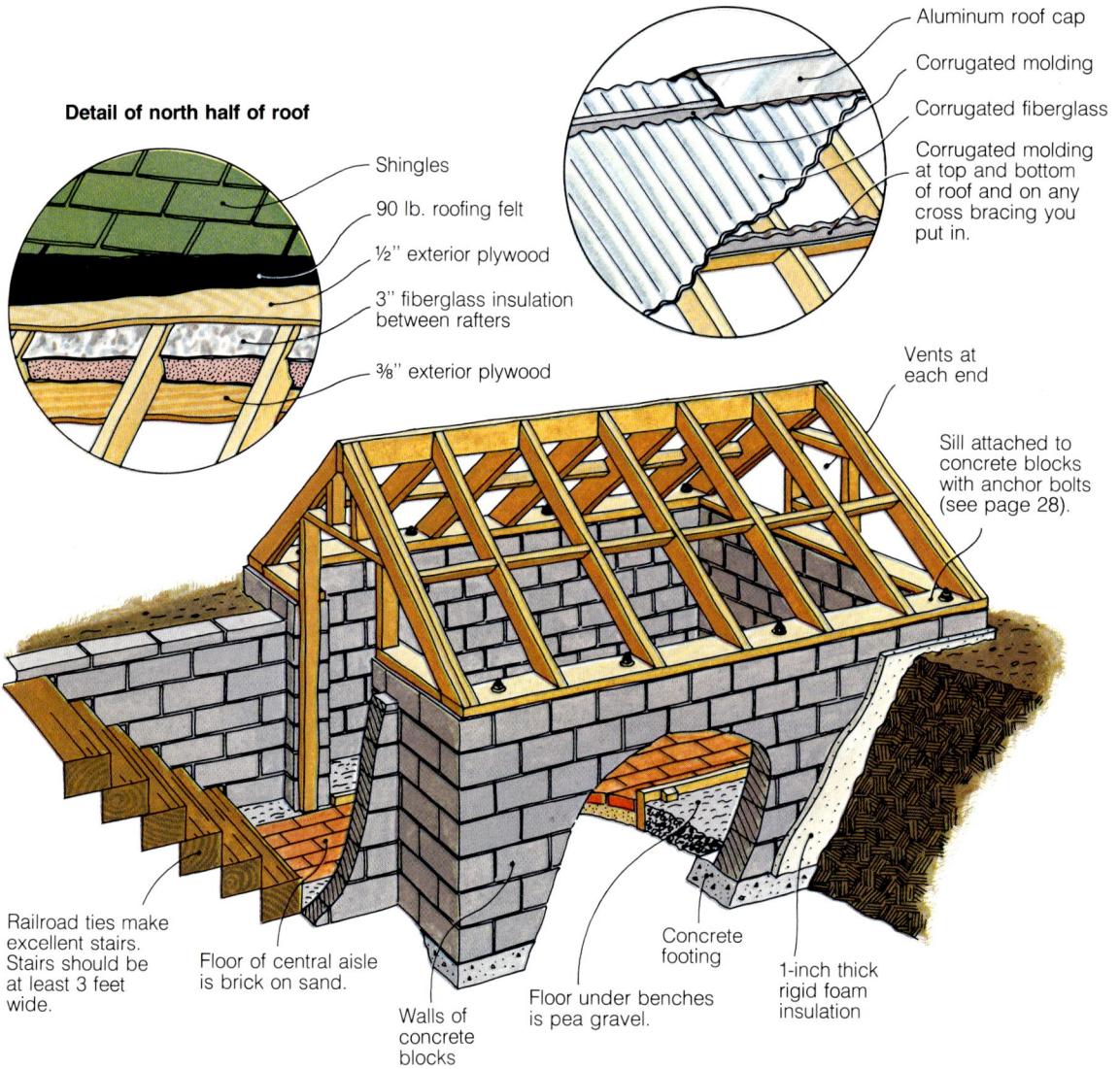

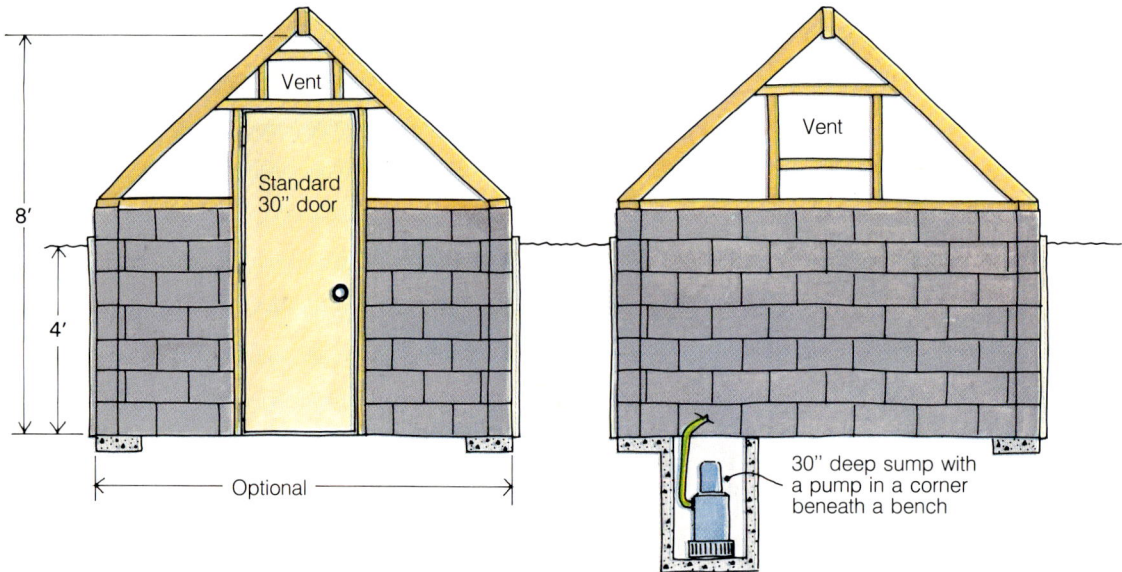

- Shingles
- 90 lb. roofing felt
- ½" exterior plywood
- 3" fiberglass insulation between rafters
- ⅜" exterior plywood

Detail of south half of roof

- Aluminum roof cap
- Corrugated molding
- Corrugated fiberglass
- Corrugated molding at top and bottom of roof and on any cross bracing you put in.

Vents at each end

Sill attached to concrete blocks with anchor bolts (see page 28).

Railroad ties make excellent stairs. Stairs should be at least 3 feet wide.

Floor of central aisle is brick on sand.

Walls of concrete blocks

Floor under benches is pea gravel.

Concrete footing

1-inch thick rigid foam insulation

Vent

Standard 30" door

8'

4'

Optional

Vent

30" deep sump with a pump in a corner beneath a bench

yourself. If you can't get help, rent a backhoe, a powerful tractor with a scoop bucket on one end and a hydraulic digging arm on the other. The cost is normally under $30 an hour. A moderate-sized backhoe will probably dig the pit and remove the dirt in about 2 hours.

The pit should be 4 feet deep. Once it is dug, square the sides until they are vertical and level the floor, checking with a level on top of a straight 2×4. Around the edge, dig a ditch 4 inches deep and 12 inches wide for the footings (pour these with the aid of leveling stakes, as described on page 23), and a sump 30 inches deep and about 18 inches wide, from which irrigation and seepage water can be pumped out of the pit. While waiting for the footings to dry, dig steps at the end, away from prevailing winter winds. Bring in water and electricity lines at this time.

When the footings are cured, start laying up the cinder-block wall. It must be insulated on the outside with a minimum of 1-inch-thick rigid insulation of plastic foam or 4 inches of pumice rock.

When putting up the wall, don't mortar each block into place. Instead, lay a course of blocks, fill every other opening with concrete, then tamp thoroughly. Once the concrete has stiffened, lay up another course and fill the alternate holes. For extra strength, add a length of reinforcing rod running up the hole you are filling with concrete. Keep checking the level and plumb of the wall as you go.

The next step is to finish the flooring while you can still get a wheelbarrow in. At this depth, the ground will be relatively warm, and insulation under the floor is not necessary. You may cover the floor with 4 inches of pea gravel or the more attractive brick-on-sand. Or, as a compromise, put the gravel under the benches, holding it in place with 2×6s, and cover the walkways with sand and brick.

Once the flooring, water, and electricity have been installed, you're ready to start the roof. For the conventional A-frame style, start by erecting a 2×6 ridge board directly down the center of the pit. This should be about 8 feet above the floor, but you may adjust it to your own height and needs.

To find the angle of end cuts so the rafters will fit smoothly against the ridge board and the sills, hold one rafter in place at the end, mark it, and use it as a pattern for the other rafters. For a 12-foot-long sun pit, cut 18 rafters. This gives you double rafters on each end to provide a good nailing surface for the end walls. The studs of the end walls should be spaced 2 feet on-center, with vent openings directly under the ridge.

For a sun pit without electrically operated fans, install vent openings on the north slope of the roof near the peak. Space them at every other rafter. Make the roofs like those described on page 33 for the lean-to greenhouse.

Cover the north slope of the roof with ½-inch plywood topped with 90-pound roofing felt, then with the covering of your choice, such as shingles. Inside, staple 3-inch fiberglass insulation between the studs, and cover with 3-inch exterior-grade plywood. Paint this ceiling white to reflect light back onto the plants.

Cover the south roof with 4-foot-wide sheets of Tedlar-treated corrugated fiberglass. Fit the top and bottom of each panel over corrugated foam molding and nail on every other ridge. Cover the ridge of the roof with an aluminum roof cap, remembering to put down another layer of foam molding between it and the fiberglass for a tight seal.

Cover the end walls with glass set between the stud openings or with flat fiberglass. In really cold areas where snow is a problem, cover and insulate the end walls.

A word of caution: sun pits are difficult to heat and ventilate, and controlling plant disease can be a problem. Sun pits were once popular as commercial greenhouses, but they fell out of favor around the turn of the century. Still, with careful management, a sun pit can be an inexpensive and satisfactory type of controlled environment.

A basic, backyard sun pit greenhouse is insulated by the earth.

ARTIFICIAL AND NATURAL LIGHT

Learn how to use natural or artificial light to the best advantage for your plants.

It can't be said too often: winter sunlight, or more correctly, the lack of it, is the greatest concern of the controlled-environment gardener. No matter how well or often you give a plant its other needs, it's the light available during short, winter days that will determine whether your poinsettias will bloom for Christmas, or your forced bulbs for Valentine's Day. The pot chrysanthemum that you force into bloom in June or July is responding to the controlled day length you maintain for it. Some plants are not very particular about having long or short days or nights, but then some are very particular about when they bloom, based on the amount of light they receive.

A chrysanthemum that naturally blooms in fall forms its buds in late summer, when the days are long and the nights are short, but it flowers when the days are short and the nights are long. Therefore, to grow it in a controlled environment so it will bloom in spring or early summer, you must give it a relatively long period of light in the months preceding flowering, then reduce the daylength to initiate flowering. If you use artificial light on the plants you want to come into bloom, shade the other plants that aren't in the same cycle.

The best part of growing plants is in observing nature. If you can acquaint yourself with plants' natural cycles, you will learn to give them what they need.

All About Light

Light is crucial to healthy plant growth. It is the energizing force in the process that all green plants use to make simple sugars from water and carbon dioxide. Without light and the green plants that trap its energy, life could not exist as we know it today.

This sugar-producing process—photosynthesis (from *photo*, meaning light, and *synthesis*, meaning to put together)—is truly one of nature's miracles. It is a solar energy trap far more efficient than any yet devised by humans.

The diagram at the top of page 80 shows where light fits in the photosynthesis process.

Light is radiant energy. Technically, it is the visible portion of the electromagnetic wavelength spectrum.

Visible light is a blend of red, orange, yellow, green, blue, and violet rays. Beyond the visible blue-violet are invisible ultraviolet rays; at the other end of the spectrum, invisible infrared rays lie just beyond the visible red. Plants absorb primarily blue and red light and reflect green and yellow.

Blue and violet rays promote foliage growth. Plants grown with blue light alone tend to be compact and have lush, dark green leaves but few flowers. Red and far-red light affects several growth processes, including the elongation and expansion of various plant parts and, notably, flowering. Plant

With the addition of artificial lighting, almost any indoor space can become a favorite garden.

The Process of Photosynthesis

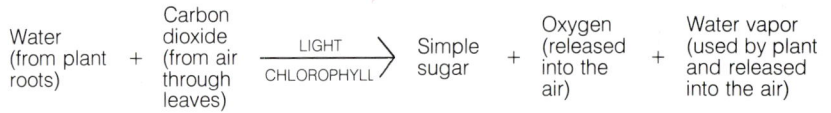

Water (from plant roots) + Carbon dioxide (from air through leaves) $\xrightarrow[\text{CHLOROPHYLL}]{\text{LIGHT}}$ Simple sugar + Oxygen (released into the air) + Water vapor (used by plant and released into the air)

1. Stomata Palisade cells
Epidermal cells

Stomata
Mesophyll cells

2.
Chloroplasts

Nucleus

3.

1. The cross section of a leaf shows the waterproof upper and lower epidermal cells with stomata (pores) through which water vapor, oxygen, and carbon dioxide enter and leave the leaf; the layer of palisade cells, just below the upper surface, where most of the chloroplasts and therefore, most of the photosynthesis occurs; and the mesophyll cells where the products of photosynthesis are stored before transfer to other parts of the plant. **2.** A single palisade cell showing the nucleus and many chloroplasts. **3.** A single chloroplast with its grana, groups of minute plates called lamellae in which most of the chlorophyll molecules are found.

scientists have identified these effects, although they have yet to discover how these occur. Research has not revealed any major effects of yellow or green rays on plant growth.

Measuring light. Measuring the amount of light available to your plants involves some work and calculation, but it's worth the effort. Providing sufficiently intense light will give you healthy, lush, long-lived plants.

Light is measured in footcandles and lumens, depending on whether you consider the light falling on the object or the source that emits the light.

Footcandles, or f.c., are the amount of light *received* on a surface. Lumens are the measure of light *emitted* by a light source.

Natural sunlight and artificial light falling on a plant are measured in footcandles, while the light emitted by such sources as the sun itself and electric lamps is rated in lumens.

One footcandle is the amount of visible light falling on one square foot of surface located one foot away from one standard candle.

For example, a clear summer day may measure 10,000 f.c., and an overcast winter day may measure as low as 500 f.c. The amount of light needed to read comfortably is about 20 f.c. The light of the full moon measures less than 1 f.c.

The most accurate way to estimate light is by mechanical means—either with a special light meter that reads directly in footcandles, a photographer's light meter, or the light meter built into a camera.

General Electric makes a light meter with a scale that gives direct footcandle readings—Model #24. It can measure up to 10,000 footcandles.

To take a reading with a footcandle meter, place the meter at the same position as the surface of the leaves. Aim the plastic-covered lens toward the maximum light source. Then, without blocking the light or casting a shadow on the meter, check the reading on the dial.

A photographic meter or camera with a built-in light meter will provide fairly accurate readings of reflected light translated into footcandles. Here are two methods.

Method 1. Set the film-speed dial to ASA 100, and aim the camera or hand-held meter at a sheet of matte white cardboard or paper temporarily placed in the proposed plant location. Orient the paper to receive the maximum light from the source. Get close enough to the paper so the meter "sees" only the white paper. Be sure not to block the light or create a shadow. The shutter speed indicated opposite stop f4, read as a whole number, will be the approximate footcandles of illumination measured. For example, if the f-stop registers an exposure of 1/250th second, there are about 250 f.c. of light playing on the white sheet.

Method 2. Set the ASA film speed at 20 and the shutter speed at 1/125th second. Focus on the white paper, as above. Adjust the f-stop until a correct exposure is shown in the light meter in the camera. Use the accompanying table to convert the f-stop value to the number of available footcandles.

The camera's photographic meter measures the same spectrum of visible light as the footcandle meter, but the latter registers intermediate readings and is also more accurate.

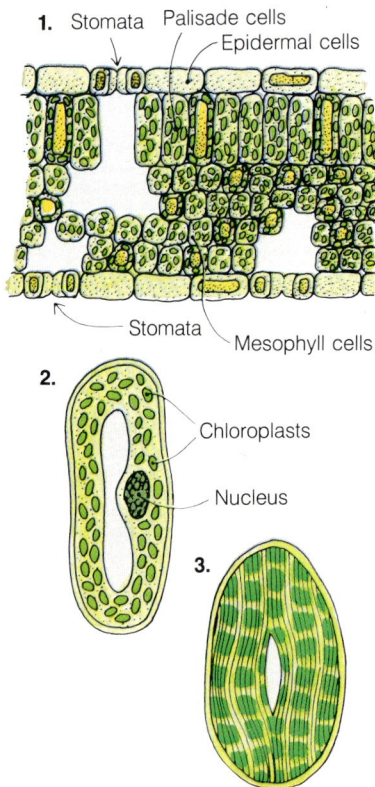

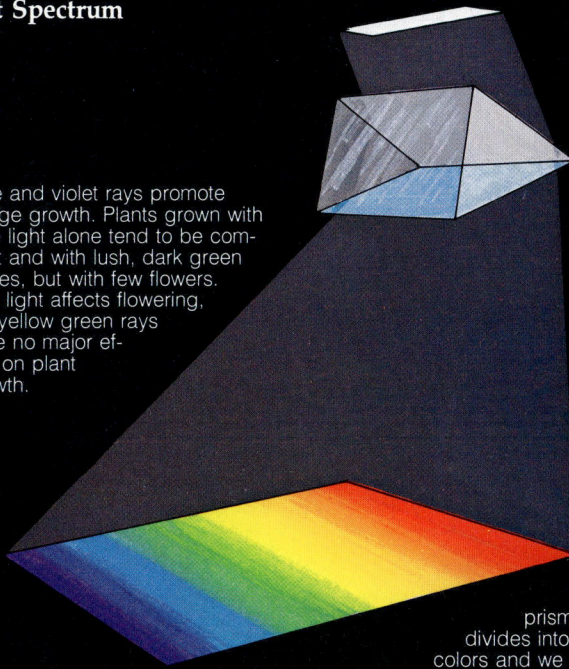

The Light Spectrum

Blue and violet rays promote foliage growth. Plants grown with blue light alone tend to be compact and with lush, dark green leaves, but with few flowers. Red light affects flowering, but yellow green rays have no major effect on plant growth.

White light passing through a prism (or raindrops) divides into its component colors and we see a rainbow.

Light meter

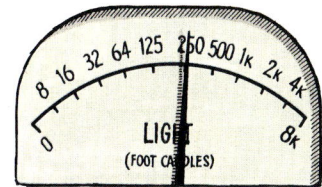

Camera

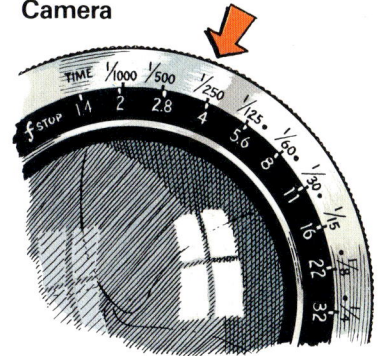

Effects of light. Light has many and varied effects on plants. Its most important qualities are intensity and duration. Measuring the light as described above is a guide to intensity.

Generally, a plant given low light-intensities only *maintains* itself; if it receives more light, it *grows*. When intensity dips below the minimum a plant can tolerate, the plant slowly weakens and dies. A plant in this state may appear healthy for some months, but in fact it is living on stored energy and is slowly declining.

Scientists use the word *etiolation* to describe plants grown in very low light or darkness. It is a French word meaning "to blanch." Etiolated plants are typically spindly and actually grow taller than they would if they had had adequate light. The color is pale, and the leaves are poorly developed. Many gardeners have experienced etiolated seedlings that grow tall quickly, then fall because of their own weight. Such seedlings are the result of being grown in low light levels.

Plants exposed to overly high light intensities exhibit variable symptoms. The leaves may wilt during the hottest part of the day, curl downward, and develop brown, burned spots. The foliage may undergo color change. Lush greens may bleach to unhealthy yellow. Plants can also experience leafburn. For instance, orchids exposed to excessive light intensity will develop blackened areas on the leaves.

Plants should never be subjected to drastic change of light without first being conditioned. A plant adapted to shade conditions can suffer fatal burning when moved to a sunny location; with conditioning, however, it might tolerate this move. It's as if a person pale from spending the winter indoors went to the beach and became severely burned by too much sun. Conversely, many plants that become accustomed to low light levels die when shifted rapidly from an area of much higher light.

Photoperiodism. Many plants are light-programmed to their own native environment and perform best in the rhythmic light/darkness cycle found there. For such plants, the length of nights and days helps determine the time required to reach maturity—that stage in a plant's life when reproduction becomes possible.

Conversion Factor (Method 2)

f-stop	Footcandles
2.8	32
4	64
5.6	125
8	250
11	500
16	1000
22	2000

A footcandle meter measures the amount of light falling on this piggyback plant (*Tolmeia menziesii*).

A wide angle-view of a growth chamber. Here, plant scientists control and study the effects of light duration and intensity.

Some plants flower when the days are long and the nights are short; these are called *long-day* plants. Some long-day plants are calceolaria, tuberous begonia, cineraria, azalea, coleus, gloxinia, stephanotis, and African violets.

Conversely, other plants produce blooms when days are short and nights long; these are the *short-day* plants. Common short-day plants are gardenias, kalanchoe, chrysanthemum, Christmas cactus, poinsettia, some cattleya orchids, aphelandra, and fuchsia.

Many plants, however, have no definite response—they are *day-neutral*. They will flower independent of the daylength.

Armed with this knowledge, you can bring plants into bloom any time of year. Long-day plants can be given supplemental light in the form of artificial lights. Short-day plants requiring 12 hours or more of darkness can be shaded with black cloth before the sun goes down. But the shading must be complete: even if tiny quantities of light leak through, flowering won't occur.

Artificial Light

Artificial light has greatly expanded the flexibility and capability of gardeners. It can provide the sole energy source in which plants can grow, or, more naturally, it can be used to supplement sunlight.

Incandescent light. Common light bulbs used every day in the home give off incandescent light. These bulbs consist of a tungsten filament wire that has high resistance to electricity. The heat caused by the resistance of the filament results in the emission of visible light.

This is a light source rich in red and far-red light necessary for flowering and other plant processes. In fact, incandescent light possesses the same proportion of these colors as sunlight, although to a vastly less intense degree. However, the total energy output is insufficient among the blue and violet rays of the spectrum. Therefore, incandescent light alone is not suitable for complete plant growth.

Incandescent lighting is the primary light source for these foliage plants.

Heat. Incandescents also give off a considerable amount of heat. This, of course, can damage plants growing too close to the light. In general, the solution is to keep the tops of plants at least a foot away from incandescent sources. However, if your hand feels warm when you put it on the foliage closest to the light source, move the plant even farther back.

Don't place the lamp too far away from the plant, either. The light reaching the plant decreases with the square of the distance that it is removed. That is, a plant 2 feet away from a light source will receive only one-fourth as much light as it would if it were 1 foot away.

Reducing heat. The easiest way to reduce heat of incandescent bulbs is to use 130-volt types. These are "industrial" grade—they burn cooler and longer than standard 120-volt bulbs, but they give out less light.

Another way is to use a greater number of smaller bulbs instead of fewer larger ones. This distributes the heat over a large area, allows you to place the lamps closer to the plants, and provides more even distribution of light.

A third method is to use reflectorized incandescent lamps. These have names such as Cool Beam or Cool Lux. They contain a reflecting surface that allows light to pass but directs heat upward. Use a heavy-duty ceramic socket with these bulbs.

The most reliable way to reduce heat is to place a shield of glass or transparent plastic between the lights and the plants. This shield will absorb or reflect a large amount of heat, yet allow nearly all the light to pass through to the plant. Put the shield several inches away from the lamp. Be sure to have good air circulation above the heat shield to carry away the excessive heat.

Fluorescent light. Fluorescent lamps are the favorite of most gardeners because they are more efficient. They supply 2½ to 3 times as much light and only a fraction of the heat of an incandescent bulb with the same wattage. Also, the lifetime of a fluorescent tube is 15 to 20 times that of an incandescent.

The glass tube of a fluorescent lamp is coated on the inside with a chemical called a phosphor. The type of phosphor determines the "color" of the light given off. Mixing various phosphors determines the "mix" of the various color wavelengths. The visible color of the light emitted, however, is not indicative of the proportion of blue and red waves given off. Remember that plants do not "see" light as we do.

The bulb also contains a blend of inert gasses such as argon, neon, or krypton, and a minute quantity of mercury vapor, sealed in low pressure. Electricity causes a current to flow between the electrodes at each end of the tube. This current is in the form of an electrical arc, which stimulates the phosphor coating to emit energy in the form of light.

Although initially more expensive than incandescent bulbs, fluorescent lamps form the backbone of gardening with lights. They can be positioned as close as 1 inch to many plants, although 6 to 9 inches is more common. They should not be placed more than 18 inches away from the top of a plant unless they are of the high-output type.

High-output tubes are used by scientists and advanced light gardeners. Their higher light intensity permits greater tube-to-plant distances as well as the greatest possible flexibility for successful artificial light gardening. These tubes are available from all the major electric companies.

Page 80 describes how to measure light to ensure adequate intensity for plant growth. The amount of fluorescent light needed can also be figured out in terms of total wattage per square foot. Experience indicates that about 20 watts per square foot is adequate for plants that normally require low light-levels, and 40 watts per square foot is adequate for high light-level plants. Of course, intensity can be further manipulated by adjusting the distance between the lights and the plants.

Most light gardeners leave lights on for as few as 10 to as many as 18 hours

Two versions of easily moved light gardens. Below: Lights and shelves suspended from the ceiling take up little space. The distance between the lights and the plants is simple to regulate. Bottom: A completely portable, self-contained, double-decker unit.

Growing chrysanthemums under artificial lights allows you to lengthen the "nighttime" hours and produce blooms at any time of the year.

a day. It makes little difference with foliage plants, but flowering plants have more specific needs. Learn the requirements of the plant you want to grow.

Fluorescents, like incandescents, "blacken" with age and lose light efficiency. For the best plant growth, therefore, replace fluorescents when they reach 70 percent of their stated service life. By that time, they'll be delivering about 15 percent less light than when new.

Plant "grow lamps." These are sold under the names of Gro-Lux, Vita-lite, Agro-lite, and Naturescent/Optima, among others. They are of two types: "wide spectrum," in which the visual qualities of sunlight are duplicated; and "spectrum enhanced," in which the rays known to be most important to plant growth are maximized.

The wide-spectrum lamps include the visible blue and far-red rays, and sometimes the ultraviolet rays as well. Their light has a "daylight" quality. Not only do they aid plant growth, they also render plant colors more realistically than grow lights do. The added (but not visible) far-red in wide-spectrum bulbs gives off a reduced light, compared to the standard cool or warm white of grow lights.

The spectrum-enhanced lamps are coated with special phosphors that reduce the green/yellow rays, which are of little value to plants. The lamp's energy is concentrated on the blue/red parts of the spectrum. Because of the missing portion of the spectrum, the light given out tends to be purplish or pinkish.

Fluorescent and incandescent combined. Ordinary fluorescent light, in the right intensities, can promote lush foliage growth, even bring some plants to flower. Like incandescent, it is short on certain parts of the spectrum. All common fluorescent output is very high in the blue light, which in general promotes foliage growth, and low in red and far-red, which are important in the flowering process.

Many artificial-light gardeners claim that the best solution to the dilemma is to combine fluorescent and incandescent, a combination that is usually expressed in terms of ratios of watts. However, many varying ratios are used. What is common to all of them is that the quantity of fluorescent light is always greater. Various gardeners have recommended anywhere between 1:2 and 1:5—in other words, 200 or 500 watts of fluorescent light to 100 watts incandescent. Other gardeners suggest 1:3 for wattages below 1,000 f.c., increasing the ratio to 1:2 above 2,000 f.c.

Researchers at the United States Department of Agriculture in Beltsville,

Water from the filled trough is drawn by the capillary mat to provide an even amount of moisture to each pot.

Maryland, have long studied the relationship of light quality to plant growth. Recently, two of their scientists—H. Marc Cathey and L. E. Campbell—summarized their research on the effects of light sources on plant growth. Their findings are summarized below.

Fluorescent (cool white and warm white).

☐ Green foliage results, which expands to parallel the surface of the lamp.
☐ Stems elongate slowly.
☐ Multiple side shoots develop.
☐ Flowering occurs over a long period of time.

Fluorescent, enhanced spectrum (Gro-Lux).

☐ Deep green foliage expands, often is larger than on plants grown under cool white or warm white.
☐ Stems elongate slowly; extra-thick stems develop.
☐ Multiple side shoots develop.
☐ Flowering occurs late; flower stalks do not elongate.

Fluorescent, wide spectrum (Vita-lite, Agro-lite, and others).

☐ Light green foliage tends to grow toward the lamp.
☐ Stems elongate rapidly.
☐ Development of multiple side shoots is suppressed.
☐ Flowering occurs early; flower stalks elongate; plants mature and age rapidly.

Incandescent.

☐ Foliage pales, grows thinner and longer than on plants grown under other light sources.
☐ Stems elongate excessively and eventually become spindly and easily broken.
☐ Side shoot development is suppressed; plants expand only in height.
☐ Flowering occurs rapidly; plants mature and become senescent quickly.

Building Artificial Light Gardens

A good place for lights is under kitchen cupboards. Here, a splash of colorful plants year-round can prove restful to the eyes. In the drawings shown here, two 40-watt bulbs were placed under a kitchen cabinet. Small staples hold the cords out of the way. The lights, however, were visible from the nearby dining table, and cast an uncomfortable glare. To hide them, a 1 × 4 board was screwed to a 2 × 2 and cut off to fit under the cabinet, shielding the glaring lights.

Windows. If you have a kitchen window that faces north and receives little light, or a bathroom window that receives almost no light, brighten them with a combination of overhead lights and plants. They can dramatically change the room's appearance.

If you have wooden window frames, you can screw the fluorescent light directly to the underside of the frame. If you don't already have a valance to shield the light, you will have to install some form of shield. To determine how deep the protective shield must be in order to hide the light fairly well, experiment with a strip of cardboard. If 8 inches, for instance, provides good shielding, cut a 1 × 8 board the width of your window, paint it to match, and screw it in place.

If you can't hang a light inside the window, use this shelf-bracket method: screw short lengths of heavy-duty shelf standards to both sides of the window frame at the top. Then, using brackets at least 2 inches longer than your light fixture is wide, bolt 1 × 8 boards to the outside of the brackets. Use glue and 6d finishing nails to attach the 1 × 8 front piece that will shield

Incandescent bulbs are used with fluorescent lights to provide a balanced system of light. The plastic sheeting helps retain heat and moisture.

Fluorescent Lighting Ideas

Here are three simple light gardens to alter "day length" or start seedlings. The fluorescent fixture on the adjustable shelf brackets can be moved up or down to give your plants more or less light.

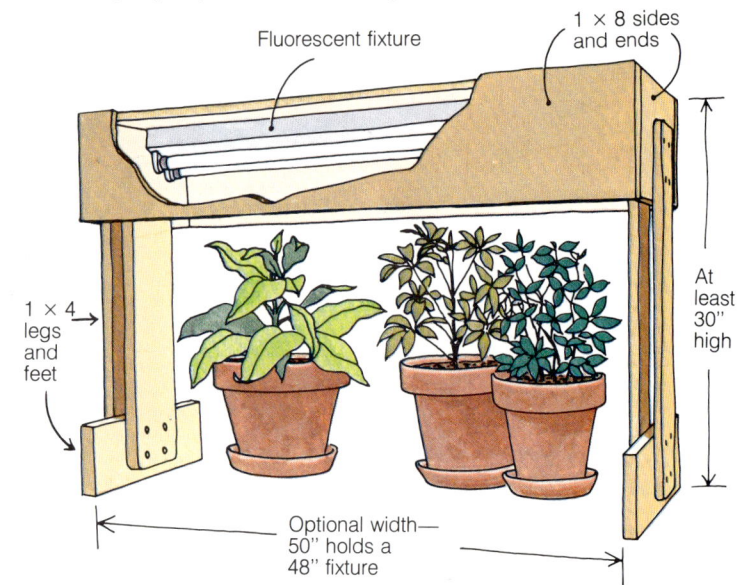

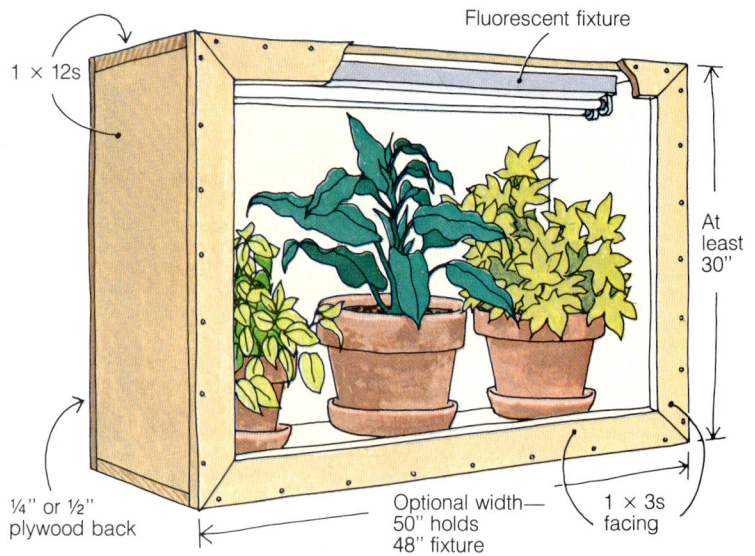

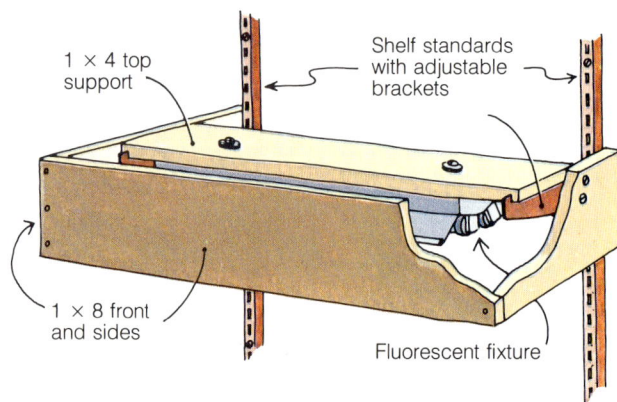

Fluorescent fixture

1 × 8 sides and ends

1 × 4 legs and feet

At least 30" high

Optional width— 50" holds a 48" fixture

Fluorescent fixture

1 × 12s

At least 30"

¼" or ½" plywood back

Optional width— 50" holds 48" fixture

1 × 3s facing

1 × 4 top support

Shelf standards with adjustable brackets

1 × 8 front and sides

Fluorescent fixture

the light. Across the top, nail a 1×4 down the middle, and hang the light from that. When it is all assembled and painted, hang it from the shelf standards. This should provide ample support for the light fixture and the shield. For windows that are wider than 4 feet, however, you should use a center support.

You can use the same shelf system to make a light garden that will grow along with the plants. Start the lights out as low as 2 inches above a seedling bed, then raise them to keep pace with the growth of the plants. This technique is particularly useful for starting tomatoes indoors before transplanting outdoors for early production.

Table-top units. These are both useful and attractive on narrow tables in long, dim hallways. Since fluorescent lights and fixtures come in a great variety of lengths, they will fit over almost any table.

For a simple but effective table-top model, start by constructing a three-sided box. It can be up to 8 feet long, with no center supports. Use a 1×12 for the top and 1×6 for the sides. If you can, miter all the joints at a 45° angle for a smoothly finished exterior that has no end wood showing. Paint the inside of the box white for added reflection; then screw the light fixture to the inside top of the box.

For the supporting legs, use four 1×4s cut 28 inches long. Bolt two legs together over each end of the box, clasping the 1×6 end pieces. To make the feet of the legs, clasp and bolt an 11-inch length of 1×4.

Instead of using decorative bolts, you can use wood screws, countersinking them all. Then fill the holes either with wood putty or small wooden buttons designed for this purpose.

Cabinet light garden. You can make a dramatic light garden for a dark side of the room by constructing a basic cabinet frame. It's nothing more than a large box on its side, with the front open. It can also double as a bookcase. You can alter the following dimensions to fit your needs.

Using 1×12 wood that is kiln or air dried so that it won't warp, cut the two end pieces 3 feet long and cut the top and bottom pieces each 5 feet long. Miter the ends if you have the tools; otherwise, use butt joints. Use white glue and 6d nails to put the frame together. Cut a piece of ½-inch plywood to 3×5 feet and then glue and nail it to the back of the frame.

Inside each end piece, drill a parallel row of holes 4 inches apart for the metal shelf holders. Cut a shelf 4 feet 10½ inches long from 1×12.

To hide the fixtures and give the cabinet a finished appearance, face all the outside edges with 1×4, including the shelves. Miter the corners of the edging on the cabinet frame to fit together at a 45° angle. Paint the interior and the underside of the shelf white to give added reflection. Paint the top of the shelf to match your decor. Fasten the 4-foot fluorescent fixtures under the top and the shelf, then place your plants. If you need to increase the humidity, put the plants on pebble trays.

Basement gardens. If you have a little-used basement in your house, consider turning it into a major light garden.

Get started by building a series of shelves along one wall, running them from the floor to the ceiling. If your basement is unfinished, you can nail vertical 2×4 supports right to the floor joists overhead. Or use 2×4 posts for the uprights and tie them together all around with 1×4s. Using ½-inch plywood, make each shelf section 3 feet wide and up to 8 feet long. Tie them together all around with 1×4s.

Solariums

Solariums, or "sun rooms," are attached greenhouses or sun porches that provide ample light for plants, as well as beauty. The examples of solariums on the following pages may inspire you to build something similar.

A capillary pad watering system and fluorescent lighting help maintain a collection of about 200 varieties of African violets in a basement garden.

The Locatell solarium. Mr. Bob Locatell of Atlanta, Georgia, has built an
8 × 19-foot solarium next to his living room/dining room/study complex. "I
leave the sliding doors open all winter long so that, in effect, this becomes an
extension of the living room." The solarium is constructed from a frame of 4
× 8-foot removable panels of ⅛-inch-thick clear plexiglass. This material is
lighter weight than "Thermopane" or other plate glass, and each panel can
be easily handled by one person.

Mr. Locatell says that "the sloped roof is a single sheet of 'Kalwall,' 1¾
inches thick, which is a plastic material that has been on the market for a
number of years. It cuts excessive glare but transmits 60 to 70 percent of the
light that falls on it. It has an insulating value equivalent to that of an
insulated stud wall, which conserves heat." Although heat is conserved in
winter by the low angle of the sun, he uses a 1,200-watt electric heater with a
fan, set at 60°, to prevent night temperatures from dropping too low. He
positions the panels in late fall, then removes them in late spring, making
the area an open patio for warm-weather use. He uses an indoor-outdoor
carpet in winter, which he rolls up and stores in summer.

Mr. Locatell sprays malathion in early spring for pest control, and again at
the start of fall. He then closes the sliding doors for two days. Even with a
large number of plants, watering takes only 30 to 60 minutes daily.

The Love solarium. Mrs. Davis Love of Marietta, Georgia, has a solarium
for the primary purpose of adding extra living and entertaining space. "We
live in it year-round and use it every day. We eat breakfast there, and, most
of the time, dinner. In fact, the changing seasons have their impact on the
mood of the solarium." The walls, which are windows and sliding glass
doors, open up halfway to convert to a screened porch in the summer. At
Christmas, Mrs. Love changes the green and yellow decor to all green,
reflecting the season.

Maintenance isn't much of a problem. The floor is covered with
Armstrong "Solarium," which takes water and high humidity. Pots catch
the water so there is no dripping. In one corner, under a staghorn fern, is a
3 × 3-foot area filled with pebbles, which drains to the outside. This area is
used for plants that require deep soaking, which, in turn, helps create high

Right: In Marietta, Georgia, Mrs. Davis Love uses this enchanting solarium primarily for relaxation and entertaining, but also starts vegetable seeds early in the year here.

Below: This orchid room of Richard Marrel in San Francisco, California, has wall panels of flat fiberglass which screen out 70 to 80 percent of the sun's ultraviolet rays.

humidity. Orchids and bromeliads are kept nearby to take advantage of a very suitable corner microclimate.

In winter, heat is provided by five electrically heated baseboards (two might be enough). Mrs. Love sets the thermostat down to 60° at night; this, she believes, explains the success of her plants. "My geraniums bloom all winter when it is 40° to 50° outside. The sun on the windows gets the daytime temperature up to 80°."

Mrs. Love has grown tomatoes and cucumbers in her solarium, getting a jump on spring. "By the time I can put plants outside, they're almost ready to eat." She has successfully started plants from seed but plans to build a separate working greenhouse to move the clutter away from the living space.

The Marell greenhouse. Mr. Richard Marell, a San Francisco attorney, has built a greenhouse that opens off his deck adjacent to the living room. It is constructed of redwood members with flat fiberglass panels designed to eliminate between 70 and 85 percent of the ultraviolet rays. It houses his prized orchid collection, which creates an ever-changing panorama from the living room.

Traditional in design, it has slatted wood benches. These provide the air circulation necessary for healthy orchids. His equipment consists of two small whisper fans running 24 hours a day (for constant air movement), one vaporizer, and one thermostatically controlled exhaust system, set at 78°.

The Gibbs solarium. Mr. Jim Gibbs of Atlanta, Georgia, has built a "Thermopane"-paneled solarium off his dining room. Designed for low maintenance, it has a slate floor, which is ideal for a wet greenhouse. Since not all pots need watering and the ground beds retain moisture, he spends only a few minutes a day watering.

A slate floor makes for easy maintenance in this solarium adjunct to the living room of Jim Gibbs in Atlanta, Georgia.

The solarium is used as a family eating area and for entertaining. It is enormously popular with visitors, who are drawn to this area. Many friends have had similar structures of their own built since seeing his solarium.

The Freeborn "green room." Mr. and Mrs. W. E. Freeborn of Atlanta, Georgia, enclosed the small back-porch area off their kitchen door with a corrugated fiberglass roof and adorned the side with a stained glass window. They call it the "green room." Mr. Freeborn comments:

"In the first place, the 'green room' does not have permanent heat in it because it gets heat from the house, and the door stays open practically year-round. We have found a few days in some winters when it was necessary to have additional heat, but there is electricity in the 'green room' and we use an electric heater for this purpose.

"The bench is warmed by a cable. It gets used mostly for green plants, although we do have some blooming things there. The things that have done best have been Thanksgiving cactus, begonias, and bougainvillea.

"The grow-and-bloom lights on the table give excellent results and are used for violets and a few annuals. We also think that this helps both cuttings and seedlings.

"Of course, that area gets a great deal of sunlight.

"The things that Mrs. Freeborn has enjoyed most are (1) growing seedlings, (2) growing plants from cuttings, and (3) caring for friends' plants that aren't doing well."

The Freeborns' "green room" proves that glass houses need not be large or elaborate to be effective. There is a whole range of ready-mades on the market, from small window units to large commercial-sized, fully equipped greenhouses. If nothing available suits your needs, an architect can provide a custom solution. Page 93 suggests some types of glass houses you might want to consider.

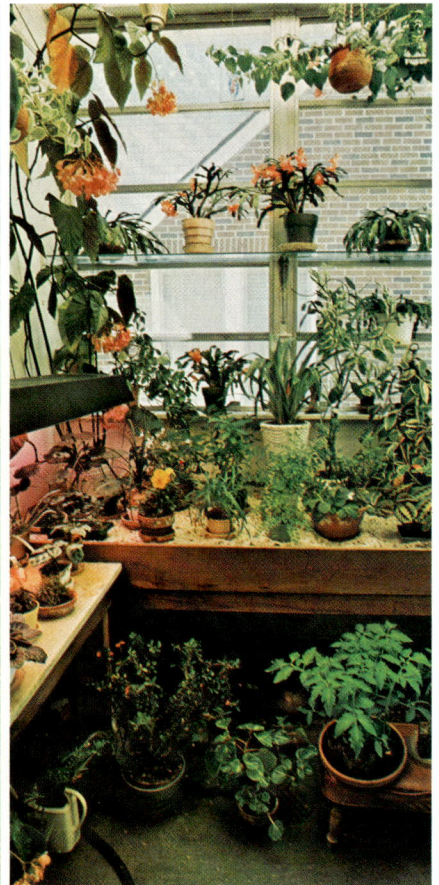

Far right: Artificial lights supplement the sunlight received through the corrugated fiberglass roof of this small back porch transformed by Mr. and Mrs. W. E. Freeborn of Atlanta, Georgia, into a greenhouse complete with cable-warmed benches.

Right: The exterior of the greenhouse.

Types of Greenhouses

Window Extension
This unit fits into the window, utilizes indoor heating, and provides extended growing space.

Lean-to
The lean-to creates a walk-in nook. It allows the introduction of larger plants than the window extension and permits the use of benches and some maintenance equipment.

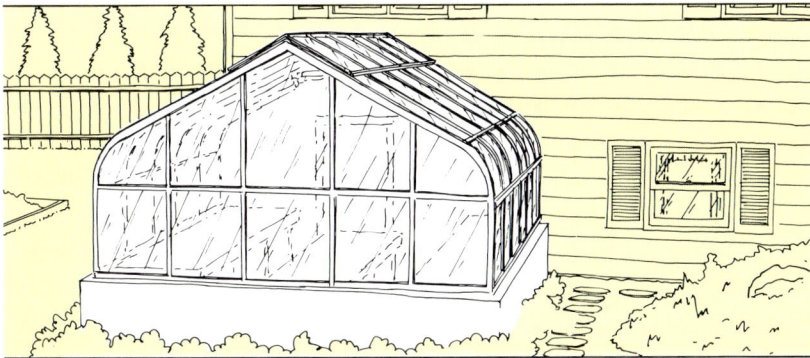

Greenhouse Extension
This type is a complete greenhouse appended to the house. There are usually doors or vents for control of humidity and heat.

Sun Room
Like the greenhouse extension, the sun room is a separate room, yet has a true feeling of space and light. It normally has glass walls and a shaded ceiling for controlling direct light. Often these rooms have tile floors to minimize maintenance problems.

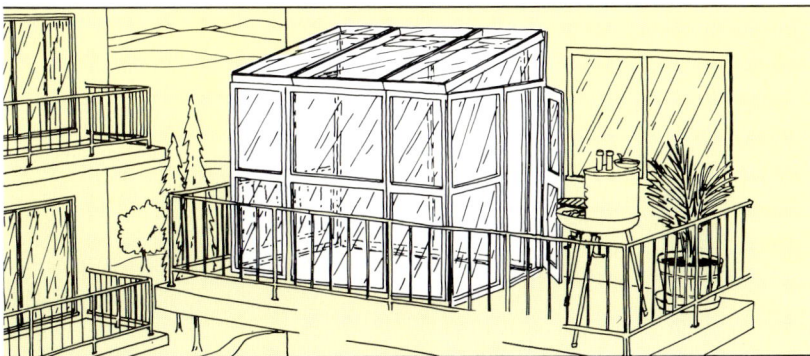

Deck Greenhouse
For city-dwellers, deck greenhouses may be the only gardening possibility. Otherwise unusable decks can often be transformed into a pleasant garden area adjacent to the living room. There are mobile greenhouses available that can be easily dismantled and reassembled elsewhere.

Deck (or Balcony) Greenhouse

1. To avoid problems, get your landlord's permission and check local building code regulations to see if this kind of structure is permitted on a balcony or patio.

2. Planning. If your balcony or patio is 4½ feet × 8 feet or larger and your outside door frame 77 inches wide or smaller, you can use the dimensions shown here. If not, or if you prefer a larger or smaller greenhouse, you will have to modify the plan and material sizes.

3. Basic construction. This greenhouse consists of ten prefabricated frame panels,

covered with plastic, and screwed together on a freestanding wood foundation. Construction of all panels is the same, only the sizes change, and the roof panels have an extra 2 × 2 on one end for added length. The door panel is optional, of course, but nice to have if your balcony is larger than the greenhouse. If you opt for no door you'll have to provide for easy removal of the covering on the lower half of one panel so you can crawl in and out during assembly and whenever else you need to work on the outside of the greenhouse.

Materials Needed

Wall and roof panels

14 pcs. 1" × 2" × 72"	2 pcs. 2" × 2" × 24"
16 pcs. 1" × 2" × 22½"	2 pcs. 2" × 2" × 36"
4 pcs. 1" × 2" × 34½"	2 pcs. 2" × 2" × 24"
6 pcs. 1" × 2" × 48"	1 pc. 2" × 2" × 36"
8 pcs. 2" × 2" × 22½"*	1 pc. 1" × 1" × 87"
2 pcs. 2" × 2" × 34½"*	

*These pieces may be 1" × 2" if you are not using rigid plastic covering material.

Foundation

2 pcs. 2" × 4" × 87"	2 pcs. 2" × 4" × 46"
2 pcs. 2" × 4" × 80½"	

Door

2 pcs. 1" × 3" × 70"	4 pcs. ¼" × 6" × 6"
3 pcs. 1" × 3" × 17"	plywood triangle corner braces

Hardware

1 pc. 1" × 1" × 87" aluminum "angle-iron"	40 3" × 3" metal "L" mending plates with screws (optional)
4 doz. 1½" × #8 wood screws	52 ¾" × #6 wood screws
9 — 3" × #12 wood screws	2 lbs. galvanized 6d box nails
6 — 2" × 2" metal "L" brackets and screws	1 pr. 3" butt hinges with screws (for door)
2 doz. 3" metal mending plates and screws	1 screen door hook to latch door
2 pcs. 8' long vinyl baseboard	

Panels

Assemble top wall and roof panels like this.

Note: Optional metal "L" mending plates are recommended if using plastic film or shade cloth.

Nail additional 2" × 2" to three roof panels.

Prefab Units to Build
5 — 24" × 72" wall panels
1 — 24" × 72" door panel
1 — 36" × 72" wall panel
2 — 24" × 48" roof panels
1 — 36" × 48" roof panel
1 — 84" × 51" foundation frame

22½" or 34½"

24" or 36"

72" to 48"

This piece must be 2" × 2" if your covering is rigid plastic—1" × 2" will do for other coverings. Leave it out of door panel.

Use ¾" #6 screws to hold ¼" × 6" × 6" corner braces.

Door

Assemble door of 1" × 3"s laid flat with ¼" × 6" × 6" plywood corner braces. Use ¾" #6 wood screws to hold corner braces. Fit door into panel and attach hinges and hook.

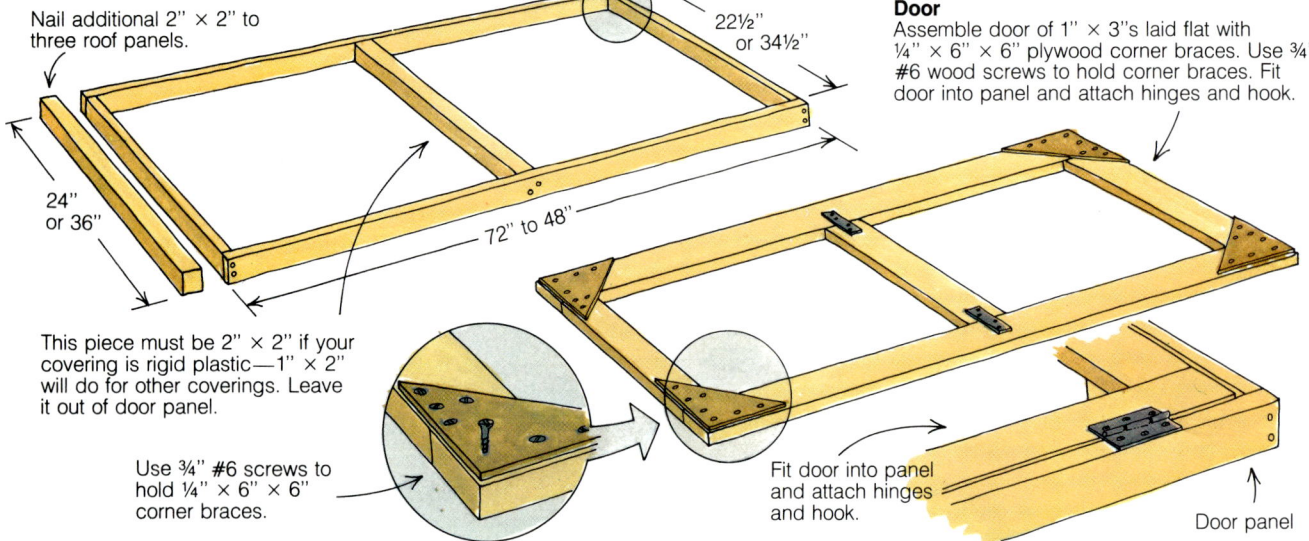

Fit door into panel and attach hinges and hook.

Door panel

Foam tape

Screws and washers

6"

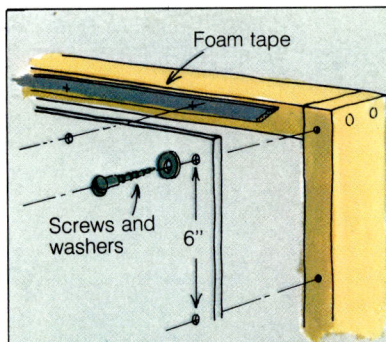

Rigid plastic. Drill holes as indicated and screw the plastic sheets gently, not too tight, to each panel. Foam tape or a bead of putty or caulking compound will seal the edges and allow for some expansion and contraction of the plastic.

Materials needed

Plastic
2 pcs. 36" × 36" (sides)
10 pcs. 24" × 36" (sides) (12 if no door)
1 pc. 36" × 48" (roof)
2 pcs. 24" × 48" (roof)
2 pcs. 34" × 34" (door)
1 pc. 15" × 48" (vent)

Insulation tape, caulking compound, or putty
2 gross galvanized ¾" #6 round head screws and washers
Aluminum screen, 1 pc.

Thick foam tape

Corrugated fiberglass. Drill holes as indicated and screw the plastic to each panel with the foam tape in position—especially at the top and bottom to fill in the spaces between corrugations.

Materials needed

Fiberglass
1 pc. 36" × 72" (side)
5 pcs. 24" × 72" (sides) (6 if no door)
1 pc. 36" × 48" (roof)
2 pcs. 24" × 48" (roof)
1 pc. 34" × 70" (door)

1 pc. 15" × 48" (vent)
Foam tape
2 gross galvanized ¾" #6 round head screws and washers
Aluminum screen, 1 pc. 15" × 50"

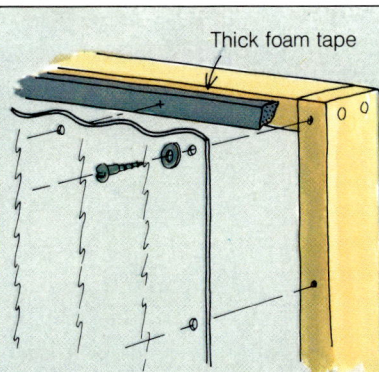

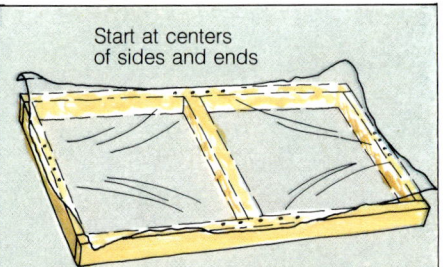

Start at centers of sides and ends

Plastic film or shade cloth. Cut sheets of material somewhat oversize. Lay the panel frame on the floor and lay the covering over it. Put a tack or staple in the center of one end, pull tight toward the center of the other end and tack it. Tack the centers of the sides the same way, then alternate stretching and tacking each end and side toward the corners as you move around the panel. When it's all tacked trim off excess material. This method gives you a tight, wrinkle-free covering.

Materials needed

200 sq. ft. of film or cloth (about 60 linear feet of 40" width)
Staples and staple gun or tacks

4. Covering. You have several choices for covering your greenhouse, depending on your climate, the appearance and durability you want, and the amount of money you want to spend. Rigid, clear plastic storm window material or plexiglas is best for cold climates. It's durable and transparent, like glass, and also the most expensive covering discussed here.

Filon or corrugated fiberglass is also good for cold climates and is very durable, but it, too, is expensive. Also, it is only translucent so you can't see out and your neighbors are unable to see into your beautiful garden. It comes in a choice of colors.

Plastic film is fairly transparent and inexpensive, but tears easily and may last only one season, especially where wind is a factor.

In extremely cold climates you may want to double-glaze your greenhouse. Adding plastic to both sides of each panel increases insulation greatly.

In subtropical climates you may want to cover your greenhouse with nursery shadecloth (Saran cloth) for shade, air circulation, and insect protection.

2" × 2" "L" brackets

Wooden turn-buttons

Vinyl baseboard flashing

Aluminum screen on outside

Removable plastic panel on inside

1" × 1" × 87" stick

Use 1½" × #8 wood screws, drill 3/16" hole for guide.

36" panels in center of front and roof

vinyl baseboard flashing

5. Assembly. When the panels are finished, the structure can be put together.

The foundation of 2 × 4s is next—build it so it looks like the drawing. You may need a temporary brace until you get the first panels in place. Use a level or framing square to be sure the joints are all square so the panels will fit snugly.

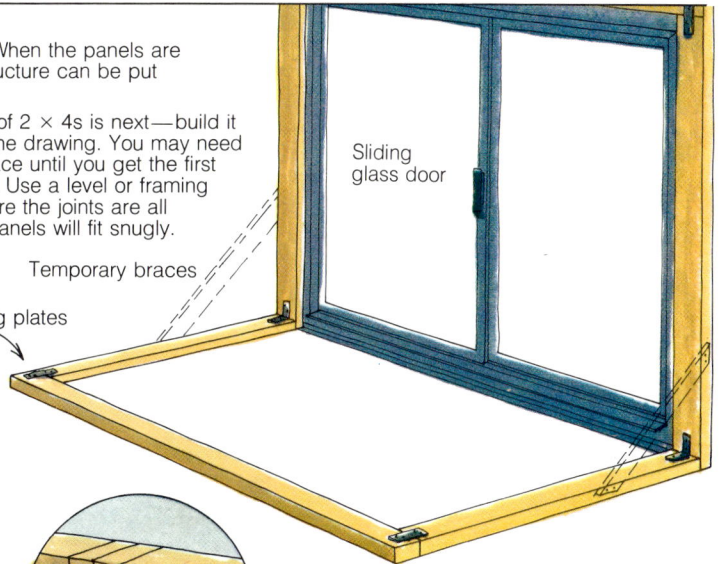

Temporary braces

Metal mending plates

Sliding glass door

Next come the wall panels. Set them in place and attach them to the foundation and each other with the 1½" × #8 wood screws as shown. A 3/16" guide hole and a little wax or soap on the screws will make this job much easier.

Now nail the 1" × 1" × 87" stick to the front edge of the front wall, attach the six 2" × 2" "L" brackets to the 2 × 4 above the sliding door, and set the roof panels in place. Secure them above the sliding door with the nine 3" × #12 wood screws.

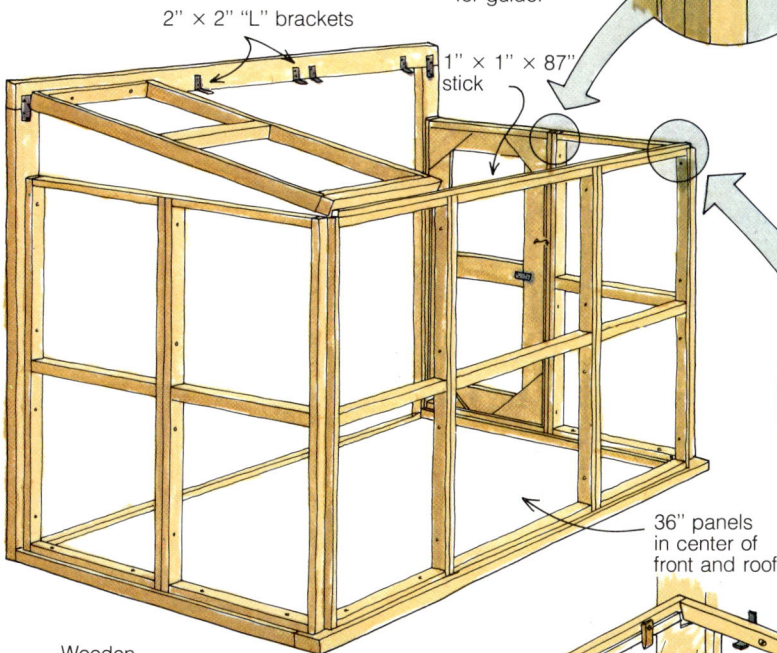

Note: If you double-glaze your greenhouse (see step 4), you'll have to use wooden strips or metal mending plates to hold panels together.

6. Finishing touches. Add flashing of vinyl baseboard pieces to back and front of roof.

Cut aluminum screen diagonally to cover the triangular spaces between the roof and walls, and tack or staple it in place.

Cut the 15" × 48" piece of plastic diagonally and shape the pieces to fit these same triangular spaces. Attach them to the inside with wooden turn-buttons and screws so you can remove them easily for ventilation (see drawing).

7. Shelves. Standard metal shelf strips and brackets attached to wall panels seem to be the best bet. They are easy to move when you want to rearrange your shelves and you may leave the strips attached if you ever want to disassemble and move your greenhouse.

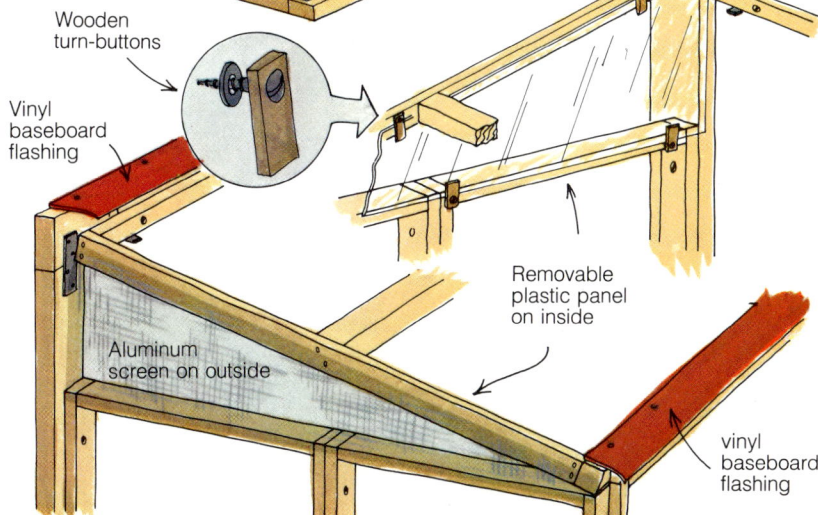

Anchored in their light gravel aggregate,
sweet peas, marigolds, tomatoes, and Swiss
chard live in a temperature-moderated
environment. The control box times the flow
of water and nutrients to the plants and
regulates the temperature of the greenhouse.

HYDROPONICS

This easy and exciting way of gardening works equally well outside for the summer or inside for year-round production of vegetables and flowers.

For many people, hydroponics—also called aquaculture, soilless gardening, and nutriculture—is a strange method of gardening. The very word conjures up images of alchemy, of convoluted systems of tanks, pipes, and strange bubbling solutions that make plants grow mysteriously—without soil. Even worse, it requires complex formulas that trigger bad memories of high school chemistry.

In fact, growing plants by hydroponics is an exciting way to produce vegetables for your table and flowers for your home. A hydroponic unit can be especially productive—year-round—in a greenhouse or other controlled environment. In addition, using hydroponics in a controlled environment makes sense in terms of size: the compactness of the system allows you to get a yield from a small space. The growing medium also benefits from being housed in a controlled environment because it stays cleaner and moister than it would outdoors.

More people are turning to hydroponics because it is becoming easier. There are commercial systems on the market, but you can make your own—it is not complex. Nutrient mixes are also readily available from nurseries or garden supply stores.

What Is Hydroponics?

To put it simply, hydroponics is growing plants in a solution of nutrients rather than in soil. In the garden, plants are anchored in the soil and draw water and nutrients from it. In hydroponics, a water solution that is rich in the necessary foods is washed or pumped through a mix of light gravel that anchors the plants and retains the solution.

Advantages. Hydroponics is one way to deal with the increasingly limited space available to many gardeners. For those people who lack a garden but who still want to grow plants and vegetables, hydroponics provides a compact means of growing abundant, large, and high-quality plants.

Plants and crops can be grown almost anywhere hydroponically, from a greenhouse to a small apartment. While the system works best in a greenhouse that has ample light and humidity, surprising success can also be achieved on a window sill.

Hydroponics requires less work than a conventional garden. There's no need to be out every day tilling the soil, pulling weeds, or chasing the neighbor's dog out of your lettuce patch. Usually, about 20 minutes a day will keep your nutriculture garden flourishing. An automated system demands even less time.

Advocates of hydroponics claim that their yields are bigger, and that their vegetables taste better. Weather damage is nonexistent. Disease is minimized if proper procedures are followed.

Finally, in these times of shortages, which include clean water, hydroponics offers the virtue of conservation: most systems use the same

This patio hydroponic container holds tomatoes, squash, and sweetpeas.

nutrient solution repeatedly for one to four weeks. When the solution is finally depleted, don't dispose of it even then—pour it around trees or plants outside to give them a lift.

Disadvantages. Although hydroponics eliminates some of the work of gardening, it doesn't eliminate it all. Hydroponically grown plants respond to poor growing conditions even more rapidly than to good ones. So you need to inspect plants closely and frequently to ensure against loss.

Setting up the system takes time. You have to build or buy boxes to hold the aggregate mix, install pipes, and hook up pumps.

Background. Plants have been grown in different water cultures for hundreds of years. The first big advance came nearly three centuries ago, in 1699. At that time, John Woodward, an English chemist and Fellow of the Royal Society, began using mint plants to learn whether plants receive their food through the soil or through water. He used three kinds of water (rain water, tap water, and river water from the Thames) and found that the more soil he added, the better the plant grew.

His experiments did not extend much beyond that, however. It wasn't until 1804 that Nicholas de Saussure proved that plants need a combination of air, soil, and water. Shortly thereafter, French scientist Jean Boussingault raised crops in beds of sand and charcoal, which he periodically flooded with nutrient solutions.

Modern hydroponics began as late as 1929, when William F. Gericke, a professor at the University of California at Berkeley (and the coiner of the word "hydroponics") set up a successful hydroponic system, growing plants without any soil whatsoever. As word of horticultural "miracles" began to spread—tomato plants that reached 20 feet in height, plus other spectacular results with flowers and vegetables—commercial hydroponics began to develop. It still is expanding today, and it is used widely in many parts of the world because of its speed and efficiency in vegetable production.

The Basic System

You can make a simple hydroponic system in an hour, from items you probably have around the kitchen. Despite its simplicity, it has all the elements of a more sophisticated system, and it works well.

You need nothing more than a dishpan, clean gravel or coarse sand, a length of plastic or rubber hose, and a bucket.

Cut a hole in the side of both the dishpan and the bucket, right near the bottom, for the hose. Make sure it fits tightly and seal it with epoxy glue. Fill the dishpan with 6 to 8 inches of pea gravel. Move the system to a sunny, protected spot and pour the nutrient solution into the bucket.

Plant 4 to 6 pepper plants in the dishpan, then raise the bucket until the growing bed in the pan is submerged by the solution. Next, lower the bucket and let the solution from the tilted dishpan drain back into the bucket. Do this once in the morning and once at night. The result will be more peppers than you can eat.

An Automated System

While the above system works well, it does require your attention twice a day. If you want to spend less time and also make sure that you don't forget to run the solution through, use a more advanced system—one that has a small electric pump and timer. The principle, however, remains the same: saturate the growing medium, then let it drain. The root hairs will find the needed moisture and nutrients on the damp gravel and will still receive air.

This larger automated system requires a growing bed and a nearby sump. A large plastic trash can or bucket works well for the sump. An electric pump that is plugged into a timer runs the nutrient solution into the growing tray

Simplest Hydroponic Garden

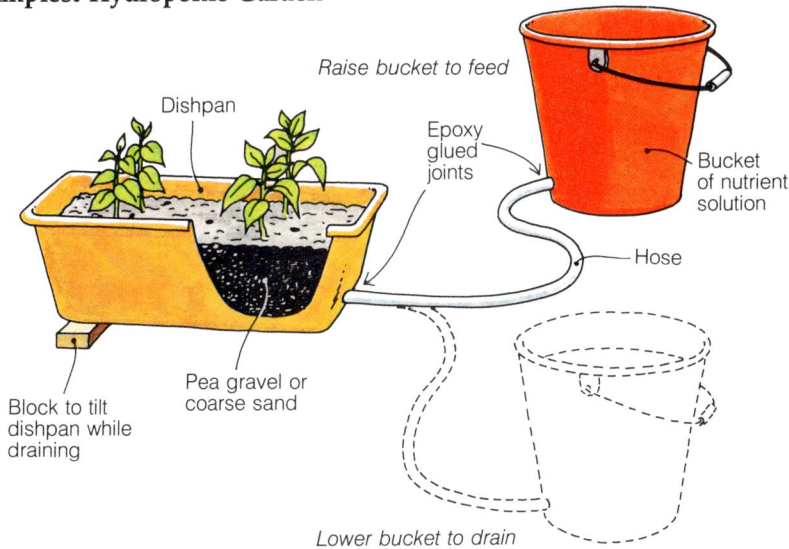

Raise bucket to feed

Dishpan

Epoxy glued joints

Bucket of nutrient solution

Hose

Block to tilt dishpan while draining

Pea gravel or coarse sand

Lower bucket to drain

Simplest Automatic Hydroponic Garden

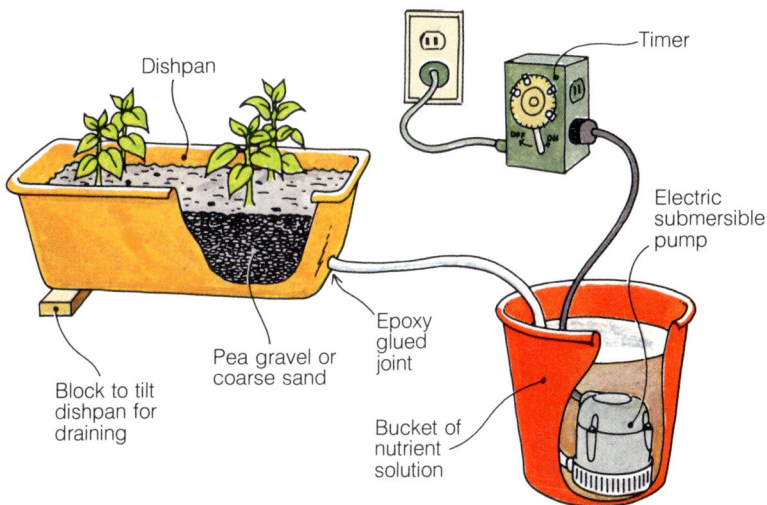

Dishpan

Timer

Electric submersible pump

Epoxy glued joint

Pea gravel or coarse sand

Block to tilt dishpan for draining

Bucket of nutrient solution

at the prescribed hour in the morning. The solution drains from the tray back into the sump. The process is repeated that afternoon.

Aggregates

Although flowers and vegetables have been grown with their roots suspended in just a mist of nutrient solution—the easiest and most practical way is to use some kind of a "soil." This allows the plants to anchor themselves and grow as if they were in the garden.

The most common form of aggregate is pea gravel, the medium-coarse grade of about ¼ to ⅛ inch in size. Any larger than that and the solution drains too rapidly and the roots dry out too quickly. The aggregate should be free of calcium or limestone. You can use ordinary sand, but by itself it is heavy and slow to drain. It also increases the risk of fungi and drowning of the roots.

Mixtures of sand and light gravel or sand and a little vermiculite are acceptable. Vermiculite alone retains too much water. Sawdust has been used, but it absorbs too much solution and does not drain properly. Some

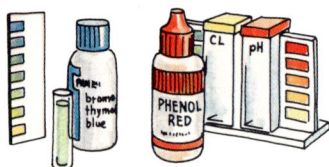

Kits for testing the pH of swimming pool or fish aquarium water work on hydroponic nutrient solutions, too.

advanced systems avoid the drainage problem by using no rooting medium at all, but instead periodically spray the nutrient solution onto the roots. The main problem with this system is one of mechanical support for the growing plants.

If you are a beginner, stick with the proven success of light gravel. Not only does it fill and drain at the right speed, it is also easy to sterilize.

Solutions

One advantage of hydroponics is that you know your plants are receiving all the nutrients they need—provided you have the right mix.

Numerous formulas for solutions are available, but unless you are inclined to chemical experimentation or you plan a large-scale operation, you should buy one of the premixed commercial formulas.

Whether you mix your own or buy a commercial solution, you will have to check its pH level after you have poured it over the aggregate. The pH tells you whether the solution is acid or alkaline. Most garden supply stores have various kits and indicator paper strips for measuring this. The pH scale runs from 1 to 14, with 7 being neutral. The ideal growing level is slightly acid, or 6.5 on the pH scale.

Check your growing solution every three days while it runs through the aggregate. In most cases you will not have to make adjustments. However, if it gets above 7, it is too alkaline. To reduce the alkalinity and increase the acidity, use an eye dropper to add sulphuric acid to the solution in the holding tank. Add a few drops (be careful not to spill any on yourself) and recheck. The next time you run the solution through the aggregate, check it again until it is adjusted. If it becomes too acid, add sodium hydroxide to raise the pH. You can also add white vinegar to increase acidity, and baking soda to increase alkalinity.

Sanitation

The hydroponic gardener in a greenhouse must take several precautions against disease. Some root fungi can spread with alarming rapidity because the solution moves from root system to root system. This is usually not a problem, however.

More serious gardeners change their shoes and slip on clean coveralls before entering the greenhouse to minimize the risk of infecting their plants.

One common disease is the tobacco mosaic virus. In spite of its name, it can affect tomatoes and many other plants. To prevent it from becoming established, do not allow tobacco or smoking in your hydroponic greenhouse.

Growing Beds

A wide variety of containers will hold the growing bed and nutrients, ranging from the simple dishpan and bucket mentioned on page 99 to wooden or fiberglass frames. No matter what the details, the essentials are the same: the container must be leakproof and fill and drain rapidly.

Some people make growing beds by cutting 55-gallon drums in half lengthwise and coating the interiors with an epoxy paint or lining with a heavy sheet of polyethylene. Others simply build a 2 × 4 frame on the floor of the greenhouse, line it with a plastic sheet, and fill it with gravel. You can even use lengths of rain gutter. You can also buy commercially made fiberglass growing beds. Choose the kind that suits you best—but follow this method, adjusting the measurements to fit your own needs.

For a completely homemade arrangement, start by making a box 8 feet long and 2 feet wide from 1 × 8s. Make the bottom from a sheet of exterior-grade plywood. Fasten a 1 × 2 across the top center to prevent the sides from bowing out. Glue all the joints with epoxy glue and caulk the seams. Then paint the interior with epoxy paint—three coats for best results. Or you can use a horticultural asphalt-base paint.

Instead of protecting the wood with some kind of paint, you can line the box with two layers (in case one layer has a pinhole leak) of 4 mil black polyethylene sheeting. Anywhere a pipe enters the box, gather a little of the plastic around the pipe and use a screw-type hose clamp to make it tight and leak resistant. You can use a piece of half-round molding to hold the plastic around the top of the box, or you can draw the plastic over the top edge and staple it to the outside of the box.

A Pumalite rooting medium in the upper box is filled with nutrient solution pumped from the lower box. This timed, submersible pump system is designed by Pacific Aquaculture, Sausalito, California.

Basic Home-Built Hydroponic Garden

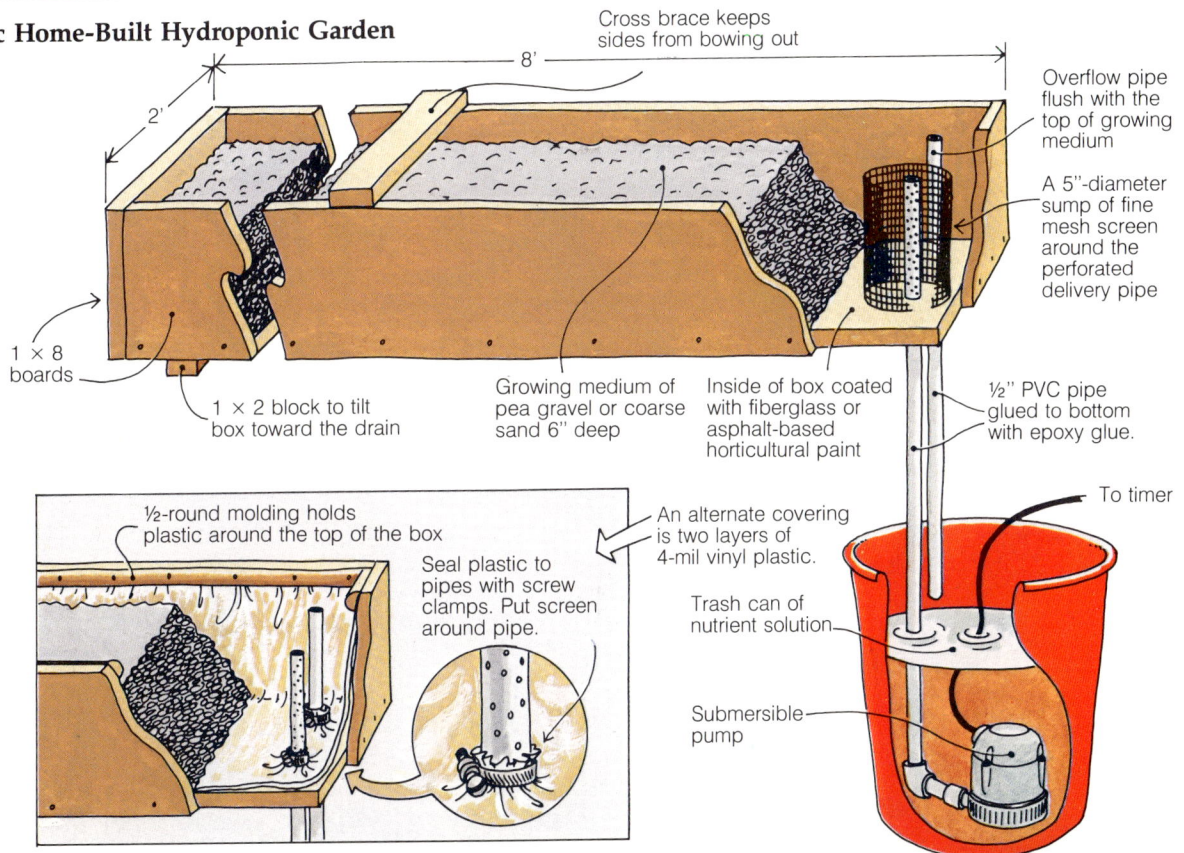

Cross brace keeps sides from bowing out

8'

2'

Overflow pipe flush with the top of growing medium

A 5"-diameter sump of fine mesh screen around the perforated delivery pipe

1 × 8 boards

1 × 2 block to tilt box toward the drain

Growing medium of pea gravel or coarse sand 6" deep

Inside of box coated with fiberglass or asphalt-based horticultural paint

½" PVC pipe glued to bottom with epoxy glue.

To timer

½-round molding holds plastic around the top of the box

An alternate covering is two layers of 4-mil vinyl plastic.

Seal plastic to pipes with screw clamps. Put screen around pipe.

Trash can of nutrient solution

Submersible pump

The yield from this hydroponic greenhouse includes corn, broccoli, cucumbers, beets, and chard. Many of a family's fresh vegetables are grown here.

Raise the end of the bed opposite the drainhole about ¾ inch by nailing a strip of 1 × 2 across the bottom. Once the box is up on a bench, this slope allows the solution that is pumped into the bed to drain back to the sump by gravity flow.

The nutrient solution can be delivered to the bed in several different ways. In one, the PVC pipe is part of both the pump and drain system. To accomplish this, simply run a pipe the length of the growing bed beneath the medium, punching ¼-inch holes in this pipe every few inches. Or, as shown in the drawing, use a perforated pipe about 6 inches long, protecting the pipe from the growing medium with a sump of wire mesh. The wire mesh lets you clean the holes in the pipe periodically, without having to dig up the medium. The solution is thus delivered to the bed and then drained back through the pump.

Other delivery systems route the pipe over the top of the bed and use small spaghetti tubing to deliver the solution to all parts of the bed.

It is advisable to add an overflow pipe at the lower end. Run the pipe through a hole next to the drain and make the top of it flush with the top of the growing medium. It should either tie into the drain pipe or run directly back to the sump.

Pumps and Sumps

Once the box is completed, the next step is to supply it with nutrient solution so that you can start planting. Since the growing box is generally on a bench for easy gardening, the other apparatus can go under the bench. This apparatus consists of a small plastic trash can or bucket to hold the solution, and a small electric pump. The amount of solution will vary with the type of growing medium used. Experiment to find the amount you need.

The pump is submersible and sits at the bottom of the solution container. Use a length of plastic hose or more PVC pipe to hook the pump to the PVC pipe in the growing box. PVC offers these advantages: it is readily available; it can be cut with an ordinary saw; and the joints glue together in seconds.

Now connect the pump to a timer plugged into a nearly socket and set so that the box will be flooded once in the morning and once in the evening.

The box will fill to the top and should drain in 10 or 15 minutes. Faster draining is all right, but the roots must not be submerged for more than 30 minutes, or they will drown.

A system in which the solution is fed to the roots from below is termed "subirrigation." There are other systems, including those that mist and pump water on top of the aggregate, but they are more complex, whereas the subirrigation method is a proven success.

Once the growing bed, the pump, and the sump are set up, you can run several boxes at the same time with a manifold hook-up, or if you can, arrange your boxes so that the solution from each one flows into the next until the last box finally flows back to the sump.

Nutrient Flow Techniques

One of the new developments in hydroponic gardening is called the nutrient flow technique (NFT). First developed by British scientist Dr. A. J. Cooper and then modified by Dr. Paul A. Schippers of Cornell University, this new approach calls for a continuous flow of nutrients—slow but steady—rather than the more commonly used method of periodic flooding. The NFT is simple and, barring a power failure, able to run by itself for days at a time.

The system incorporates the sump, pump, and growing beds described on pages 100–101. The big difference is a nutrient solution container mounted at one end and slightly above the growing bed. The solution is released from the high container into the growing bed through a small rubber hose. A screw clamp on the hose adjusts the amount of nutrient flow.

The growing bed is angled at a slope of 1:100 or more to keep the nutrients flowing through the growing medium.

The solution runs from the growing bed into the sump, where a submersible pump runs the solution back into the upper holding basin.

Nutrient Flow System

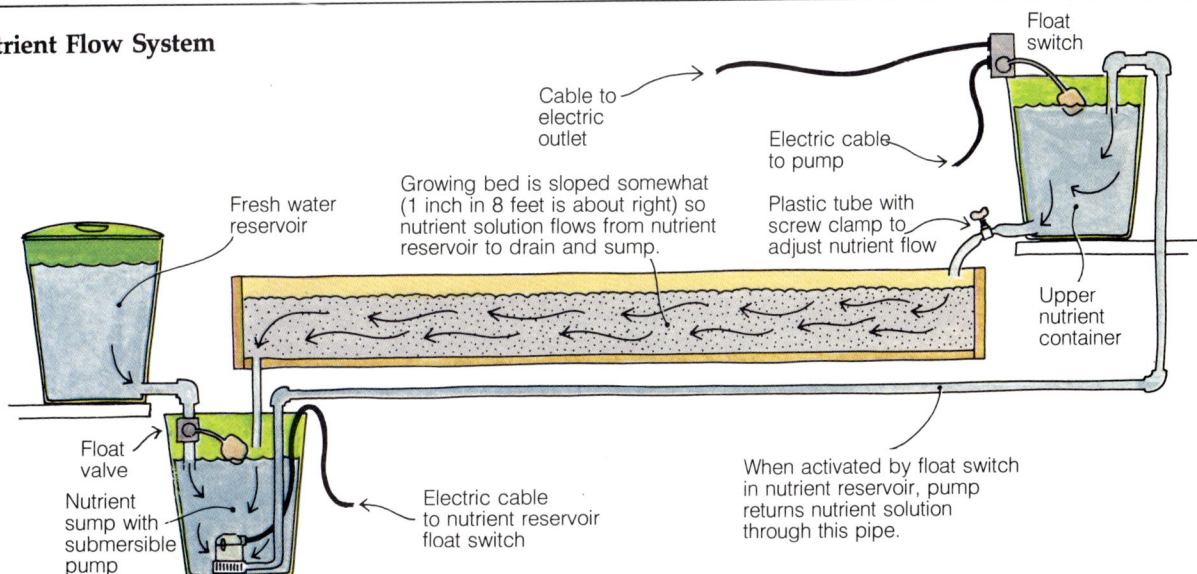

Float switch

Cable to electric outlet

Electric cable to pump

Fresh water reservoir

Growing bed is sloped somewhat (1 inch in 8 feet is about right) so nutrient solution flows from nutrient reservoir to drain and sump.

Plastic tube with screw clamp to adjust nutrient flow

Upper nutrient container

Float valve

Nutrient sump with submersible pump

Electric cable to nutrient reservoir float switch

When activated by float switch in nutrient reservoir, pump returns nutrient solution through this pipe.

The pump is controlled by a float switch mounted in the upper basin. When the solution drops enough, the pump is activated until the float rises enough to shut off the pump.

A float valve in the lower holding tank admits fresh water from a barrel when the solution level drops too low because of transpiration and evaporation.

Dr. Schippers has also devised a simple channel-bed system for growing smaller plants, such as lettuce, spinach, or Chinese cabbage. To make this type of bed, nail 2 × 4s about 6 inches apart to a 4 × 8-foot sheet of plywood, then cover it with black polyethylene to form the troughs. At the top, the nutrient solution is put in each channel through a manifold system. It is drained from the other end back to the sump.

Planting

Once everything is set up, you can plant. Larger seeds that will not wash away can be sprouted directly in the growing box. Set them in the aggregate by making a small hole with your finger or using a short length of PVC pipe to place them. For tiny seeds, you can remove the bottoms from small paper cups and fill them with a mixture of gravel and vermiculite to hold more moisture. Set these cups directly in the growing bed.

You can transplant seedlings directly to the growing mix—but even if you wash the roots, the risk of transplanting a fungus as well is increased. You can also germinate seedlings between two damp paper towels and then transplant them.

Normally, you should fill and drain the planting bed twice a day. During the summer months, however, when it is hot and dry, you may have to increase this to three or even four times a day. It won't hurt the plants to be flooded more often, as long as there is proper drainage, but letting the roots dry out may do irreparable damage. This is why the nutrient flow technique promises better growing conditions.

The growing medium should remain damp, like a wrung-out washcloth, at all times. Once the operation is underway, you and your hydroponic garden will adjust to each other, and you will know almost instinctively if the plants are doing their best.

During the hot months, the water in the solution will evaporate more rapidly. Check periodically to see that the solution level is kept at 90 percent

Detail of the Pacific Aquaculture system. Water of nutrient solution is added to reservoir through the end slot. Nutrients are added twice monthly and changed once a month. The solution, delivered by a timed pump, is checked weekly for pH level.

Channel-Bed System

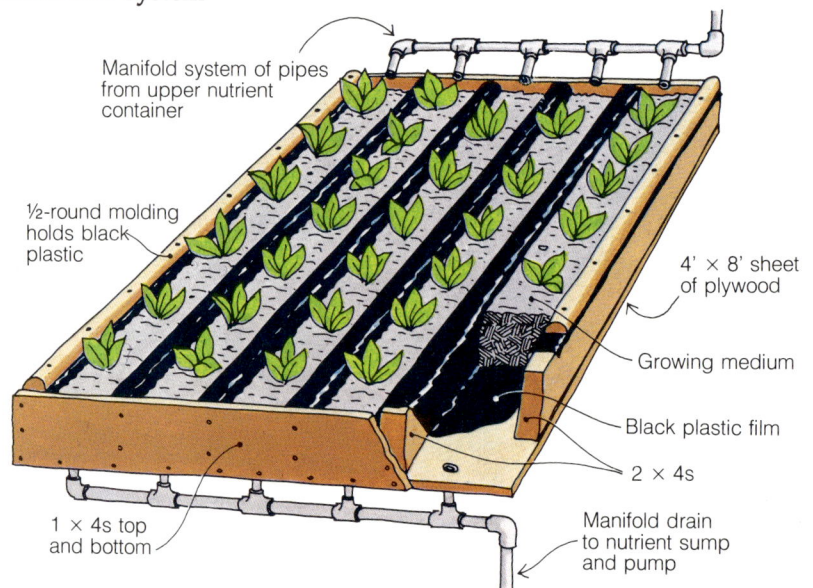

Manifold system of pipes from upper nutrient container

½-round molding holds black plastic

4' × 8' sheet of plywood

Growing medium

Black plastic film

2 × 4s

1 × 4s top and bottom

Manifold drain to nutrient sump and pump

or more of the original level. Otherwise the nutrient salts may become too concentrated and burn the roots. Unless it is time to change your nutrient solution, make up for evaporative loss by adding plain water. If you add nutrient solution, you will be constantly increasing the concentration of nutrients and will eventually kill your plants.

You will also learn quickly how well the plants are doing on the nutrient mix you give them. For best results, start by changing this solution every week. Then—gradually—extend the changing time, while watching to see whether your plants show any signs of reduced growth. Gardeners commonly go two, even four, weeks on each batch; but there are many variables, so experiment and watch the plants carefully.

Finally, be sure to flood the growing container with fresh water every time you change the solution. This washes away the build-up of residual nutrient salts that could eventually damage the roots.

Sterilizing the Bed

Even if diseases never invade your hydroponic garden, it is a good idea to sterilize the bed at least once a year. However, if your plants are attacked and killed, you will have to remove them and sterilize the bed completely. Here are two good methods.

The first is to use a mixture of chlorine and water. This is the same solution that is used to bleach clothes or keep swimming pools clean, but your mixture is considerably stronger. Mix 1½ ounces of liquid chlorine in 10 gallons of water. Plug the end drain hole and fill the box until the growing aggregate is fully submerged. Let it soak 24 hours, then drain and throw away the chlorine solution. Flood and drain the box with fresh water three times a day for the next two days; then you're ready to plant again.

Final Reminders

The plants in a hydroponic garden cannot survive on nutrients alone. They must be in balance with the complete growing cycle. They also need:

☐ *Ample light.* Plants must have light in order for photosynthesis to take place. If they can't get enough sunlight, supplement it with fluorescent lighting, or grow the plants entirely under fluorescent lights.
☐ *Correct temperature.* A plant's response to heat regulates its rate of growth. Most plants do well in the 65° to 75°F. (18° to 24°C.) range, while others require a more extreme temperature.
☐ *Balanced nutrients.* By checking the pH level and watching how plants respond the longer you let the solution remain, you will keep your operation a success. The pH balance must be maintained, however.

You can probably grow almost any plant you like in your hydroponic tank, but some grow more easily than others. Some grow so luxuriously, in fact, that you may find you've planted too closely. When you start your first crop of any plant, give the individuals lots of room. Interplanting works very well for some of the slower-growing crops. For instance, spacing your tomatoes on 18-inch centers will encourage top production. Interplant with fast-maturing crops, such as lettuce and radishes.

Be careful to follow the manufacturer's directions when changing the growing medium. Salt build-up and toxicity problems can develop if you do not circulate the medium properly or change it soon enough. You can avoid most disease problems entirely by following directions carefully. Don't use too much or too little of the mineral mixture: the plants need the proper balance.

Experiment with different varieties of a crop until you find the one that does best in your unit. You may want to try new crops every year—for example, tomatoes, green peppers, or strawberries. You can also use different methods of support for your plants—strings, stakes, and trellises.

OTHER CONTROLLED ENVIRONMENTS

To get the most out of your garden there are ways to lengthen the growing season by controlling temperature, moisture, and light.

Some gardeners are especially determined to harvest a crop in spite of weather, season, or such handicaps as excessive shade. They may not always succeed in harvesting tomatoes or corn—late crops—but their ideas are always interesting and worthy of attention.

The goal of the determined gardener is to find a way to "beat the season"—whether by lengthening it, making it warmer or cooler, making it wetter or drier, adding or reducing sunlight, or providing protection from the wind.

If you are one of these determined gardeners, this chapter is for you. It discusses old and new techniques used in various gardens—specifically, coldframes, row covers, hotbeds, hot caps, and an array of unique, home-made season cheaters.

Coldframes

Structurally, a coldframe is a bottomless, usually glass-covered, box that's heated only by the sun. It should be airtight, rotproof, and sunk into the ground. Its hinged transparent window can be stock coldframe "sash" (available from greenhouse supply firms), an old window or glass door, fiberglass, or polyethylene film.

The term "coldframe" actually applies to many types of structures. Around the turn of the century, no farm garden was complete without one. Their biggest disadvantage is that they don't have the room to accommodate both the gardener and the plants.

Orient the coldframe to the south in order to receive maximum winter sunlight. (See illustration, page 18.) A fence or wall on the north side provides wind protection. White or silver paint on the inside walls helps reflect more light to the plants. If you want to adapt an old door frame or window, notch the bottom mullions or pane dividers (as it sits on the coldframe) so that water will run off.

Place a thermometer inside the frame and shield it from the direct rays of the sun. If you watch it for a few weeks, you'll learn how the temperature fluctuates. When the temperature is high, open the sash to permit air circulation. When it starts to drop, close the sash again to conserve the radiation that's absorbed by the soil.

In actual practice, you usually open the frames in the morning and close them as soon as the sun's direct rays have passed over. Or you can equip the frame with a small, thermostatically controlled fan.

During hot weather, consider keeping the coldframe cool with shade-cloth, a lath, a mist sprayer, or other methods similar to those used in a greenhouse.

Coldframe uses. Here are some of the ways you can use coldframes.

Root cuttings. Try softwood cuttings of geraniums, fuchsias, and chrysanthemums. Evergreen and semi-evergreen azalea cuttings will root within a

Interchangeable panels on this coldframe allow varied use of the structure. The fiberglass panels (top) retain heat. Lath (center) permits maximum air circulation, and shade cloth (bottom) protects tender shoots from wind and strong sunlight.

month. (Take the current season's growth around midseason, before the wood has turned red or brown.) Many other deciduous and evergreen trees and shrubs are easily propagated by cuttings.

Start seeds early. Vegetable garden seeds and flowers can get started as much as eight weeks sooner in a coldframe.

Grow salad greens in winter. In mild climates, a coldframe adds just enough extra warmth to help lettuce, chives, and other salad greens grow right through winter. In cold climates, a well-insulated coldframe enables you to do the same thing. In some cases, bottom heat may be necessary. (See hotbeds, page 112.)

Force flowers. Early spring flowers such as primroses, pansies, and candytuft can be forced into bloom in pots placed inside a coldframe. Bulbs also can be forced in a coldframe—for example, daffodils, hyacinths, and tulips.

Old-fashioned coldframes. Coldframes, hotbeds, and other "season cheaters" have been in use for many years. In 1911, L. H. Bailey had this to say about coldframes:

"The common type of coldframe is twelve feet long and six feet wide, and is covered with four three-by-six sashes. It is made of ordinary lumber loosely nailed together. If one expects to use coldframes or hotbeds every year, however, it is advisable to make the frames of two-inch stuff, well painted, and to join the parts by bolts and tenons, so that they may be taken apart and stored until needed for the next year's crop.

"It is always advisable to place coldframes in a protected place, and especially to protect them from cold north winds. Buildings afford excellent protection, but the sun is sometimes too hot upon the south side of large and light-colored buildings. One of the best means of protection is to plant a hedge of evergreens.

"There are three general purposes for which a coldframe is used: (1) for the starting of plants early in spring; (2) for receiving of partially hardened plants which have been started earlier in hotbeds, and (3) for wintering young cabbages, lettuce, and other hardy plants which are sown in the fall."

Even earlier, in 1897, Edward J. Wickson wrote:

"A coldframe is simply for the purpose of concentrating sun heat and protection from low temperatures and heavy rain storms. It is a convenient receptacle for seed flats, or it may be put over seeds sown in the ground. The frame is made of one-inch boards, the front board about twelve inches wide, the back board or boards eighteen inches wide and the sides sloping from eighteen to twelve inches to meet the widths of the front and back.

"The frame is usually made three feet from front to rear. This frame is then covered with either glazed sash, cloth frames, or lath frames, or first one then another, according to the amount of protection and heat or shade desirable. The arrangement is called a 'coldframe' because no provision is made for bottom heat. There are many modifications of the coldframe; lath or slat houses or lath covers for beds with raised edging boards, etc., are all on the coldframe principle, and in warm climates, . . . the arrangement serves an excellent purpose."

Construction. The traditional coldframe is a rectangular box with a clear top that is angled to directly face the low winter sun. It is often made with scrap lumber found around the house, and either a glass sash or a plastic top.

For the frame, use 2 × 12 redwood or a wood that's been treated with preservative. The back is made from two 6-foot lengths of wood joined with 1 × 4-inch cleats spaced every 4 feet. Cut each of the two side pieces 2 feet 8 inches long. When they are nailed inside the front and back lengths, they will allow the sash a 1-inch overhang to permit water runoff. Complete the ends by cutting two more lengths 2 feet 8 inches long, and saw them diagonally from one corner to the other.

Drafts must be avoided in the coldframe, because they would either stunt or kill the seedlings. To minimize drafts, seal all the joints with a flexible sealant. Tack weatherstripping all around the frame where it joins with the sash. For even more protection, nail 1 × 4-inch lengths around the front and the sides, letting them extend up flush with the top of the sash. Only the front, which overhangs for water runoff, cannot be further protected in this manner.

Put the top in place by hinging it in back so it can be raised or lowered for ventilation. On the front, use two hooks and screw eyes to keep it from blowing open in strong winds.

To support the sash when it is open, use hinges to fasten lengths of 1 × 1 to the inside of the sash. When the sash is closed, these will fold up and out of the way. Notch the support stick every 4 inches so it will fit snugly over a 16d nail driven in each end wall of the frame. This deep notching will allow for adjustable opening of the sash and will support the open top and keep it from blowing over backwards.

Instead of buying a glass sash for the cover of the coldframe, you can make one from either 2 × 2 redwood or from wood that's been treated to resist the moisture build-up inside the frame. Like the glass sash, the top is 3 × 6 feet, with lap joints for a tight fit all the way around. The two center braces are 2 feet apart on-center. This will allow you to use lengths of clear corrugated

This familiar design of coldframe is treated with a wood preservative to prevent decay. The 2 × 12-inch stock frame faces south and is covered with glass.

Top: A fiberglass-enclosed, raised coldframe holds a thriving out-of-season sweet potato crop. While ventilation was a daytime necessity, night temperatures in the coldframe were from 2 to 5 degrees warmer than the night air.

Right: In this end view of the above coldframe, note details of fiberglass end panels which increase light, rubber buffers at the cover's bending stress point, and the hook and eye latch to hold the cover open.

Above left: Spring transplants harden off under the coldframe cover which has been removed from its raised bed.

fiberglass. The top can also be covered with clear plastic film, which can be replaced when necessary.

If you use corrugated fiberglass, use corrugated molding, either redwood or rubber, on the top and bottom to prevent drafts. Use aluminum nails with neoprene washers to fasten the fiberglass.

For glass covering (this allows the maximum amount of light), use a router or dado saw blade to rabbet the edges of the frame ½ inch in and ⅛ inch deep. Lay a bead of sealant around the rabbeted edges before laying in each pane of glass. Use strips of 1 × 2 over the glass to hold it in place. Be sure to lay an additional bead of sealant around the edges of the glass before putting the strips on.

Raised Garden Covers

As raised gardens become more popular, there's no reason why they can't be turned into mini-hothouses, allowing you to get an early start on your gardening season.

Build a wooden frame of 2 × 3 to fit directly on top of your raised bed. Use steel corner braces to strengthen it. Hinge one side of the frame to the raised bed, spacing the hinges 2 to 3 feet apart. Now take a sheet of corrugated fiberglass and screw it vertically to the hinged side of the frame. Use washers with the screws, and predrill every hole 8 inches apart. Leave a ½-inch clearance around the bottom so the fiberglass will not hit the raised bed edge when the frame is tilted up.

Bend the fiberglass down to the other side, making as near a half-circle as possible. Trim off any excess, then screw the fiberglass to the frame. Enclose the ends with ½-inch exterior-grade plywood cut to fit snugly just inside the fiberglass. Glue a strip of molding to the fiberglass.

This style lets you prop up the whole frame so you can work in the raised garden.

Another way is to cover the plywood ends with foam molding, then screw the fiberglass to the ends—but only halfway. Because the screws go only to

Protection from wind, excess rain, and hail is afforded nine different carrot varieties being tested in this raised bed under a fiberglass cover. A solar collector (just visible at the far right) heats water that flows under the bed, making it into a hot bed (see pages 113 and 114).

Semicircle row covers stabilized with heavy gauge wire prove to give better protection to young plants than do sharply angled row covers.

the top of the ends, you can flip open one side for ventilation and access. When it's open, it is held with a hook and eye bolt in the rear of the frame.

If snow is a problem in your area, you can make the raised garden cover more rigid by supporting the center with an additional end piece.

Hotbeds

A hotbed is a coldframe plus bottom heat. In the past, many elaborate methods of supplying bottom heat were devised. The most common was fermenting or composting organic matter, but steam pipes, heated flues, and similar systems were sometimes used as well. Today, of course, electrical and solar systems are available along with the more traditional methods.

A hotbed more closely approaches the capabilities of a greenhouse. Many seeds germinate readily only when supplied with bottom heat. In addition, a hotbed usually enables cuttings of all types to root more quickly.

Sources of heat. Heat can be supplied to a hotbed from many sources, including decaying organic matter, fires, electricity, and the sun.

Manure. Prior to the wide use of electricity, manure was the common way of heating a coldframe so that it could function as a hotbed. At one time, manure was a readily available resource; for many people, it still is. Horticultural writer L. H. Bailey found this a common practice. He wrote:

"It is important that the manure be as uniform as possible in composition and texture, that it come from highly-fed horses, and is practically of the same age. Perhaps as much as one-half of the whole material should be of litter or straw which has been used in the bedding. The manure is piled in a long and shallow square-topped pile, not more than four or six feet high as a rule, and is then allowed to ferment. Better results are generally obtained if the manure is piled under cover.

"The first fermentation is nearly always irregular; that is, it begins unequally in several places in the pile. In order to make the fermentation uniform, the pile must be turned occasionally, taking care to break up all hard lumps and to distribute the hot manure. It is sometimes necessary to turn the pile five or six times before it is finally used, though half this number is ordinarily sufficient. When the pile is steaming uniformly throughout, it is placed in the hotbed, and is covered with the earth in which the plants are to be grown.

"Hotbed frames are sometimes set on top of the pile of fermenting manure. The manure should extend for some distance beyond the edges of the frame; otherwise the frame will become too cold about the outside, and the plants will suffer. It is preferable, however, to have a pit beneath the frame in which the manure is placed.

"Manure which has too much straw for the best results, and which will therefore soon part with its heat, will spring up quickly when the pressure of the feet is removed. Manure which has too little straw, and which therefore will not heat well or will spend its heat quickly, will pack down into a boggy mass underneath the feet.

"The amount of manure which is to be used will depend upon its quality, and also upon the season in which the hotbed is made. The earlier the bed is made, the larger should be the quantity of manure. Hotbeds which are supposed to hold for two months should have about two feet of manure, as a rule.

"The manure will heat very vigorously for a few days after it is placed in the bed. Use a soil thermometer that reaches into the manure to watch its temperature. When the temperature is passing below 90°F., seeds of the warm plants, like tomatoes, may be sown, and when it passes below 80° or 70°F., the seeds of cooler plants may be sown."

As you can imagine, the manure-heated hotbed entails considerable labor for a rather inexact result. However, if properly prepared and handled as Mr. Bailey describes, it is a workable and reliable source of heat.

Other fermenting organic material can be used—for example, a portable coldframe on top of a compost pile will benefit from the additional heat.

Flue-heated hotbed. This type of hotbed is more complex, but it works well if you have a large supply of firewood or coal and want a large hotbed.

Picture the flue-heated hotbed: a fire pit at one end, with 4-inch flues or stove pipes running the length of the bed. The hot gasses exit through chimneys at the opposite end. The chimney should be high in order to provide good draft. Generally, there should be a rise in the flues of at least 1 foot in 25. A steeper rise will ensure good draft. The flue pipes should occupy a space beneath the beds, and should never touch the bottoms of the beds unless the pipes are insulated.

For a hotbed roughly 50 feet by 10 feet, lay three flues, evenly spaced, under the bed. The end closest to the firebox should be about 2 feet under the bed. The firebox end must be deeper to prevent that area from overheating.

For the fire pit, make it 4 feet square and about 4 feet deep. The firebox can be a 55-gallon drum on its side with three vent pipes welded on the back to connect into the three flue pipes. A door cut in the end with hinges welded on is the opening to feed the stove with wood or coal. An oil heater could also be used.

Start the first fires about three days before seeding to ensure that the ground is warm enough. Check the temperature of the soil with thermometers. From then on, one fire in the morning and one in the evening should be enough to maintain warmth in the hotbeds.

Electric hotbeds. The electric cable is by far the simplest and most common method of heating a coldframe today. Such cables are available in a variety of forms—with and without built-in thermostats, plastic and lead coated, and single or double wire. The "propagation mat" is probably the most convenient. It resembles an electric heating pad, but is waterproof and made to be buried in the soil. With electric heat and a thermostat, precise control of bottom heat is obtained, therefore broadening the gardener's capability.

How long should the soil cable be? This depends on the size of the area to be heated. Also, the same length cables offered by different manufacturers may have different capacities. As a rule of thumb, plan to use 2 to 4 linear feet of cable per square foot. For example, a 3 × 6-foot frame is 18 square feet. Depending on the manufacturer's recommendations, between 36 and 72 linear feet of cable will be required. Another way to determine how much cable you need is to allow 10 to 15 watts for every square foot. (In a sunny, wind-sheltered location, a well-insulated hotbed would use only 10 watts.) Naturally, propagation mats heat an area equal to their dimensions.

Lay the cable on the level bottom of the frame, being careful not to overlap. If the cable is as stiff as a cold hose, plug it in and allow it to warm slightly. Clothespins or something comparable may help hold the cable in place. Then cover the cable with about an inch of sand. (Do not use peat moss—it may dry and insulate the cable, and thus cause it to overheat.) Putting hardware cloth or screen on top of this will protect the cable from being damaged by hand tools. Directly on top of the screen, place a 5- or 6-inch layer of rooting medium such as sand, peat, or perlite. For safety, check to make sure that all connections are moisture proof. Also, be sure that the assembly is properly grounded.

Solar-heated hotbeds. The solar-heated bed shown on page 111 is a new and ingenious invention. This particular solar panel, intended for heating swimming pools, is available commercially. Eight ¾-inch plastic pipes were evenly spaced at the bottom of the bed. The direction of flow is from the top of the panel into the visible end of the bed. The 1¼-inch return pipe visible beneath completes the cycle.

These tender lettuce plants were nurtured through early spring by (top) a screen for protection from birds, and (bottom) an outer sheet of insulating plastic.

Warming Cable Placement

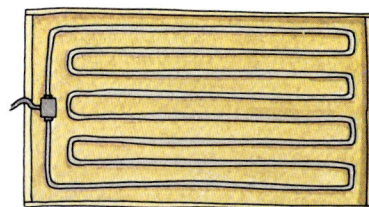

Warming cables should be arranged like this one. Spaces should be of equal widths, and the cable must never cross itself.

Below: The clear plastic over these tomato plants significantly increased daytime temperatures of the air around the plastic.

Center: Experiments showed that switching to black plastic for nighttime insulation maintained a higher temperature inside the coldframe.

Bottom: This divided coldframe experiment showed that clear plastic maintained higher daytime temperatures but lower nighttime temperatures than the black-covered side, which, at 10:00 PM, was 9 degrees warmer than the outside air.

This system uses no pumps, relying instead on the rising hot water to give motion to the system. For it to function properly, all air must be removed from the pipes. This is why there are hose spigots with which to flush the system.

Many such systems are possible. Adding a coldframe like the one shown on page 110 makes the solar-heated hotbed a reality. Some other basic solar-heating techniques can help transform a coldframe into a hotbed.

Line the outside of the frame with 1-inch-thick pieces of rigid insulating material, and extend this 12 inches into the ground. This insulating material will keep out the surface cold, yet trap the natural warmth of the deeper earth.

Stack dark-colored bricks against the back of the frame on the inside. During the day, these bricks will be heated thoroughly by the sun; during the night, the stored heat within the bricks will slowly be released back into the coldframe.

Large cans painted black and filled with water will do the same. For more on solar energy, see page 65.

Test Garden Reports

Many experiments were conducted at a test garden in Los Altos, California, where the coldframe/greenhouse principle was combined with commonly available materials.

In an attempt to determine the swing of temperatures and how to moderate them, the researchers measured not only maximum and minimum temperatures, but how much heat retention each type of covering material could provide. They also explored ways of utilizing the simple principles of solar energy, as well as ways to speed seed germination.

The following questions were posed:

☐ Will a coldframe make it possible to grow a vegetable crop, such as sweet potatoes, that usually does not adapt well to the climate?
☐ Will a coldframe improve the setting of fruits on tomato and pepper plants?
☐ How much frost protection will a coldframe provide?
☐ What is the difference in reradiation between clear and black plastic? Since the researchers knew that clear plastic allows unimpeded transmission of radiation to the plant and soil during the day, they hypothesized that black plastic would slow reradiation on a cold night.
☐ In what ways can seed germination be improved? Seed row covers were tried (see page 107), as well as modified styrofoam picnic boxes.

These pages show some of the experiments. By observing the soil and by using maximum/minimum thermometers, the researchers kept track of the temperatures (both inside and out) of the "black and white" experiment, the

Day	Daily Maximum Temperature	Daily Minimum Temperature	Polyethylene Cover 10p.m.			Fiberglass Coldframe 10p.m.		Automatic Coldframe 10p.m.	
			clear	black	outside	inside	outside	inside	outside
1	95	49	66	68	60	62	58	64	60
2	86	48	62	63	58	59	55	60	57
3	77	54	59	62	57	60	55	59	57
4	73	56	60	61	58	62	58	61	59
5	70	54	63	64	60	61	58	62	60
6	77	51	65	67	63	64	61	65	63
7	82	49	67	69	63	64	61	65	63
8	89	56	62	64	58	64	60	60	58
9	84	50	65	66	62	65	59	62	60

fiberglass coldframe, and the automatic coldframe (see photograph, below). The results are charted on the opposite page. The daily maximum and minimum are as reported by the local weather station. All temperatures are reported in degrees Fahrenheit.

Season-stretching Ideas

Before you use any kind of season-stretching device—whether plastic jugs, plastic draped over an A-frame, or a simple coldframe—there are a few things you should know.

It matters *where* you use such early-season growing aids (for example, row covers and plastic jugs). In areas where temperatures are consistently cool, such aids fulfill their function very well. But if you live in an area where a stretch of cool spring weather may be broken by temperatures equal to a hot summer day, your plastic-covered plant may be killed by the heat.

Good ventilation is the key to avoiding disaster. A row cover that has both ends open should provide enough ventilation to let the excessive heat escape. If there is no ventilation through plastic covers of any kind, you'll have to remove the covers on a warm day and replace them again at night.

One way to keep plastic row covers warm at night is to put large plastic bottles or plastic tubes filled with water inside the covers. During the day, the sun warms the water. Then at night, the water slowly gives off heat and keeps the plants inside the cover a few degrees warmer. Even slight temperature increases can be enough to make a considerable difference in plant growth.

The A-frame. The A-frame is an extension of the trellis idea. Vegetables that once were considered "space wasters" in the small garden can now be grown vertically. Just about anything that vines, including the small-fruited watermelon, winter squash, and melons, can be trained skyward.

Above: A styrofoam picnic box can be used for a miniature greenhouse.

Below: This commercial coldframe opens 6 to 7 inches when air temperatures exceed 72°F. It closes at air temperatures of 68°F. and below. No electricity is required—the automatic device is a simple thermal piston.

Top: Seeds get an early start in this miniature greenhouse.

Above: Plastic sheeting on this portable A-frame makes an effective early spring row cover.

The A-frame can be positioned to take advantage of maximum sunlight and heat on one side, leaving the opposite for growing crops that demand a cooler environment.

It also can be converted into a tent to protect plants from early spring frost. Try making a row tent out of the frame by covering it with plastic.

The "Hatch Patch." Plastic mulches are proven season stretchers. They are particularly valuable for increasing yields and speeding up ripening of melons, eggplant, peppers, and summer squash. In areas where early-season temperatures are cool for these warm-weather crops, plastic mulch used in experimental plots increased yields of muskmelon up to four times.

How does this work? One theory is that the temperature of the film, especially black plastic, soars high on a warm, sunny day and transfers a great deal of heat to the air above it, rather than to the soil. Insulating air pockets between the film and the soil surface retard heat transfer from the black film to the soil.

The "Hatch Patch," a demonstration garden run by Oregon State University, has come up with some interesting and useful research findings. Duane Hatch, an Extension Agent in Eugene, Oregon, and the originator of the "Hatch Patch," reports on his experience with plastic mulches:

"A layer of plastic over the soil aids greatly with warm season crops such as tomatoes, melons, peppers and squash. The warming of the soil will promote 10 to 14 days earlier maturity and higher yields with tomatoes. Melons, seeded about the 10th of June, gave us ripe cantaloupe and watermelon by mid-September.

"We demonstrated that clear plastic is better than black plastic because the sun's energy is expended on the soil rather than on the top part of the plastic. The weeds were not a major problem under the clear plastic if temperatures of 90° or more occurred to burn off the weeds. In 1974 we weren't getting enough heat to burn off the weeds, and we had to lift the plastic and do some hand weeding.

"The hills of squash and melons were planted through an X cut in the plastic. With the amount of water that goes through the planting hole and around the edge of the plastic, no special watering was necessary."

In another experimental planting in Oregon, several tomato varieties were tested. According to the *Oregon Vegetable Digest:*

"In 1973, 13 tomato varieties were tested at the North Willamette Experiment Station for their adaptability to the northern Willamette Valley.

"One of the growing beds was covered with black polyethylene plastic (1½ mils thick). Three plants of each variety were set 4 feet apart in the center of the bed. For irrigation, a porous wall tube ('Viaflo' by DuPont) was placed

Below: This experiment is testing the effectiveness of black plastic mulch on corn plantings.

Photographs taken several weeks apart show the rapid growth of various vegetables in the Plastic Garden at Dixon Springs Agricultural Center in Simpson, Illinois. A sawdust mulch is used between rows.

on the bed surface near the plants. Tubing was placed beneath the plastic mulch. A hole cut in the mulch permitted plants to be set. Plants were tied to a trellis of woven wire, which was installed soon after planting.

"Earliest tomatoes were from unmulched plants, but the yield of marketable fruit from plants grown with the plastic mulch was increased by an average of 114 percent over that of unmulched plants. In addition, plastic mulch also increased fruit size an average of 13 percent, saved on irrigation, and prevented weed growth."

When installing plastic mulch, make sure the soil is damp before you put down the mulch, so that the mulch has moisture underneath to retain.

To water under a plastic mulch, cut short slits in the plastic. This lets you water with sprinklers, a hose, or a soaker hose. Or, if you already have a drip-irrigation system, this works well with plastic, too.

Hot caps. These are another means of providing plants with the protection of controlled climates. They are excellent in areas where plants are in the ground and coming up but are still subject to cold snaps or frost in late spring or early fall.

The easiest way to make a hot cap is to cut off the bottom of a 1-gallon plastic milk jug. Leave the cap off during the day and replace it at night.

Bottomless plastic jugs are individually staked for stability. While effective for cool days and nights, hot caps left on during hot days can roast young plants.

If the daytime weather is warm, however, check the covered plants periodically. Heat can build up quickly, even with the top off, and cook young plants.

There are larger structures that will trap the sun's heat during the day and protect against frost at night. They do not have to be elaborate to be efficient.

A simple one is nothing more than a large, clear plastic bag supported by three sticks placed over a plant. Sheets of polyethylene film, draped over wire frames stuck in the ground and anchored with rocks, will help provide a temporary greenhouse for young plants. If the plant is entirely covered, cut several vents in the plastic to prevent the plant from baking.

To cover whole rows at a time, bend 4 × 8-foot sheets of clear corrugated fiberglass and stake them at the sides. At night, for added protection, drape the ends with polyethylene film or cut end blocks from plywood to fit. This type of cover was recently tested to see whether increasing the temperature in the early evening would speed the growth of peppers. The panel was put in place at sunset and removed the next morning. Soil and air temperatures, which were checked at 11 p.m. nightly, were higher in the covered rows than in the open rows, and the covered peppers grew faster and larger than the exposed peppers.

The plant cover, or row cover, widely used in England and France around the turn of the century, is still popular in these countries. A *cloche*—a glass bell jar—was used. A simple *cloche* can be made of two panes of glass clipped together at the top. You can devise your own, or buy specially made clips from gardening equipment suppliers.

The Shady Retreat

Plants need sunshine for maximum growth, but many are too delicate to withstand extended exposure to direct sunlight. The lath house offers an ideal solution—a cool and shady retreat where plants can receive a proper balance of light and fresh air. Many lath houses become retreats for people who want to be outside but who also want to escape the sun's direct rays.

If you have a sun-baked patio that is often too hot or too wet to use during summer days, you can use a variety of shade structures to convert it into a garden of filtered light. The shade possibilities range from extending the roof line of your house to building a complete shade/lath house, which serves as a refreshing area for people and plants.

Most people cover a shade structure with wood strips, which are both esthetically pleasing and long lasting. Lath is the standard cover, but you can also use grape stakes or 1 × 2 furring strips, both of which are effective and inexpensive. When your covering material goes up to 2 × 2 or larger, your costs also go up sharply.

Another alternative is to put fewer lath strips overhead and use a bamboo screen or saran cloth for really hot days. Saran cloth, which is generally used to shade greenhouses, will screen anywhere from 30 to 90 percent of the sun, depending on how tight the weave. In areas where excessive summer rain limits outdoor activities, you can cover shade structures with canvas, polyethylene, or fiberglass.

Just how much shade you want and how large a shade structure you need depends on your personal taste.

Lath house. One of the most attractive additions to a yard is the lath house, either freestanding or attached to an existing structure. Build it with the idea that it will be a summer retreat not only for plants but also for people. Make it large enough to house a table and chairs; once you decorate it with hanging plants, you and your friends will want to sit down and enjoy the new atmosphere. You also can cover the roof with panels of corrugated fiberglass to add the benefit of rain protection and extend the lath house's use in areas where the climate is unpredictable.

The simplest and most practical variety is the attached lath house. Its

Above far left: Detail of lath construction.

Above left: Removable lath sections with a 2 × 2-inch end brace fit snugly against the 2 × 6-inch joist.

Above center: Two people can easily handle these sections of lath.

Above right: A 4 × 4 lath support post is attached to a pier.

Left: The completed lath house; shaded coolness on a summer day.

Far left: The harsh glare of the sun is softened by lath.

shade will modify the climate not only for your plants but also for your home. Build this attached structure with two considerations in mind. First, slope the roof slightly; if you cover it later, you will have runoff. A ¼-inch drop per foot is generally sufficient. Second, build in removable modules if you want to catch the sun to help heat the house during the winter months.

Here's how one lath went up on a south-facing deck that was too hot and exposed during hot summer days. The lath was designed to be removed during the winter.

This deck already had a concrete footing in which to place the four redwood 4 × 4 posts that would be the outside supports. Holes were drilled with a concrete bit at the measured points, and steel post anchors were fastened with ½-inch expansion bolts. The uprights were put in place and bolted to the sides of the deck for additional bracing.

The shade porch rafters were attached to the house with 2 × 6 joist hangers on the ledger board. These 16-foot rafters were attached to the posts with ½ × 4 lag screws. The rafters extended 4 feet beyond the posts for additional sun protection.

With the skeleton in place, a double row of 2 × 2s was nailed on top of the rafters 12 feet out from the house to tie the unit together and minimize any swaying.

The removable shade panels were made by nailing 1 × 2 furring strips onto 2 × 2s spaced the width of the rafters. Each panel is light enough for one person to handle.

The western end of this lath house admitted too much late-afternoon sun for comfort during the summer months. To counter this, panels similar to those on the rafters were built, but here the furring strips ran vertically, to give the impression of more height. These panels were screwed in place during the summer and removed in the winter, along with the overhead panels, to admit more sunlight.

Wooden lath allows shade-loving plants to flourish in this narrow space.

In the more likely event that you will have to put in your own foundation for the shade porch, you can use precast concrete piers or pour your own footings. These should be spaced 4 feet apart. If you pour your own, embed steel anchor straps in the concrete while it is still wet.

Once the footings are dry (wait at least 48 hours), put the 4 × 4 posts in place and bolt the cases to the anchor straps. Provide temporary bracings with 2 × 4s.

Instead of clasping each upright between two 2 × 6s, as in the previous example, run a 4 × 4 bond beam across the top of all the posts. Cut the posts so that when the bond beam is in place, the rafters will slope slightly away from the house for runoff, in case you want to cover it later on.

It's best to tie the bond beam to each post with a steel T-brace. Once it is in place, extend the rafters and toenail them to the bond beam. Finally, nail on the shade strips of your choice.

Whether a lath house is latticed and has a corrugated fiberglass roof (left), or more spacious and open as are the patios below, the resulting modified environment can expand both the home and the garden.

Attached shade structures offer two distinct advantages: the house wall gives excellent support, eliminating half the posts needed; and the shade structure is more convenient to use, since the porch becomes an extension of your house. It's advisable to build the framework of all shade structures strong enough to support at least the weight of one person. Anticipate the possible addition of solid roofing at some later date.

The tops do not all have to be covered with laths, particularly if you are in an area where direct, hot sunlight is not a real problem. You might also consider the egg crate construction, which gives the sense of overhead protection but keeps it very open. An excellent way to create the egg crate effect is to lap joints wherever overhead pieces cross. It takes time to cut and chisel out each lap joint, but once cut, the pieces will form the structure quickly and have great strength. You can also lay out the stringers every 2 to 3 feet apart, then toenail in each crosspiece. Later on, you can quickly cover egg crate overheads with bamboo screens, shadecloths, or fiberglass panels if you need more protection. The open egg crate style also lends itself well to supporting natural coverings, such as grape vines, wisteria, or bougainvillea.

Terrariums

Terrariums are the bottled jewels of indoor gardens. They range from exquisite miniatures inside pill bottles to fully landscaped gardens inside fish tanks. Terrariums are ideal for plants that require warmth, high humidity, and ideal soil conditions.

There is no limit to what you can plant in terrariums. Even cacti will grow under glass if planted in a sandy soil and kept dry. Most terrarium plants, however, are selected for their small size, tropical nature, and slow growth.

History. The terrarium was invented in 1829 by Dr. Nathaniel Ward, a surgeon interested in natural history. While studying the life cycle of the sphinx moth in sealed jars, Ward noticed within a few days that condensation was running down the sides of the bottle. Shortly thereafter, he was astonished to see tiny ferns sprout. The ferns lived four years in the bottle without a drop of added water. In 1832, he packed ferns and moss into two large glass containers and sent them to Australia—a trip that took eight months. The plants flourished, as did the ones that Australians shipped back under glass.

Dr. Ward immediately began producing what became known as "Wardian cases." These were partly responsible for the successful shipment of plants to botanical gardens around the world. The great tea plantations of northern India were established by 20,000 tea plants in Wardian cases that were shipped from Shanghai. All previous attempts to ship live plants had failed. Today the Wardian case is called a terrarium, and it is just as much at home in your livingroom as it was on a 19th-century clipper ship.

Planting. First, make sure the container is clean and completely dry. If it is a long-necked bottle, leave it open overnight, or dry it in the oven at a low temperature for a few hours. This will help prevent the soil from sticking to the insides when you begin to plant.

Make the first layer of fine gravel or crushed rock, for drainage. This material allows excess water to flow into the gravel and keep roots from rotting or drowning. Too much water is the common problem in terrariums.

On top of the gravel, add a fine layer of activated charcoal. Next, put down a thin layer of sphagnum moss to keep the soil from sifting into the gravel. Finally, add soil mix through a funnel.

When placing the plants, whether in a bottle or in an open container, plant the largest ones first. There are two reasons for this: (1) you will not dislodge the smaller plants, and (2) arranging the larger plants first gives a good focal point for the garden.

Maidenhair fern and a parlor palm in an antique glass and brass container.

Far left: This floor-model terrarium houses maidenhair fern, bird's nest fern, and ivy.

Left: Several fern varieties can be easily cared for in this fish-tank terrarium which has the advantages of both sunlight and fluorescent lighting.

Below: The glass jar provides a terrarium environment for this sprig of ivy.

Prepare the hole with a stick. Then, using a grasping tool or wire, lower the roots into the prepared hole and tamp the plant in place.

Next, place a piece of driftwood, a rock, or a small statue that you might want in your garden. Add additional plants, and finish with small pebbles or pieces of live moss.

Watering. Once your terrarium garden is in place, it is time for the critical task of giving it the right amount of water. The soil should be damp but not soaked. Excess water in a terrarium, particularly in a bottle, is difficult to eliminate because there is so little loss by evaporation, but you must have enough water to start the rain cycle in the bottle. This rain-forest effect will keep your terrarium lush.

Add lukewarm tap water carefully, in order to not dislodge the plants. In open containers, a fine-holed sprinkling can or mister will work well. In bottles, tip the container slightly and let the water trickle down the sides; it will also wash away any soil stuck there.

If you have doubts about how much water to provide, water less than you think you should. Watch the container. If condensation builds up in a few hours, the terrarium is probably all right. If you think you underwatered and the plants begin to droop in a day or two, add a little more.

Extreme fogging and condensation inside are signs of overwatering. If this happens, remove the top and let the excess moisture evaporate.

Maintenance. Once the proper rain-forest effect is established, your terrarium should be largely self-sustaining. It will probably not need water for one to two months. You will be able to spot its needs by looking for lack of condensation and possible wilting.

Lighting is vital to any successful garden, including the terrarium. In the winter months, keep the plants near windows so that they can receive all the light they need during the shorter days.

Reminders. Be sure to turn your terrarium periodically so that all sides receive equal amounts of light. This will keep the plants growing straight. Every month to six weeks, you can add a few drops of liquid houseplant food, mixed at one-fourth the listed strength for standard potted plants.

Window Greenhouses

The window greenhouse is a big step up from gardening along a window sill or putting plants in a bay window. A real window greenhouse closes on the inside so that the plants are not subjected to the drying effects of the house.

This creates a problem, however. Because these little greenhouses are small, they can heat up rapidly when hit with sunlight. They can also cool down markedly at night. Therefore, vents that connect to the outside and from your room into the window greenhouse are important—they keep the air relatively constant. Although this is not a serious problem, it is one to be aware of.

Location. Almost any window in the house will do. It depends on what effect you wish to create and what plants you want to grow. To get maximum sunlight, especially during the winter months, choose a south-facing window. The next choice is the east, which gets the morning and midday sun. A western window will get late-afternoon sun only, and a north-facing window will get minimal light and direct sunlight only in the early morning and late afternoon during the summer.

However, with the help of fluorescent lighting, you can put a window greenhouse anywhere you wish—even in a bathroom window that opens into an air shaft.

Once a window greenhouse is installed, the room suddenly seems larger, more open, and spacious. So put your window greenhouse where you think it will look the best and do the most for your room. Then, make it flourish with plants for that exposure.

Window types. Before you start building or buying a window greenhouse, consider the kind of window you have and how to remove it. There are six basic types of window: awning, jalousie, fixed, casement, double-hung, and sliding.

Fixed awning and jalousie windows. These are normally in steel or aluminum frames. Simply unscrew and lift out.

A window greenhouse is not difficult to install. (1) The greenhouse will be installed in the window to the left of center. (2) Remove the existing window and install new framing. (3) Seal the framing with weatherstripping. (4) You will probably need help to lift the greenhouse into place and attach it with the first couple of screws. (5) You may then finish the other attachments. You may wish to install silver screen shade cloth, which shields out about 35 percent of the sunlight. It reflects light on the outside (6), but can be seen through from the inside (7). Apply it to the greenhouse glass (8) using spray adhesive or two-sided adhesive tape.

The installed greenhouse—but without the shade cloth.

Double-hung window. First pry loose the inside stop on one side of the window frame. Once that's out of the way, pull that side of the window toward you and out from the groove on the opposite side. Then lift out the sash cord.

Casement window. First unscrew the crank and operating bar. Next, unscrew all hinges on the inside of the window doors. To remove the steel casement frame, unscrew it on the sides, then remove the inside stops, as for a double-hung window, and lift out.

Sliding window. Loosen the release screw at the inside top of the sliding window. Then lift up and pull out at the bottom.

Fixed window. The fixed frame will come out the same way as the sliding window, although it is fitted more tightly. In some instances you may have to remove the center frame piece.

PROPAGATION

*Knowing a few basic facts will
enable you to start your own plants
from seeds or cuttings.*

Once your controlled environment is ready—after the odor of bleach and
paint have faded away—you can start planting. Nothing is so encouraging
as success, so start with seeds or cuttings from easy-to-grow plants. Observe
them and use them to learn about your controlled environment.

Seeds

Nature's primary method of reproducing plants is with seeds. Most seeds
that you purchase for a controlled environment need only planting, constantly moist soil around them, gentle warmth (55° to 75°F., or 13° to 24°C.),
and light to become healthy seedlings.

All seeds must absorb water before they can begin to grow, so soaking
them overnight in warm water will always speed the germination of any
seeds you buy. However, it will make very small seeds harder to sow
because they will tend to stick together.

Getting seeds started. A soil mix that can be used for almost all seeds is
shown on page 59.

How deep should you plant the seeds? A good rule is: not more than twice
their thickness. If seeds get lost or germinate poorly, it is almost always
because they were planted too deeply or because the soil was not kept
uniformly moist. Plant the seeds in rows, and label the rows even if you're
sure you'll be able to identify the seedlings.

You may want to grow seedlings from the seeds of trees or shrubs in the
neighborhood. Then you'll want to be able to identify good ripe seeds and
also know where the parent plants originated.

A seed has three basic parts:

1. *The coat,* which keeps out moisture to prevent premature germination.
2. *The food storage,* which gives the seedling a good start.
3. *The embryo* or tiny, immature plant, which you can usually see at one
   end of a seed when you open it.

You can help the germination of seeds with very hard coats if you file
or nick them gently. This lets moisture enter and triggers the germination process.

If the parent plant originated in the tropics, there's a good chance that the
seeds will germinate almost as soon as you plant them in the greenhouse.
But if the plant is native to a cold or temperate zone, you may have to
simulate the cold springtime that the seeds would have gone through in
their natural setting. Storing the seeds for about 40 days in a household
refrigerator at about 40°F. (4°C.) will break the dormant period. Mix the
seeds with some slightly damp perlite or peat moss, put them in a jar or
a plastic bag, and place them in the back of the refrigerator. When the 40
days have passed plant them in the greenhouse as you would any other
kind of seed.

Plant cuttings and germinating seeds do well in this high-humidity propagation box.

Once you've planted, be patient; leave the soil alone. The seeds of some plants will germinate in five to seven days, while others may take three weeks. Some cactus seeds may take a year or more to germinate. The expected period for germination is usually noted on the seed packet.

Transplanting. Transplanting a seedling once or twice before you give it a permanent home is often necessary. The growing container should always be in proportion to the size of the seedling. A plant in too large a container may be just as difficult to care for as one in a container that is too small.

Cuttings

Planting cuttings is an ancient way to propagate many trees and vines. From the Middle East come the olive, grape, pomegranate, date, and many other fruit-bearing plants that can be grown from cuttings of stems or roots.

It is helpful to consider some general rules that govern the ease or difficulty of getting stem cuttings to take root:

☐ The younger the cutting, the more likely it is to root. Take cuttings of most plants from shoots that are less than a year old. There are a few exceptions, such as the olive, that may do better if the cutting is from second-year wood.
☐ The more leaves on a cutting, the better it will root. This is because plant food and plant hormones, which stimulate root growth, are produced in the leaves. On the other hand, if the leaves are too numerous or too large, they'll give off more moisture than the cutting can take in, and the cutting will die.
☐ The more light the cutting gets, the faster it will root as photosynthesis builds up the carbohydrates. Of course, too much direct hot sunlight will shrivel it up even faster. Ideally, the high light level without heat of an artificial growing area is best for rooting cuttings.

After a few days in moist sand, these *Sedum* leaf cuttings (below) readily take root and produce tiny new plants (bottom).

The rooting medium can be almost any mix that has good drainage and lets air penetrate, yet retains moisture. It should also be sterile, if possible, and support the cuttings well. Horticultural perlite is one commercial product that seems to fill the bill. For greater moisture retention or a lower pH, add some ground sphagnum plant. Commercially available rooting hormones can benefit some plants, but a great many plants produce enough hormones on their own. (The hormone compounds available commercially are organic and relatively unstable. Keep them in a closed container and away from light—preferably in a freezer.) If you notice that the bottom of a cutting is turning black, chances are the rooting hormone is too strong.

Just where to take a cutting and how to handle it depends on the type of plant, as described below. But here is a good general plan:

☐ Take a 4-inch cutting from young wood.
☐ Strip the leaves or needles from the lower half, and cut away a portion of any very large leaves in the upper half.
☐ Bury the lower part 2½ inches deep in perlite or soil mix.
☐ Water once or twice a day, or use a misting system if your controlled environment has one. You can maintain high humidity around the cutting by inverting a glass jar over it or placing the cutting and pot in a clear plastic bag.
☐ Keep the cutting in a place that gets bright light but no direct sunshine at a temperature of around 60° to 65°F. (16° to 18°C.).

The surrounding temperature can be cooler if you have a heating cable that can keep the bottom of the seedling bed at about 70° to 75°F. (20° to 23°C.).

Stem cuttings. There are several types to note.

Hardwood. Cuttings are considered to be hardwood when they come from shoots that have grown through an entire season and the mother or stock

Far left: For most cuttings, the rooting process is accelerated by heat from small electric cables.
Left: These are vigorous cuttings of shefflera (*Brassaia actinophylla*).

plant is either approaching or in a dormant period. Hardwood plant cells are fully formed, and lignification—strengthening into woody tissue—has taken place. Of all the types of cuttings, hardwood is the least likely to dry out, get wounded, or becomes sick before you can plant it.

Not all *deciduous* flowering shrubs can be propagated from stem cuttings, but a surprising number can. One technique is to take the cuttings in the fall—just after the leaves have dropped—from shoots that grew during the spring and summer of that year. Discard the top 10 to 12 inches (this wood is not likely to be fully mature), then cut the remainder in 12-inch lengths. As you gather up the lengths, keep them all running in the same direction (one easy way is to cut the bottom of each piece at an angle and the top straight across). Each length should have several nodes—the junctures where the leaves were joined to the stem. Discard those that don't. Scratch or slice the bark up 2 or 3 inches from the bottom and, if you have some rooting hormone compound, rub a little into these wounds. Then tie about 10 to 25 cuttings—all pointing the same way—in a loose bundle, and label each bundle. Pack the bundles loosely, top ends up, in a 5-gallon or other container that is 5 or 6 inches deeper than the cuttings and has many drainage holes in the bottom. Then fill the container with coarse perlite, set it in a cool place away from the light—under a bench, perhaps—and water it once or twice a week.

If you take the cuttings in November or December, they should be ready to plant by mid-February. By then, most species will be well healed, some may already show roots, and a few may even have some white top growth. Plant the cuttings in pots or trays about 6 or 8 inches deep and 6 inches apart, and put them in a cool place with plenty of light. As the spring gets warmer and the days get brighter, move the containers into a shady location outside. By July or August, you'll have lots of young shrubs to replant in the garden.

Narrow-leaved evergreen hardwood cuttings are among the easiest to grow. These are the yews, junipers, arborvitae, cypress, and some cedars and pines.

Take shoots from the past season's growth; discard a few inches of the less mature wood at the tip; cut the rest into lengths of about 4 inches; dip the lower half in a rooting hormone; and plant about 2½ inches deep in perlite. If you have a heating cable, set it at 65° to 75°F. (18° to 24°C.) and place the cuttings' container on it. Water daily. In 10 to 16 weeks, most of the cuttings should be rooted; but wait patiently if they're not. Then transplant them into pots or a transplant bed, leaving 6 inches between each. They should grow into bushy plants in their first summer, and can be transplanted to their permanent places in the second or third summer.

Broad-leaved evergreen cuttings are perhaps the most difficult to handle. These are the hollies, evergreen viburnums, rhododendrons, azaleas, and

In a controlled environment, vegetable garden plants such as corn, cucumbers, and beans are easily started from seed, providing vigorous seedlings to be planted in the ground when weather permits.

other plants that do not lose their leaves in the winter. The first and biggest problem is to get cuttings of the right maturity. Experiment by taking a few cuttings from the tips of branches every week and watch for rooting. You should then be able to decide which growth from the mother plant seems best for the variety and your area. If the tip of the branch snaps when you bend it, the wood is probably too mature. If it bends double without breaking, it's probably not old enough and will start to wilt as soon as you put it in the rooting mix.

Try to choose shoots that are plump and have full-sized leaves. If the species has large leaves, reduce the leaf area by cutting away half of each leaf. Follow the rooting procedure described for narrow-leaved evergreens. Even if the old stock plant from which you took the cutting is perfectly hardy, its offspring will need the protection of a greenhouse or coldframe during their first winter.

Softwood. Softwood cuttings are the quickest of all to take root—or to die. Swedish ivy can take root in a week or less, and many other houseplants need only two or three weeks. Get the cuttings from the stock plant into the rooting mix quickly; a bit of rooting hormone powder may help, but you won't usually need it. If the cutting has many or very large leaves, remove some. Water regularly and fertilize with a good houseplant food or liquid manure.

Some philodendrons can be rooted easily from a short piece of stem with a single leaf. This is often called a mallet, or club cutting, because of its appearance. Be sure not to plant such a cutting more than 1½ inches deep. Care for it as you would any other softwood cutting.

Left: This flat of leaf cuttings is fitted with a plastic cover to provide young seedlings with extra warmth and moisture. The cover must be removed for a short time each day to provide air circulation.

Below: A small flat of fern spores, enclosed in a plastic bag, produced these new ferns.

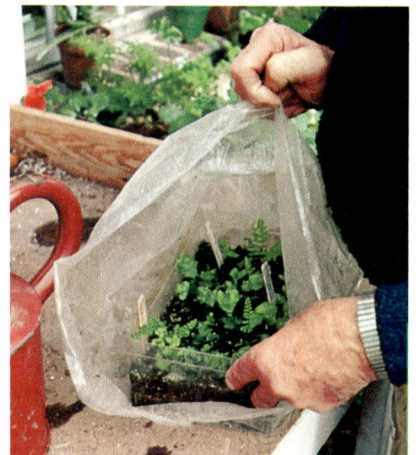

Herbaceous This last type of stem cutting is actually two groups—plants with fibrous or succulent stems, and perennials. Cuttings from plants in the former group—succulents, cacti, and geraniums—have to be air dried so that the cutting wound will start healing before they are planted. Geraniums need about half a day exposed to air, and succulents and cacti need two or three days. While drying, the cuttings should be kept in bright light but *not* in direct sun. After planting, be careful not to overwater succulents or cacti; just once every week or two is enough.

An herbaceous perennial is a plant whose top dies in winter but whose roots live on. Cut 6- to 8-inch-high shoots from the stock plant at ground level, and root them in perlite or a mix, as if they were softwood cuttings. As soon as they are well rooted, transplant them directly to the garden.

Leaf cuttings. A single leaf is sufficient to root African violets, some of the begonias, and many other plants. The leaf has to grow shoots as well as roots. Most plants that have this ability are characterized by thick, fleshy stems and leaves.

Begonias will root from a leaf petiole (stem) or from breaks in the veins of a leaf if it is laid flat on the rooting mix and pegged down with a toothpick. When two little leaves have formed on the parent leaf, you will see tiny rows of red or black spots on their undersides. These are the root initials. Put them down in the soil mix about ¼ inch. A good mix for these kinds of plants is half perlite and half potting soil. They should be lightly fertilized after a week or ten days.

The African violet and gloxinia take a little longer but usually root easily. Drops of cold water will mark their leaves, so water carefully and don't expose them to mist. If you don't need many new plants, you can root these leaves in a glass of water and move them to pots as soon as you see the little plantlets form at the base of the leaf stem.

Root cuttings. Since the roots of a plant aren't often visible, we usually don't think of them as material for cuttings. But in fact, almost any species of plant that grows out of the ground in 2 or more stems can be rooted from roots. This is an especially good method for lilac and quince, which can't be rooted easily from stem cuttings.

The best time to take root cuttings is just before an active period of growth—usually, very early in spring. Dig up all or part of the mother plant to get the cuttings, then replant the parent. Cut lengths of root of 3 or 4 inches from just under the ground's surface. Be sure to keep the top end up when you plant them in rows about ¼-inch under the surface of the rooting mix. Keep them watered; a few weeks later, you should see the shoots coming through the mix.

Propagation by Stem Cuttings

Different types of plants vary in their ease of propagation by stem cuttings, as well as by the time of year cuttings are taken and the methods used to prepare the cutting.

Herbaceous

Geranium

Coleus

Impatiens

Succulents

Carnation

Fibrous begonia

Ficus

Chrysanthemum

Herbaceous plants are among the easiest plants to propagate; a selection of them is illustrated above. Cuttings from plants with fibrous or succulent stems should be air dried before planting. This helps prevent the transmission of disease from the soil.

Basic techniques

Make cuttings 3 to 5 inches long; cut just below a node (where the leaf joins the stem).

Strip off the bottom leaves. The top leaves are necessary for root formation.

Dust the end with hormone powder. This is not absolutely necessary, but helps promote vigorous root growth.

Stick and firm the cutting in the soil mix with the leaves just above the soil.

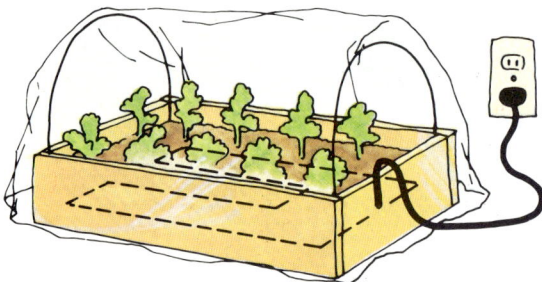

Herbaceous cuttings root readily if given bottom heat and constant high humidity. An electric heating cable (see page 113) in the bottom of a flat, plus a plastic cover, works well.

For propagating just a few cuttings, a pot in a plastic bag or a cutting box with a glass cover will provide the high humidity beneficial to the root development of the cuttings. Be sure to open the bag or remove the cover for a few hours every day to allow fresh air to circulate.

Softwood

Pyracantha

Oleander

Softwood cuttings are taken in late spring from new growth. They should be from stems that are flexible, but still mature enough to break when bent sharply. Some examples of softwood plants are hydrangea, spirea, lilac, forsythia, pyracantha, and oleander.

Wounding

Some cuttings are wounded when the leaves are stripped away.

A wound may also be made by slicing a strip of bark from the base of the cutting.

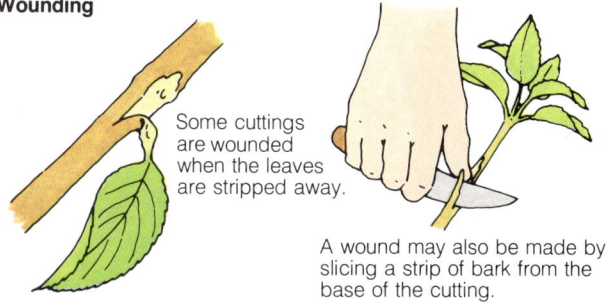

Wounding the cutting strips a portion of the bark away, exposing the cambium layer. This helps broadleaved evergreens and evergreen hardwoods root more readily.

Broadleaved evergreen

Azalea

Gardenia

Holly

Rhododendron

Broadleaved evergreen cuttings are usually taken during the summer months from new shoots that have partially matured. Cuttings should be made in the cool, early morning when the stems are firm. Wounding is beneficial. Some broadleaved evergreen plants are azaleas, boxwood, euonymous, gardenia, xylosma, jasmine, and holly.

Evergreen hardwood

Juniper

Yew

Chamaecyparis

Thuja

Evergreen hardwood cuttings of such plants as junipers, arborvitae, or yew are usually taken between late fall and late winter, after a frost. Cuttings are made 4 to 8 inches long with the bottom leaves removed. They respond well to wounding, relatively high light intensity, bottom heat, and the use of a root-promoting hormone.

Deciduous hardwood

1. Cut 6" to 8" of dormant stem.

2. Cover half of a sheet of plastic with moist planting mix.

3. Lay the cuttings in the mix. Fold the other half of the plastic over the mix and roll it fairly tightly.

4. Secure the rolled plastic with rubber bands. The plastic will help the soil mix retain the moisture necessary for rooting.

Hardwood cuttings from deciduous plants can be taken any time the shrub or tree is dormant, from late fall to midwinter. They may be propagated in a number of ways: by placing them directly in the ground, in a soil mix in a container, or in a plastic roll-up (as illustrated above). Insert the cutting deep enough so that only one bud is above the soil mix. Examples of some plants that use this method of propagation are deutzia, grape, honey locust, mock orange, poplar, and viburnum.

SPECIAL PLANTS

A greenhouse is an ideal controlled environment for growing tropical fruits and flowers as well as out-of-season vegetables.

The Tropicals

As long as you have a controlled environment, you can grow pineapples or papayas, for example, in any climate. Just plan ahead—that way you'll have the exotic fruits you want in time for Thanksgiving or any other occasion. Seeds are available from many seed companies, or you can buy young tropical plants from nurseries in southern areas of the country.

Pineapple. Despite its name, this fruit is not the result of a union between a pine tree and an apple tree. Rather, the pineapple is so named because it was once much smaller and resembled a pine cone.

To make a little pinery in your controlled environment, reserve a sunny spot for a 12-inch pot, then buy a ripe pineapple at a fruit stand or market. You can eat the fruit and start a new plant from the leafy top. Twist, rather than cut, the top off and leave it to air dry for about a week in any warm, dry place. The pineapple is a bromeliad and the fruit will stay alive for many days after it's picked.

After the top has cured, plant it in a 6-inch pot in very porous soil. A good mixture is ⅓ manure and ⅓ garden soil, mixed in turn with an equal quantity of perlite.

When you see that the pineapple top has rooted and is beginning to grow, give it a little fertilizer. You can work about a tablespoonful of blood meal into the soil around the base of the leaves, or use any liquid plant food. If you use a liquid, sprinkle it generously over the leaves as well as the roots of the plant. In either case, be careful not to snap or injure the new leaves; they are surprisingly brittle.

After about 18 months, move the pineapple plant to a 12-inch container and keep it in the warmest and brightest part of the greenhouse. At about 30 months, a lovely flower spike will shoot above the leaves. As it matures, you'll see the little immature pineapple. The more food, water, warmth, and light you can give the parent plant, the larger the fruit will grow. The plant is now strong enough to be shown off in the house for a day or two at a time. As the fruit comes of age, it will turn slightly yellow and begin to get soft. You can then pick it at any time. The parent plant will continue to grow offshoots and suckers for many years. Keep on fertilizing and watering it, and your next crop may yield two or three fruits. Without dividing, the plant will produce for six or seven years, but the fruit will get progressively smaller.

Passion fruit. *Passiflora edulis* is a beautiful vine to grow in a controlled environment, although it can stand a bit of frost. The seeds germinate easily. Sow them about ⅛ inch deep in regular potting soil. They will germinate in two or three weeks. When the second set of leaves appears, transplant the seedling to a 12- or 14-inch tub that has a trellis attached. If you want a larger vine, transplant three of the seedlings into a 16-inch tub. The tub can be

moved outside to a semishaded area each summer. The vine is not likely to flower the first year, but it should flower during the following winter in the greenhouse.

Passion fruit is seedy but delicious. Even without the fruit, the leaves and flowers make this easy-to-grow tropical splendor a worthwhile plant to have.

Papaya. There's little comparison between store-bought and tree-ripened papaya. Only the finest and sweetest melon from the market begins to approach the quality of one fresh from the tree.

The papaya is a very tender plant and must be kept constantly at temperatures of about 60°F. (16°C.) if you're to have a vigorous tree. Like other tropicals, it will thrive on nighttime temperatures of 70° to 75°F. (21° to 24°C.). It will usually die if the temperature drops below 40°F. (4°C.), even for a short time.

You can buy the seeds of many varieties of papayas, and you can even grow a tree from seed saved from a fruit you've bought at the market. Unfortunately, many varieties of papaya have separate male and female trees, so unless you have room to grow enough seedlings to ultimately select a pair, it is best to grow only varieties known to have flowers of both sexes on the same tree. Wash the seed well in a strainer, and plant it immediately, following the procedure for passion fruit. Give them a heavy application of organic fertilizer at two-week intervals, after the plant is well started. As the tree grows, transplant it to a larger pot until you ultimately end up with a 16- or 18-inch tub as the final container.

A papaya seed sown in January or February should produce fruit about 24 months later. The plant is lovely, growing straight and upright, with the fruit appearing near the trunk just under the leaves.

Guava. *Feijoa sellowiana* is best purchased as a plant because the seeds are very small and sometimes difficult to germinate. Grown in a greenhouse tub, the guava will develop handsome gray-green leaves that are nearly silver underneath; beautiful red and white flowers; and the small, oval fruit.

The plant has to be pollinated. If you don't want to let a few bees in the greenhouse, hand-pollinate with a soft, small paint brush. Go from blossom to blossom, brushing the center of each with a couple of gentle strokes. Do this every other day until the petals fall.

Citrus Fruits

Any of the endless varieties of citrus fruits you find in the market can be grown in a greenhouse. Many citrus are on dwarf rootstalk, and others are naturally small. Many of the best varieties are grafted, so you'll have to buy the plants rather than planting seeds. If you have room for only one tropical fruit tree in your greenhouse, consider a dwarf lemon of a variety that will bloom and fruit year-round.

Growing citrus in a tub differs from growing other greenhouse plants in two ways: first, the soil should not be kept constantly moist; instead, let it dry out at regular intervals in order to stimulate the roots. But don't let the plant wilt, and do give the foliage a good, regular spraying with water. Second, citrus plants need fertilizing monthly to produce good fruit. If the fruit is sour or the skin is very thick, this means that the plant probably has not been getting enough food.

Tomatoes

While tomatoes hardly qualify as an exotic plant, they do grow wonderfully inside a controlled environment such as a greenhouse. You can benefit from the experiences of commercial greenhouse tomato growers by reading about the four accepted methods of tomato culture:

Bed culture. Plant tomatoes directly in the soil on which the greenhouse

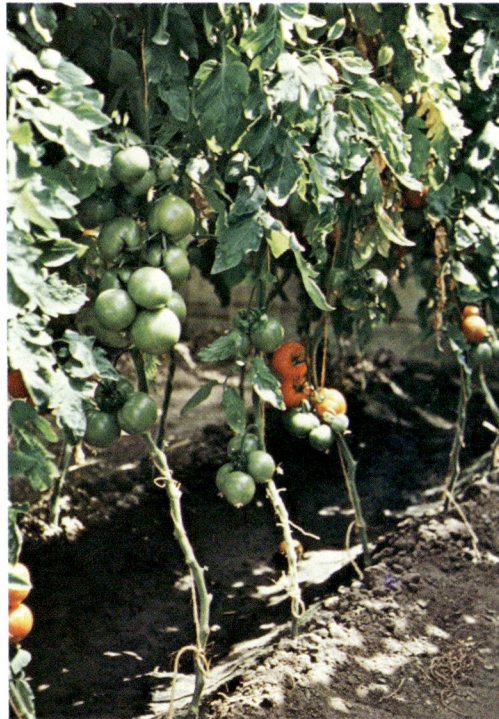

Left: Greenhouse tomato plants trained to a single stem, supported by plastic twine knotted loosely to the base of each plant, then clipped to a supporting overhead wire.

Below left: Even a greenhouse which requires hand-watering can result (right) in a month-to-month supply of fresh edibles.

structure is built. Enrich the soil with organic matter and fertilizers, much as you would for outdoor gardening. However, you have to sterilize the soil each year to control soil-borne diseases that are particularly harmful to tomatoes.

Newer methods of growing greenhouse tomatoes involve either a trough, a ring, or hydroponics. These were introduced commercially to eliminate or reduce the need to sterilize all the ground beds in the greenhouse. The principles, which apply equally well to home gardeners, are to use a sterile growing medium, and to confine the roots to a relatively small area.

Trough culture. In this method, you grow tomatoes in long, narrow, plastic-lined beds filled with a lightweight soil mix. In order to be effective, the plastic liner must be impermeable to roots. You can make the troughs out of concrete blocks, 1 × 6- or 2 × 6-inch lumber, or similar building materials. The troughs should be 5 to 6 inches deep, and about 24 inches wide to accommodate two rows of tomatoes. Cut drainage holes, 1 inch in diameter, on each side of the plastic liner, 1 to 2 inches from the bottom, about 10 feet apart.

Ring culture. Set the tomato plant into an 8- to 10-inch-diameter ring, or sleeve, of plastic film or tar paper. The rings have no top or bottom. Fill these with a sterile growing medium and place them 4 to 6 inches deep into a troughlike bed of water-absorbing aggregate. Ring culture allows the to-

A winter planting of hanging tomatoes can provide a succulent spring yield of fruit.

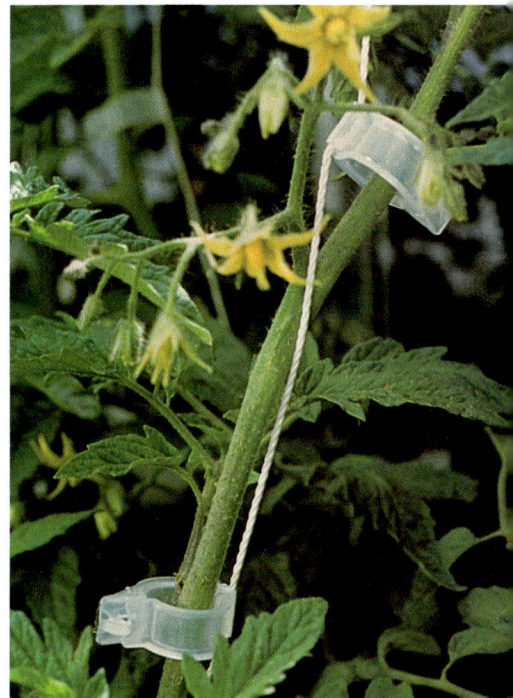

mato plant to form two separate root systems. Advocates claim that using an artificial mix in the ring and allowing the roots free access into the water-charged underlayer combines the advantages of both soil culture and hydroculture.

Hydroponic culture. This method works well for tomato plants. The tomatoes are grown in specially designed tanks on beds filled with aggregate, or similar material. An automated battery of pumps irrigates the plants and applies nutrients at regular intervals.

Timing. The late-spring single crop is by far the easiest to produce. Plant seeds of greenhouse varieties in late winter, and set the plants permanently in the beds in early spring. Flowering, fruit setting, and fruit growth occur during the increasingly longer and sunnier days of spring and early summer. Harvest begins much in advance of field-grown varieties, and extends into the season until the field varieties are commonly available. You can grow excellent crops of high-quality fruit: plants produce from 8 to 12 clusters, with 1 to 2 pounds of fruit per cluster.

Pruning and training. Regardless of the growing method, train tomato plants to a single stem. Remove all side shoots at least twice a week. Support the plants with plastic twine, tying one end with a small, nonslip loop to the base of the plant, and attaching the other end to a wire supported 6 to 8 feet above the plant row. As the plant grows, twist it around the twine in one or two easy spirals for each cluster of fruit.

Far left: Stake-trained tomatoes in plastic containers produce heavily in this fiberglass greenhouse.

Center and right: Tomatoes, such as this indoor favorite 'Floradel', can be supported by using plastic StemGem clips to keep twine and stems aligned.

Greenhouse Sources

Aladdin Industries
P. O. Box 10666
Nashville, TN 37210

Aluminum Greenhouses, Inc.
14615 Lorain Avenue
Cleveland, OH 44111
Freestanding and lean-to lightweight models.

American Leisure Industries
Box 63
Deep River, CT 06417

Casa-planta
9489 Dayton Way
Beverly Hills, CA 90210
Inexpensive, modular, vinyl covered.

Environmental Dynamics
P. O. Box 996
Sunnymead, CA 92388
Fiberglass prefabs with steel frame.

Feather Hill Industries
P. O. Box 41
Zenda, WI 53195

Gothic Arch Greenhouses
Box 1564
Mobile, AL 36601
Freestanding prefabs.

Greenhouse Specialties Company
9849 Kimker Lane
St. Louis, MO 63127

Hansen Weather-Port
300 South 14th
Gunnison, CO 81230

Ickes-Braun Glasshouses
P. O. Box 147
Deerfield, IL 60015
*Complete supplies for building your
own design.*

Lorn and Burnham
Irvington, NY 10533
All sizes and types.

Maco Home Greenhouses
P. O. Box 109
Scio, OR 97374
Inexpensive greenhouses.

McGregor Greenhouses
P. O. Box 36
Santa Cruz, CA 95063
Fiberglass prefabs.

National Greenhouse Company
P. O. Box 100
Pana, IL 62557
Hobby and professional prefabs.

J. A. Nearing Company
10788 Tucker Street
Beltsville, MD 20705
Aluminum greenhouses.

Redfern Greenhouses
55 Mount Hermon Road
Scotts Valley, CA 95060
Prefab lean-to and freestanding.

Redwood Domes
P. O. Box 666
Santa Cruz, CA 95060
Geodesic dome greenhouses.

Peter Reimuller
P.O. Box 2666
Santa Cruz, CA 95060
Inexpensive vinyl-covered models.

Santa Barbara Greenhouses
390 Dawson Drive
Camarillo, CA 93010
Inexpensive fiberglass prefabs.

Sturdi-Built Manufacturing Co.
11304 S.W. Boones Ferry Road
Portland, OR 97219
Prefab home units.

Texas Greenhouse Company
2717 St. Louis Avenue
Fort Worth, TX 76110
Prefab aluminum and redwood units.

Turner Greenhouses
P. O. Box 1260
Goldsboro, NC 27530
Inexpensive greenhouses.

Vegetable Factory, Inc.
100 Court Street
Copiague, L. I., NY 11726
*Aluminum frame, double-pane acrylic
glazing. Several models.*

Verandel Company
P.O. Box 1568
Worcester, MA 01611
Inexpensive lean-to greenhouses.

The controlled environment of this glass,
brick, and aluminum greenhouse not only
bursts with life but also greatly expands the
working space of this dwelling

Index

Italicized page numbers refer to illustrations.